ON
SF

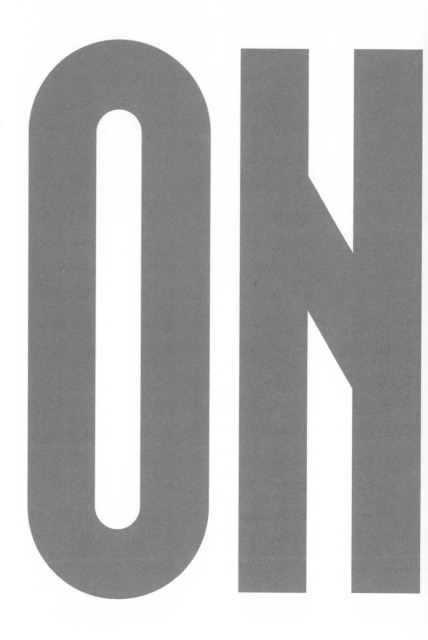

THE UNIVERSITY OF MICHIGAN PRESS ANN ARBOR

THOMAS M. DISCH

Copyright © by Thomas M. Disch 2005
All rights reserved
Published in the United States of America by
The University of Michigan Press
Manufactured in the United States of America
⊗ Printed on acid-free paper

2008   2007   2006   2005   4   3   2   1

A CIP catalog record for this book is available from the British Library.

Library of Congress Cataloging-in-Publication Data

Disch, Thomas M.
    On SF / Thomas M. Disch.
        p.   cm.
    Includes index.
    ISBN 0-472-09896-9 (cloth : alk. paper) — ISBN 0-472-06896-2
(pbk. : alk. paper)
    1. Science fiction, American—History and criticism.   2. Science
fiction—Authorship. I. Title.
PS374.S35D57   2005
813'.54—dc22   2004026268

Contents

PART ONE ON SF The Forest

The Embarrassments of Science Fiction

Embarrassment is in itself an embarrassing subject. Like beauty, it is all too apt to have its source in the sensibility of the beholder. Why should I be made uneasy by someone else's faults unless I fear to see my own mirrored in them? A capacity for embarrassment implies, at the very least, a lack of that loftiness and high cool that we all try to pretend is natural to us. No one, for instance, blushes at the blunders in a school play, for it is easy to see children, even one's own, in their eternal aspect. The point of having them on stage is for the charm of their inevitable failure in filling out their grown-up roles. If it were, instead, one's husband or wife who were so publicly failing, embarrassment would be hard to avoid—though there might still be charm for others in the audience.

Sophistication requires one to have no friends, or only those who can be counted on either never to fail or never to venture forth. In the quintessentially sophisticated world of Proust's novels there are no moments of embarrassment: his artists are first-rate, his aristocrats know better than to *do* anything, and everyone else is a provincial. A provincial is any person who *would* be embarrassing if he were a friend or a member of the same club.

Science fiction writers are the provincials of literature. We have always been able to embarrass each other, but to the world at large our gaucheries are generally accounted a major (if not the entire) part of our charm. If the critic Leslie Fiedler could end a speech in praise of science fiction with the sincere hope that sf should not lose "its slapdash quality, its sloppiness, or its vulgarity," so might a countess lavish praise on the ruddy health and unaffected manners of milkmaids. Samuel Delany wrote a long and satisfying essay taking Fiedler to task for his condescensions and pointing out that milkmaids acquire their complexions and their fetching rags as a consequence largely of the conditions they must work in and the pay they receive. I can't do better, by way of moving on, than to quote Delany: "Slapdash writing, sloppiness, and vulgarity are, no matter how you catch them, fat, diseased lice."

So much for our relations with the mainstream. While we remain provincials, it will not be possible to command any other kind of attention from the capitals of art. It is for us to take ourselves seriously and to consider the uncomfortable question of whether we ought to be permitted out into company. Many of the failings of provincials—their clothes, their manners, their accents—are easily correctable or else forgivable, but others, such as ignorance and complacency, are rooted in the provincial condition. My purpose in this essay is to consider the degree to which science fiction has its source in its own most flagrant faults.

Late in 1970, I made a suggestion in the bulletin of the Science Fiction Writers of America that I thought satisfactorily accounted for most of what is radically wrong with sf, as well as a good part of what is right. I suggested that science fiction is a branch of children's literature.

Let me count the ways.

In my own case, and in that of almost all my contemporaries who admit to a taste for it, that taste was acquired at around age thirteen. Often earlier; seldom much later than fifteen (though I have met a woman of mature years who became an avid reader of sf at age forty, during a long period of hospitalization). The taste may persist throughout life, but it seldom again exercises the addictive force it possesses in early adolescence, except among science fiction fans (concerning whom I shall have more to say by and by).

Consider, too, how many classic novels and stories in the genre are about children of exceptional wisdom and power. There was an early anthology, *Children of Wonder*, which I doted on, devoted to this sole theme. There are, as well, van Vogt's *Slan*, Sturgeon's *More Than Human*, Wyndham's *The Chrysalids* (*Re-Birth* in America), Pangborn's *A Mirror for Observers*, and major novels by Clement, Clarke, Asimov, and Blish—in all of which the protagonists are children. May it not be safely assumed that one reason for this is that such books were written *for* children?

To say that a book is written for children is not a condemnation, of course, but it is a limitation. It is limiting intellectually, emotionally, and morally. To consider those limitations in that order:

The intellectual limitations of sf are the more remarkable by virtue of the degree to which many of its readers and writers seem to regard their involvement with the genre as a badge of intellectual distinction, like membership in Mensa. This sorts oddly with an engrained anti-intellectualism and repeated demands that sf should stick to its last and provide only escapist entertainment—and yet many of the elder statesmen of the field are capable of such seeming self-contradictions. In fact, if they could but state it, their position is demonstrably consistent, and in fact, like all our opinions, is essentially a rationalization of their practice. Briefly, they would allow writers to deal speculatively with whatever materials might be introduced into a beginning course in the physical sciences, while disbarring irony, aesthetic novelty, any assumption that the reader shares in, or knows about, the civilization she is riding along in, or even a tone of voice suggesting mature thoughtfulness. Sf obeying these rules is called hard-core sf, and some purists would have it that it is the only kind that matters. A classic hard-core story, many times reprinted, Tom Godwin's "The Cold Equations" concerns an eighteen-year-old girl stowaway on a space ship who must be jettisoned because in calculating the fuel needed for landing no allowance has been made for her additional mass. Much is made of the fact that at an acceleration of five gravities the girl's one-gravity weight of 110 pounds will increase to an effective 550 pounds. As a specimen of English prose, of character portrayal, of sociological imagination, the story can only be judged as puerile; yet within its own terms, as a fable designed to convey to very young people that science is not a respecter of persons, it is modestly successful.

The emotional limitations of children's literature are even more restrictive. There are, here and there, children bright enough to cope with the *Scientific American* or even the *Times Literary Supplement*, but crucial aspects of adult experience remain boring even to these prodigies. At the cinema children fail to see the necessity for love scenes, and if a whole movie were to prove to be about nothing else, then they would just as soon not sit through it. No less an authority than Kingsley Amis has pronounced sex and love as being outside the sphere of interest proper to science fiction. Other subjects commonly dealt with by mainstream writers are also presumed not to be of interest to sf readers, such as the nature of the class system and the real exercise of power within that system. Although there is no intrinsic reason (except difficulty) that sf should not venture into such areas, sf writers have characteristically preferred imaginary worlds in which, to quote Sprague de Camp, "all men are mighty, all women beautiful, all problems simple, and all life adventuresome."

The moral limitations of a literature built on such premises should be immediately apparent. Evil is seen as intrinsically external, a blackness ranged against the unvaried whites of heroism. Unhappy endings are the outcome of occasional cold equations, not of flawed human nature. There can be no tragic dimension of experience. Even a tentative expression of pessimism is regarded as grounds for dismissing a work out of hand. Compare sf to mysteries in this respect. Every mystery, however misbegotten, assumes that men are all capable of any degree of evil. That is, all characters are suspects. Such an assumption is essentially foreign to the experience of children. This is not to say that children are innocent, but only that they suppose they are.

Having put forward these reasons for considering sf to be a branch of children's literature, I must confess that something essential remains lacking—chiefly, an explanation of why it is read by so many adults. Further, science fiction has other failings and limitations that this theory fails to account for. I am left with an interesting and only partially valid observation, whose chief merit is that it has been a small annoyance to various people I don't like.

Let me approach the problem from a different direction—the problem, that is, of who reads sf and why. And let me explain, as a kind of belated preface, why the nature of science fiction's readership is so crucial a consideration.

Genre fiction may be distinguished from other kinds of writing in being shaped by the (presumed) demands of its audience rather than by the creative will of its writers. The writers accommodate their talents to the genre's established formulae. These formulae exist in order to guarantee readers the repetition of pleasures fondly remembered. It is no more reprehensible for a writer to seek to gratify such expectations than for a restaurant to do so; and it may be done, in one case as in the other, with more or less skill. This emphasis on replication rather than creation does explain why cookery—and hack writing—finally must be considered as crafts rather than as arts. Indeed, the very mention of "art" is apt to bring a manly sneer to the lips of the hack writer, who prides himself on his craftsmanship, his competence as an entertainer meeting the demands of an audience. It follows that we may learn more about any genre by examining its readership than by studying its writers.

As an example of such an approach let me quote an article in which I sought to account for the conventions of the gothic romance:

Gothics are mostly read by housewives or those who see a life of housewifery looming ahead. In gothics, the heroine is mysteriously threatened and wonders whether it was her husband/fiancé who tried to drop the chandelier on her. . . . Few of the ladies who devour gothics are in serious danger of being pushed off a cliff in Cornwall for the sake of their legacies, yet the analogue of the brand of fiction they buy to their real predicament is close. Every gothic reader must ask herself whether her marriage is worth the grief, the ritual insincerity, the buried rancour, and the sacrifice of other possibilities that every marriage entails. To which the gothic writer replies with a resounding Yes! It is worth all that because down deep he really does love you. Yet to the degree that this answer rings hollow the experience must be renewed. Poor Eleanor must return to the dark castle of her doubts, and the doubts must be denied. And then again.

Is there an analogous model of the representative reader for the much broader and more complex genre of science fiction? I believe there are probably several. One such might be a precocious fourteen-year-old, impatient with his education, anxious for economic independence, with a highly developed faculty for daydreaming and little emotional or moral sophistication concerning the content of his daydreams. That is a fairly accurate portrait of myself at age fourteen, when my passion for sf had reached its height. Now, not just any daydream will serve for such a reader. It must be one to suit his circumstances. Try this, for instance. I quote from the back cover of a paperback:

> Somewhere in this world there are six people who—together—can do anything. Some day, perhaps tomorrow, they will put their power to work and the world will be transformed. In the meantime they are waiting quietly. They look—and often behave—like people you know. But with a difference: they think of themselves as "I"—not "we"—because in a curious way they are One.

Add to this that the central figure of the book is a schoolboy of prodigious intellectual gifts desperately trying to pass himself off on the world as the boy next door. This book, as every sf reader will recognize, is Theodore Sturgeon's *More Than Human*. It is a book that even today I cannot praise highly enough. Among its many excellences is the fact that it uses its considerable power *as a daydream* to inculcate ethical values and spiritual insights usually entirely absent from genre writing. For instance, the book's insistence on mutual interdependency (and, by implication, on psychic integration) is in sharp contrast to the legion of stories in which the hero discovers the fate of the world to rest in his sole power. Another theme of the book—the need to bide one's time—is of obvious utility to any fourteen-year-old. But the largest subliminal lesson is latent in the fantasy of possessing secret mental powers. What this represents, I believe, is an assurance that there is a world of thought and inner experience of immense importance and within everybody's grasp. But it is only there for those who cultivate it.

So long as one stands in need of such assurances and exhortations, so long will sf remain a source of solace and of strength. That is why sf is *par excellence* the literature of students, and why, usually, once you've got your degree and begun to lead a livelier life in the wider world, your need for the intellectual cheerleaders of sf slackens. However, if for any reason you don't get the degree, or if the degree doesn't get you what you thought it would, then you may be doomed to spin the wheel of this one fantasy forever. These, the second especially, are large qualifications. Few expectations worth the having are likely to be entirely fulfilled, and so there remains in every foolish heart appetites that only fantasy can assuage.

That is one model of the science fiction reader, and essentially it is an elaboration of my first theory—that sf is written for children. There is, however, another kind of science fiction reader, more typical formerly than now, who is drawn to the genre by distinctly different needs. His preference is for a different sort of sf than that I've been considering till now. He regards the Golden Age of sf as the thirties and forties. He is an admirer of E. E. Smith, of Edgar Rice Burroughs, of A. E. van Vogt, and, at the farthest stretch of his imagination, of Robert Heinlein. This is the science fiction "fan," and he exercises, by the preponderant and inarguable weight of his purchases, a major influence on the genre.

Since I cannot frame a description of this reader in terms that do not betray my bias against him, I should like to defer to John W. Campbell Jr., who in 1952 wrote this description of his conception of the average reader of his magazine, *Astounding*:

> Reader surveys show the following general data: that the readers are largely young men between 20 and 30, with a scattering of younger college students, and older professional technical men; and that nearly all the readers are technically trained and employed.
>
> The nature of the interest in the stories is not economic, not love, but technical-philosophical.

Now, as an example of what Campbell's technically trained élite was enjoying in those days in the pages of *Astounding*, I'd like to quote a brief passage from A. E. van Vogt's *The World of Null-A*, which Campbell has called "one of those once-in-a-decade classics." In this passage the hero and his girlfriend have gone to a giant computer to be tested on their understanding of the principles of a new all-purpose science called General Semantics:

> "Now that I'm here," said Teresa Clark, "I'm no longer so sure of myself. Those people look darned intelligent."
>
> Gosseyn laughed at the expression on her face, but he said nothing. He felt supremely positive that he could compete right through to the thirtieth day. His problem was not would he win, but would he be allowed to try.

The story proves his doubts to be justified, for he is beset on all sides by mysterious and implacable enemies. Thanks, however, to his grasp of non-Aristotelian logic he does win through. Concerning the virtues of this new philosophy, van Vogt had this to say in his introduction:

> Every individual scientist is limited in his ability to abstract data from Nature by the brainwashing he has received from his parents and in school. As the General Semanticist would say, each scientific researcher "trails his history" into every research project. Thus, a physicist with less educational or personal rigidity can solve a problem that was beyond the ability (to abstract) of another physicist.

What can be inferred of a reader for whom van Vogt's sentiments and the situations of his fiction are persuasive? First, I think, that education is a subject of profound ambivalence. On the one hand, success is equated with passing a test administered by a computer that shares the author's reverence for non-Aristotelian logic. There is some apprehension as to one's competitors, for they look "darned intelligent." On the other hand, we (of the real world) are apparently "brainwashed" in school, and physicists with less education may be better qualified to solve certain problems than their better-educated peers. While I have my own reservations about the educational system, there is a ring for me, through all of this, of dead-end jobs and correspondence schools (whose come-ons regularly grace the back covers of sf magazines). The technical training and employment that Campbell speaks of are all too often likely to be training in the use of the soldering iron or even the crowbar. Van Vogt and Campbell speak all too clearly the language of lower-middle-class aspiration and resentment, nor are they alone in this. By far the greater part of all pulp science fiction from the time of Wells till now was written to provide a semi-literate audience with compensatory fantasies.

This aspect of the social origins and provenance of sf, though seldom spoken of, will not come as a surprise to the seasoned reader of the genre. The pulp magazines that arose at the turn of the twentieth century had, as a matter of survival, to cater to the needs of the newly literate working classes. Inevitably, it shows.

Sf is rife with fantasies of powerless individuals, of ambiguous antecedents, rising to positions of commanding importance. Often they become world saviors. The appeal of such fantasies is doubtless greater to one whose prevailing sense of himself is of being undervalued and meanly employed; who believes his essential worth is hidden under the bushel of a life that somehow hasn't worked out as planned; whose most rooted conviction is that he is capable of *more*, though as to the nature of this unrealized potential he may not be too precise.

Another prominent feature of sf that is surely related to the naive character of its audience is its close resemblance, often bordering on identity, with myth, legend, and fairy tales. Throughout the twentieth century a large part of the American urban lower classes, from which the sf audience was drawn, were recent immigrants from what is commonly called the Old Country—that is to say, from the place where folk tales were still a living tradition. Indeed, except for the stories of their religions, this was likely to have been the only literary tradition familiar to these immigrants. Thus few of the first sf readers were more than a generation away from the oral tradition at its most traditional. Think of that sense of wonder that is the touchstone of the early pulp stories: could it not be, in essence, an analogue of the sense of wonder all country mice experience at their first view of a modern metropolis? Doubtless, the twentieth century has had some surprises even for sophisticated city mice, but it is part of *their* code not to let on to this. Surely they will not erect wonder, novelty, and the massive suspension of disbelief into first principles of their aesthetics. Sophisticates require the whole complex apparatus developed by two centuries of realistic novelists in order just to begin enjoying a made-up story. But for a naive audience, as for children, it is enough to say, "once there was a city made all of gold," and that city rises up in all its simple splendor before their inner eye.

A less beguiling feature we may expect to find in a lower-class literature is resentment. Resentment, because it has its source in repressed anger, usually is expressed in indirect forms. Thus, the chief advantage of the ruling classes, their wealth and the power it provides, is dealt with in most science fiction by simply denying its importance. Power results from personal virtue or the magic of machines. It is rather the personal characteristics of the wealthy that become the focus of the readers' resentment—their cultivated accents, their soft hands, their preposterous or just plain incomprehensible ideas, which they refuse to discuss except by their own ornate rules in their own tiresome language. Most maddeningly, they hold the unswervable and utterly unfair conviction that because they've had the good luck to be better educated they are therefore smarter. In a world full of doltish university graduates, this assumption of superiority is in the highest degree exasperating to any moderately intelligent machinist or clerk. But what is to be done? To attempt to catch up could be the work of a lifetime, and at the end of it one has only succeeded in becoming a poor copy of what one originally despised—an effete intellectual snob.

Happily, or unhappily, there is an alternative. Deny outright the wisdom of the world and be initiated to a secret wisdom. Become a true believer—it matters not the faith, so long as it is at variance with *theirs*. All millennialist religions have their origins in this need for creating a counterculture. As religion loses its unique authority, almost any bizarre set of beliefs can become the focus of a sense of Election. Whatever the belief, the rationale for it is the same: the so-called authorities are a pack of fools and frauds with minds closed to any but their own ideas. Just because they've published books doesn't mean a thing. There are other books that are in complete opposition. Beginning with such arguments, and armed with the right book, one may find one's way to almost any conclusion one might take a fancy to: hollow earths, Dean drives, the descent of mankind from interstellar visitors. For the more energetic true believer there are vaster systems of belief, such as Scientology. I select these examples from the myriad available because each historically has been a first cousin of science fiction. And for this good reason: that sf is a virtual treasury of ways of standing the conventional wisdom on its head. Only sophisticates will make a fine distinction between playing with ideas and adopting them. For a naive reader the imaginative excitement engendered by a new notion easily crystallizes into faith.

As this begins to sound like an indictment of sf and its readers, I should like to point out that these class-associated features of sf should not be considered as faults. They are essentially neutral and may be employed to good or ill effect, according to the gifts and goodwill of any given writer. Fantasies of power are a necessary precondition of the exercise of power—by anyone. One cannot do what one hasn't first imagined doing. The upper classes possess a great initial advantage in discovering while still young that the world is in essential agreement with *their* fantasies of power. Princes have a great resource of self-confidence in knowing that someday they'll be kings. Self-help books, from Samuel Smiles through Dale Carnegie, all agree on the crucial importance of hyping yourself into a state of self-confidence. Without that, there is little chance of competing against the toffs who got their gleaming teeth and firm handshakes, as it were, by inheritance. As a device for schooling the mind in what it feels like to be a real go-ahead winner, a few novels by Edgar Rice Burroughs could be quite as effective as an equivalent dosage of Positive Thinking. To denigrate the power fantasies of sf is very like laughing at cripples because they use crutches. A crutch that serves its purpose is to be admired.

As to the kinship between sf and fairy tales and legends, I should not think it would be necessary to make apology. What more fertile soil could any fiction sink its roots into, after all? If individual artists have not always been equal to their materials, that is their loss. It is our gain as readers that often, even so, their botched tales retain the power to astonish us. Even in a cheap frankfurter pork tastes good.

Finally, as to resentment, who shall say that there are not, often enough, good grounds for it? Anger and defiance may he healthier, manlier modes of expression, but when the way to these is barred, we must make do somehow. "Cinderella" and "The Ugly Duckling" are fantasies inspired by resentment, and they possess an undeniable, even archetypal, power. When we are compelled to recognize that our allegiance is owing to powers, whether parents or presidents, whose character is flawed or corrupt, what shall we feel in acquiescing to those powers (as we all do, sometimes) unless resentment? The lower classes may feel their oppression more keenly because it is more immediate and pervasive, but resentment to some degree is part of the human condition.

However (and alas), this does not end the matter. Resentment may be universal, but it is also universally dangerous, for the political program of the resentful inevitably savors of totalitarianism and a spirit of revenge. Once they attain to political power the know-nothings can have a sweet triumph over the know-it-alls by *declaring* that the earth is flat, or Einstein a heretic. The books of one's enemies can be burned or re-edited. I am by no means the first to observe and deplore this fact of political life, nor yet to note its bearing on a certain variety of science fiction. For a fuller consideration of the fascist lurking beneath the smooth chromium surface of a good deal of sf, I recommend Adolf Hitler's remarkable novel, Lord of the Swastika, also known as The Iron Dream, by Norman Spinrad.

This aspect of sf is only alarming to the degree that the jack-booted variety of sf writer can make good their claim to speak for the field as a whole: which today, surely, is far from being the case. However, this side of sf does remain an embarrassment so long as sf is regarded as a unitary phenomenon, an extended family whose members have a general obligation to notice each other's existence. In the larger world of mainstream literature, matters are ordered otherwise. The better sort of writers simply ignore the productions of their inferiors, even as they crowd their own off the bestseller lists. They do this in much the same way that the gentry arrange their lives so as to be able to ignore the scowling faces of the lower orders. This has its inequalities, as when good writers have the misfortune to be tagged as "popular entertainers" and fail to receive the critical attention their work merits. But it is undeniably a convenient arrangement, and for good or ill, it is happening right now to sf. It is stratifying into the same three-deck arrangement of highbrow, middle-brow, and lowbrow. A new variety of reader has sprung up beside the older fandom and the ever-replenished ranks of juvenile readers. This new readership has its own distinctive needs and preferences. Being one of the trees, my own view of the forest is not necessarily to be trusted, and so I will not try to characterize these readers, except to call them—*us*. My only reason for bringing up the matter at all is to pose the question of what *our* relation to *them* should be.

In my first notes for this essay I had a kind of half-aphorism that I haven't been able to sneak in anywhere along the way. It was this: sf bears the same relation to fiction that Scientology bears to science. It works for some, but it won't bear looking at. Essentially the question that remains to be asked is whether such a statement—that it won't bear looking at—is justifiable or wise. When it is said that the poor shall always be with us, too often the implication is that one may therefore ignore the poor, and that listening to their grievances is a waste of time.

The alternative to letting sleeping dogs lie is to risk being bitten. That is to say, for me to speak candidly about the books of certain of my colleagues in the field is to invite their hostility and to wound the feelings of many readers who've enjoyed these books; and this without any expectation of entering on a fruitful dialogue, since I have no confidence at all that we share enough common assumptions about life and literature to enable us to undertake a meaningful discussion. "Fan," after all, is a shortened form of "fanatic." Moreover, as I've indicated, in many ways I have no quarrel with these books, just as I have no interest in reading them.

Nevertheless, I feel that my subject requires me to offer at least one specific instance. Recently I had occasion to read Robert Heinlein's *Starship Troopers*, a book that surely provided Norman Spinrad with one of his models for *The Iron Dream*. Thanks to Norman it isn't necessary to say much concerning Heinlein's politics. I'm sure that Heinlein himself would reject the label so many of his critics would pin on him, that of "totalitarian." He might, after a bit of qualifying, go along with "authoritarian" since his story does make such an issue of implicit obedience to authority.

What is embarrassing to me about this book is not its politics as such but rather its naivete, its seeming unawareness of what it is *really* about. Leaving politics aside and turning to that great gushing source of our richest embarrassments, sex, I find *Starship Troopers* to be, in this respect as well, a veritable treasury of unconscious revelations. The hero is a homosexual of a very identifiable breed. By his own self-caressing descriptions one recognizes the swaggering leather boy in his most flamboyant form. There is even a skull-and-crossbones earring in his left ear. On four separate occasions, when it is hinted in the book that women have sexual attractions, the only such instances in the book, each time within a single page the hero picks a gratuitous fistfight with the other servicemen—and he always insists on what a lark it is. The association is reflexive and invariable. Sexual arousal leads to fighting. At the end of the book the hero has become a captain and his father is a sergeant serving under him. This is possible because his mother died in the bombing of Buenos Aires by the Bugs, who are the spiritual doppelgängers of the human warriors. In an earlier captain-sergeant relation there is a scene intended to be heartwarming, in which two men make a date to have a boxing match. Twice the hero makes much of the benefits to be derived from seeing or suffering a lashing. Now all of this taken together is so transparent as to challenge the possibility of its being an unconscious revelation. Yet I'm sure that it was, and that moreover any admirer of the book would insist that it's just my dirty mind that has sullied a fine and patriotic paean to the military life.

So why bring it up at all? For two reasons. The first is that such sexual confusions make the politics of the book more dangerous by infusing them with the energies of repressed sexual desires. It may be that what turns you on is not the life of an infantryman, but his uniform. A friend of mine has assured me he knows of several enlistments directly inspired by a reading of *Starship Troopers.* How much simpler it would have been for those lads just to go and have their ears pierced. The second related reason is that it is a central purpose of art, in conjunction with criticism, to expand the realm of conscious choice and enlarge the domain of the ego. It does this by making manifest what was latent, a process that can be resisted, but not easily reversed. And so even those who dislike what I have had to say may yet find it useful as a warning of how things appear to other eyes, and be spared, in consequence, needless embarrassment.

At the beginning of this essay I pose the question whether the faults of sf are extraneous to its nature or intrinsic. In looking back at what I've said, my answer would seem to be that they are intrinsic: but then so are its characteristic strengths. Sf deals with the largest themes and most powerful emotional materials—but in ways that are often irresponsible and trivializing. Altogether too many of us, even the true giants like Philip Dick, are willing to trust our powers of improvisation untempered by powers of retrospection and analysis. We accept the interest paid to the overriding fascination of our subject matter as a tribute paid to our talents, which in few cases have been exercised to anything like their full extent. It would be gratifying to add, by way of rounding this off on a mellow note, that none of this much matters—that lousy books don't survive and good books do. And why not, after all, end on that note? It may not be entirely true, but it must be an article of faith for anyone who wants to write good books. I believe it. So should you.

Ideas: A Popular Misconception

In recent issues of *Foundation* and other magazines Ian Watson has been reiterating a notion that I finally cannot resist calling into question. His thesis, in its most skeletal form, is that science fiction characteristically treats of Ideas, and that such is the weight, wonder, and significance of these Ideas that the genre transcends mundane literary criteria, which are dismissed as "stylistics." This argument begs so many questions that it is virtually unassailable. As to his central thesis, that important Ideas are exciting, or vice versa, who will deny it? How, from this vast and fuzzy premise, he comes round to his usual conclusion that sf is the sacred preserve of a muse unlike all others varies from pronouncement to pronouncement, but that is his unchanging moral. I would like, here, to point out some of the ways in which his arguments strike me as wrongheaded, self-serving, and dishonest.

First, let me nod in passing to the old dichotomy of Style versus Content, which will go on being debated as long as there are college freshmen. Old hands at the literary game know this to be a false and spurious distinction, especially in aesthetics. The Ideas in a work of art do not exist independently of the medium that conveys them—whether that medium is language, paint, or musical notes. To plead on behalf of a writer's ideas while offering excuses for his style is tantamount to confessing a sense of at least the partial inadequacy of those ideas, to admit that the writer in question has not commanded one's entire loyalty or whole attention. A writer's strengths as much as his inadequacies prove, when examined carefully enough, to be attributable to his particular use of language—to what Watson would dismiss as "style." But this line of argument, though so established as to amount to a truism, is too abstract to be appealing. It is more comfortable to speak of books as we remember them (big urns full of Characters, Plots, Ideas) than as we experience them (a modulated flow of language). So rather than scuttle Watson's case before it's embarked on the high seas, I'm willing to talk about Ideas and Style.

Let me ask, first, what Ideas are we talking about? Whose Ideas, in which books? I particularly want to know which otherwise meretricious works (stylistically speaking) must be forgiven on account of their good

Ideas? Those of E. E. Smith, perhaps? Watson wrote, in *Arena 7*, of Smith's books:

> "Blasters roar, crypto-science jargon jangles evocatively, galaxies collide. It's gawkish stuff. Yet there is such sheer passion for science, discovery, space; such wonder (even though the human and social dimension is missing and the stuff is frankly unreadable beyond the age of 14 with its lumpy style, minimal characters and histrionic plots) that I turn with sadness to some more obviously mature, adult, artistic sf of today."

Does Watson mean to say that there are good Ideas hidden in the dreck? Does it amount to an Idea to say, "Hey, what if there were real spaceships and we could fly them to another galaxy a zillion light-years away!"? Strictly speaking, yes it does—but scarcely an original Idea, even, I would suppose, for the most naive of Smith's readers. This is not to say that it can't be made an exciting Idea, however familiar, by a dramatic presentation—but aren't we talking about "stylistics" at this point? Watson does cite a more original notion of Smith's—that his hero saves "kidnapped girlfriends from falling into dead stars by firing morse-code messages through space by machine gun." An irresistible Idea, in its way, but of the category Dumb Idea. Dumb Ideas are, indeed, the particular delight of the old pulps, and anyone can enjoy a giggle at their expense— or a sigh, like Watson's, for the supposed lost innocence (was it ever really his, though?) that could accept such absurd concoctions at face value. This is what Camp is all about, and Camp, these days, is scarcely an elitist pleasure. Even in my youth, so long ago, *Mad Magazine* was trafficking in Camp. People like Dumb Ideas, even though they know they're dumb; witness the success of *Star Wars*.

But Watson (I assume) isn't defending Dumb Ideas, or only incidentally, insofar as they may be general enough (the Idea of Space Travel, for instance) to encompass an Idea that actually has something going for it, the sort of Idea that a professional scientist or philosopher need not be ashamed of. The question then suggests itself to me—if one has got hold of such a really Good Idea, why not present it to the world in the glory of its naked truth? Why is fiction, in any form, required as swaddling clothes? The most successful Ideas have generally been disseminated in nonfictional form. (Though the fancy immediately suggests an alternative universe in which Newton and Darwin felt compelled to propose their theories in the form of novels or epic poems.) The answer is obviously that fiction is not a suitable medium for presenting Ideas for scientific or philosophical evaluation.

What it is good for, and what it often does, is to take Ideas and systems of Ideas from the cool context of the laboratory and the seminar room and demonstrate their relevance to human life. Insofar as the Ideas of sf are worth taking seriously, they belong to a community of discourse that neither originates within the field nor remains there. Truly original Ideas are few, and most intellectual activity consists in glossing them, cross-referencing them, and restating them more lucidly or more forcefully.

But already I find myself falling into the same slovenly usage as Watson in speaking of Ideas as though they were all of one generic type, like Cats. In fact, when we speak of the Ideas in a work of fiction they are of a radically different nature from the Ideas of science and philosophy.

Consider *The Island of Dr. Moreau*. What is its basic Idea? That animals might be surgically altered so as to become almost like people? Only the most naive reading yields this banality. (Though how often sf critics seem to think it is enough to catalogue the salient nuts-and-bolts of a plot by way of summing up its "Ideas"!) If the book deserves our intellectual consideration, it is rather because it examines human nature in the light of Darwin's theories and speculates on the degree to which human nature resembles that of the brute creation. Wells, however, is not under the onus of explaining Darwin's theories to his readers. Rather, he dramatizes the conflict between two views of human nature. He does this with such artistic economy that the uncritical reader is simply swept along by the story—not so much unthinkingly as thinking (with Wells's help) so quickly and efficiently as not to notice what he's about. The Ideas are there, by implication, but taken in the context of the ongoing drama they are not particularly striking Ideas. Only when Wells's art has imparted an intensity and human significance to these Ideas do they become "his" (or as a genre "ours").

In a word, Wells is mythmaking. Here, for a moment, Watson and I may find ourselves on common ground, for in his essay in *Arena 7*, he speaks of sf as the mythology of the modern age. Our difference may come down to this—that he would emphasize the material being made a myth of, while I would emphasize the process itself. But this shift of emphasis has large repercussions, for it means that Watson wants to believe his Ideas, while I am content to entertain mine.

No doubt that's disingenuous. I have the same vested interest in my Ideas as Watson has in his (or if not in my Ideas as such, in something I think of as uniquely my own; I'd probably call it my Art). The founding text of the sociology of knowledge, Mannheim's *Ideology and Utopia*, propounds a very interesting Idea. To wit—that all systems of thought (ideologies) are ultimately no more than special pleading for the ideologue's privileged position. No one, Mannheim maintains, has any Ideas but those that it is to her advantage to have.

To apply this thesis to the present case, artists, when they turn to criticism, are chiefly engaged in expounding the peculiar excellence of their own work as artists, but by proclaiming its virtues and exculpating its faults, Watson, in maintaining the primacy of Ideas in sf and denigrating the importance of "Stylistics," is telling us how we are to read and value his own fiction. It is an evaluation in which other critics have concurred, though not always with the same unqualified approbation.

More than this, however, Watson seems to be demanding that his Ideas be judged on their own merits—not as the elements of a fictional invention but on the grounds of their literal truth. He makes a distinction between science and poetry parallel to that between Ideas and Stylistics. E. E. Smith, for all his failings, is to be admired for his faith in Science, while other writers, manifestly more accomplished, are nevertheless deplored because they worship the false gods of Poetry, Irony, and Skepticism. Of the work of these writers (though he doesn't mention me by name, I trust he would include me in their number), Watson writes:

> The science ideas of genuine sf, and science itself too, become all too often a form of stylistic kitsch, reflecting a self-indulgent disillusion with science, wonder, and hope, the future and their replacement by a sophisticated Silver Age rococo.

Science, in its current usage, is that area of knowledge which does not fall under the strictures that apply to Ideology. It is certain, not relative. "Science ideas," thus, are ideas we can believe in, and that is what Watson longs for on the evidence of his own work. The consistent theme of his fiction is that of human transcendence. Transcendence is a religious preoccupation, and like many other sf writers, Watson uses science fiction as a vehicle for exploring the vast, dim, and undeniably fascinating terrain on the borderland between here and somewhere transcendentally else. Faith must be, by definition, in things unseen and unproven—but passionately longed for. There is always a temptation to insist that one has, in fact, seen those things. Gospels are written to this effect, and novels. And yet, maddeningly, doubters continue to express their doubts about one's words of witness, doubters who reflect, to quote Watson again, "a self-indulgent Western disillusion with science, wonder, hope, the future."

I am not suggesting that Watson's Ideas are Dumb Ideas on a par with those of E. E. Smith. But they are Doubtful Ideas, in that they are not susceptible of proof and so find themselves in the same boat with other Ideologies.

The Ideas of Poetry, similarly, tend to be Doubtful Ideas (and I would even suggest to Watson—and to sf writers in general—that Poetry, willynilly, is the business that they're in), but poets have a different relation to their Doubtful Ideas than do true believers. Poetry is the language Faith speaks when it is no longer literal, a language that is, of course, self-indulgent (i.e., playful, provisional, undogmatic) and that is also, perhaps, disillusioned (if the alternative is to be illusioned). It is the language of Ovid, of Dante, and of legions of other poets, and nowadays it is the language of such science fiction as I would care to make a case for. If it smacks of the Silver Age, there is no disgrace in that—for the Golden Age never did exist. Least of all in science fiction.

Mythology and Science Fiction

The sun, under which there is nothing new, also rises, and what has happened will happen again, tomorrow and tomorrow and tomorrow. This doctrine, though sanctioned by many authorities, has never found much favor among those whose trade is Novelty—gallery owners, fashion photographers, messiahs, and science fiction writers.

It can be argued that there are, in fact, new things under the sun nowadays—Concorde jets, Kellogg's Pop-Tarts, sun lamps, the Tomorrow show with Tom Snyder, and much else besides, some good, some bad, and all pouring with indiscriminate abundance from the cornucopia of technology.

What hasn't changed (so far) is the nature of the darkly wise being who must confront both old and new and make some sense of them. The forms of that sense are the structures of mythology, the forever bifurcating, often rickety architectures that support every conceivable (human) meaning.

Myths are everywhere—in every morsel of food, decorating banks and birdhouses, tingeing the blandest discourse with dire resonances, making the mildest encounter a drama. Don't take my word for it: read Freud, or Levi-Strauss, or Barthes. In this very broad sense mythology embraces the whole realm of the cultivated and the civilized, everything shaped by the hand and mind of men, which, for most of us, includes everything in sight. Indeed, even where the hand can't reach, the all-conquering imagination extends its empery, staking a claim on the stars by the simple act of connecting the dots and naming the figures formed by the lines: Orion, Cassiopeia, Hercules, Draco.

Myths are everywhere, but especially in literature. Reduce whatever tale to its atomic components and you'll find those eternal champions and heroes of a thousand farces, Mr. and Ms. Mythos. There they are, skulking in the background of even the likeliest story, disguised as people with next-door names—Steven, Edward, Anna, Emma—but recognizable for all that as Adam, Oedipus, Ishtar, or Snow White. It is not the ingenuity of critics that accomplishes this, but simple human nature. We are a species, alike not only in the morphology of the flesh but as well in that of the spirit—and limited in both. Limited, too, in the relations we can form with others. People arrange themselves in pairs, in eternal triangles, in square dances, and so on, up to about twelve. Thirteen at table is unlucky; fourteen anywhere is a mob (or, if they're our mob, a tribe). Like the Sun Himself, we are prisoners of plane geometry, and the geometers who have described and defined the configurations we are capable of forming are the makers, and remakers, of our myths.

Myths are everywhere in literature, but especially in science fiction, in which category I would (for present purposes) include all distinctively modern forms of fantasy from Tolkien to Borges. The reasons for this aren't far to seek. Myths aim at maximizing meaning, at compressing truth to the highest density that the mind can assimilate without the need of, as it were, cooking. (Extending that metaphor, natural philosophy—science—would represent truth in a less immediately ingestible form—dry lentils, so to speak.) To attain such compression myths make free use of the resources of the unconscious mind, that alternate world where magic still works and metamorphoses are an everyday occurrence. Science fiction presumably abjures magic, but only—like Giordano Bruno, Uri Geller, and other canny charlatans—in order to escape the Inquisition. In fact, sf has been trafficking in magic and mythology since first it came into existence. Mary Shelley's *Frankenstein* is subtitled *A Modern Prometheus*, and the horror-show monsters whose image continues to be emblematic of the genre are provably the descendants of "Gorgons and Hydras, and Chimaeras dire." There is scarcely a theme in sf for which a classic parallel cannot be found: try it.

As mythmakers, science fiction writers have a double task, the first aspect of which is to make humanly relevant—literally, to humanize—the formidable landscapes of the atomic era. We must trace in the murky sky the outlines of such new constellations as the Telephone, the Helicopter, the Eight Pistons, the Neurosurgeon, the Cryotron. Often enough, in looking about the heavens for a place to install one of these latter-day figures, the mythmaker discovers that the new figure corresponds very neatly with one already there. The Motorcyclist, for instance, is congruent at almost all points with the Centaur, and no pantheon has ever existed without a great-bosomed, cherry-lipped Marilyn who promises every delight to her devotees. But matching old and new isn't always this easy. Consider the Rocket Ship. Surely it represents something more than a cross between Pegasus and the Argo. What distinguishes the Rocket Ship is that (1) it is mechanically powered and that (2) its great speed carries it out of ordinary space into hyperspace, a realm of indefinable transcendence. My theory is that the contemporary human experience that the myth of the Rocket Ship apotheosizes is that of driving, or riding in, an automobile. We may deplore the use of cars as a means of self-realization and of public highways as roads to ecstasy, but only driver-training instructors would deny that this is what cars are all about. And, by extension, the Rocket Ship. The twenties and thirties, when driving was still a relative novelty, were also the heyday of the archetypal—and, in their way, insurpassable—power fantasies of E. E. Smith and other, lesser bards of the Model T. Among adolescents and in countries such as Italy, where car ownership confers the same ego satisfaction as surviving a rite of passage, the Rocket Ship remains the most venerated of sf icons—and not because it embodies a future possibility but because it interprets a common experience.

The second task of sf writers as mythmakers is simply the custodial work of keeping the inherited body of myths alive. Every myth is the creation, originally, of a poet, and it remains a vital presence in our culture only so long as it speaks to us with the living breath of living art; so long, that is, as it continues to be twice-told. Everyone pitches in—from Mesopotamian parents recounting the story of Gilgamesh to scholars translating that story into modern languages. Even Homer, probably, felt the anxiety of influence; by Ovid's time all stories were old stories. The names might be changed, the scenery altered, but the basic patterns were as fixed and finite as shoemakers' lasts. This is why Kipling can maintain that "there are nine and sixty ways of constructing tribal lays, and—every—single—one—of—them—is—right!"

Science fiction writers do not have a unique responsibility toward preserving the body of inherited myth. It is a task that we share with poets, painters, playwrights, choreographers, composers, and commentators of every description. I offer the following catalogue not so much as an Extra-Credit Reading List (though they will all get you points) but to suggest the variety, range, and universality of the undertaking. Among works that conscientiously retell discrete myths from beginning to end are T. H. White's *The Once and Future King*, Joyce's *Ulysses*, Richard Adams's *Watership Down*, Cynthia Ozick's *The Pagan Rabbi*, Mary Renault's *The King Must Die*, Mann's *Joseph and His Brothers*; any number of plays by Yeats, Eliot, O'Neill, Gide, Giraudoux, Anouilh, and Sartre; operas by Bartók, Schoenberg, Strauss, and Stravinsky. Additionally, there are writers who, instead of retelling one specific tale, retrace the underlying structures of mythology as these have been systematized by scholars like the Grimm brothers; Frazer, Graves, and Joseph Campbell. Notable among such "synthetic legends" have been Goethe's "Märchen" (perhaps the first artificial folktale), Koch's *Ko*, Barth's *Giles Goat-Boy*, Hoffmannstahl's libretto for *Die Frau ohne Schatten*, and Naomi Mitchison's *The Corn King and the Spring Queen*.

Only in the last ten or fifteen years have science fiction writers shown much interest in the preservative as against the interpretive side of myth-making. The most obvious reason is that writers for the early pulps were not notable for literary sophistication. Van Vogt's stories, at their best, have some of the charm of fairy tales, but I doubt that this was ever his aim. Similarly, the standard space opera often follows a pattern strikingly similar to that which Joseph Campbell describes in *The Hero with a Thousand Faces*, but again I would submit that the likeness was inadvertent. (Though not, of course, accidental: archetypes are hard to avoid once you've set out to tell a story.) The writers of the fifties, such as Blish, Knight, or Bester, though themselves men of undoubted literary culture, were obliged to write for a naive audience for whom almost any story was mind-blowing. The shades of irony or degrees of finesse that may distinguish one revision of a familiar story from the next are lost on readers for whom just the idea sets their sense of wonder to tingling.

What changed in the early sixties wasn't the nature of sf writers but of their audience. Simply, it had grown up. Not all readers, of course. There were still, there are still, and there will always be those for whom sf represents their first trip into the realms of gold. But now side by side with these are readers who can be counted on to know more about the life of the mind than can be discovered in the works of Edgar Rice Burroughs and Charles Fort; who have the knack of reading books in pretty much the spirit they were written.

The point, for instance, of Michael Moorcock's *Behold the Man* isn't that, gee whiz, a Time Traveler questing for the historical Jesus is involved in a case of mistaken identities. The point isn't What Happens Next because the reader is assumed to be able to foresee that. The point is, rather, how seamlessly the modern (ironic) version of the myth can be made to overlay the gospel (and so, inevitable) version. To a large degree, therefore, the point is the author's wit, his grace, and his depth. In a word, style.

Style not in the niggling sense of being able on demand to use the subjunctive and to come up with metaphors, similes, and stuff like that. Style, rather, in the exclamatory Astaire-and-Rogers sense of (in the words of Webster) "overall excellence, skill, or grace in performance, manner, or appearance."

Big Ideas and Dead-End Thrills: The Further Embarrassments of Science Fiction

In his lecture "From Poe to Valéry," T. S. Eliot characterized science fiction's most venerable American ancestor in a manner that describes the genre quite as aptly as the author:

> That Poe had a powerful intellect is undeniable: but it seems to me the intellect of a highly gifted young person before puberty. The forms which his lively curiosity takes are those in which a pre-adolescent mentality delights: wonders of nature and of mechanics and of the supernatural, cryptograms and cyphers, puzzles and labyrinths, mechanical chess-players and wild flights of speculation. The variety and ardour of his curiosity delight and dazzle; yet in the end the eccentricity and lack of coherence of his interests tire.

Eliot could have continued, even more damningly, in the same vein by noting the respects in which Poe's representations of sexuality are typical of those adolescent rakes and roués whose information on the subject derives from the library and a theoretical fascination rather than from experience or actual desire. The Poe who, in his early twenties, wrote "Berenice," wherein the soulful, aristocratic Egaeus develops a passion for the teeth of his affianced cousin Berenice, is a kind of adult impersonator, a teenager grossing out the grown-ups by reducing their lusts to an absurdity.

"The teeth!" Egaeus famously raves, "—the teeth!—they were here, and there, and everywhere, and visibly and palpably before me; long, narrow, and excessively white, with the pale lips writhing about them. . . . In the multiplied objects of the external world I had no thoughts but for the teeth. For these I longed with a frenzied desire." In the tale's denouement, with wonderful celerity, Berenice dies in an epileptic fit; she is buried, and a menial whispers to Egaeus "of a violated grave—of a disfigured body enshrouded, yet still breathing—still palpitating—*still alive!*"

I cannot resist quoting Egaeus/Poe's last breathless paragraph in full:

He [the menial] pointed to my garments: they were muddy and clotted with gore. I spoke not, and he took me gently by the hand: it was indented with the impress of human nails. He directed my attention to some object against the wall. I looked at it for some minutes: it was a spade. With a shriek I bounded to the table, and grasped the box that lay upon it. But I could not force it open; and, in my tremor, it slipped from my hands, and fell heavily, and burst into pieces; and from it, with a rattling sound, there rolled out some instruments of dental surgery, intermingled with thirty-two small, white and ivory-looking substances that were scattered to and fro about the floor.

In 1975 I gave a talk on the theme "The Embarrassments of Science Fiction," in which I developed a notion I had first advanced in 1970, in the bulletin of the Science Fiction Writers of America: that science fiction should be accounted, as best can be understood, as a branch of children's literature. I noted how often a taste for sf is acquired in early adolescence—the golden age of science fiction, our tribal wisdom has it, is thirteen. I pointed to the number of classic stories about children of preternatural wisdom and power. And I deplored, at some length, the limitations that result from the genre's readership demographics. Implicit in my critique was an agenda for an aesthetically and intellectually mature science fiction, written by grown-ups for grown-up tastes; the sort of science fiction I supposed that I and some few of my friends were writing at that time—the writers, as we advertised ourselves, of the New Wave.

Well, the New Wave is ancient history now, most of what we wrote out of print and all of it out of date—for there is nothing so ephemeral as yesterday's thoughtful predictions, whether in the op-ed page or in sf magazines. The predictive imagination is driven by archetypes; it demands Big Bangs, stunning upsets, Vistavision. History arrives incrementally and often by the side door. Consider how, in the twenty-three years since 2001, the space program has dwindled away to insignificance, a victim of public apathy, bureaucratic gigantism, and systemic corruption. Consider in that same film the anthropomorphic HAL, a melodrama villain disguised as a computer; consider all sf's failures to imagine the cybernetic age, despite the easy-to-follow instructions of Alvin Toffler and like pundits, until we were actually living in it. Consider such dreaded transformations as those that are threatened by the greenhouse effect or the destruction of the ozone layer or AIDS. Consider the new geopolitical imbalance of power. Consider all these things, and then ask what sf has had to say about them.

Almost not a word. Yet science fiction has never been more popular than in these past fifteen years. Beginning with *Star Wars*, in 1977, sf movies have been a major component of the Hollywood product—no longer grade-B entries for the drive-in crowd but big-bucks extravaganzas, which, often enough, have been remakes of earlier, drive-in movies such as *The Fly* and *Invasion of the Body Snatchers*. At the same time, sf titles have begun to appear regularly on bestseller lists, to the degree that in recent months a quarter to a third of best-selling fiction titles on both hard- and soft-cover lists have been sf or else of the kindred genres of horror and heroic fantasy.

Nearly without exception, the genre works that have enjoyed such popularity have been of the type that I characterized in "The Embarrassments of Science Fiction" as children's literature. For while I had faint-heartedly bemoaned the genre's juvenility, more farsighted souls—editors, notably Ballantine's Judy-Lynn del Rey—had taken the same estimate of the situation and seen an enormous untapped market. Del Rey and those who followed in her footsteps discovered and groomed writers like Stephen Donaldson, Terry Brooks, and Piers Anthony, who could scale down Tolkien or Asimov from the seventh- or eighth-grade reading levels of the overeducated fifties and create tetralogies suitable to the diminished reading skills of today's children.

Other publishers pioneered the sf equivalent of franchise merchandising, issuing series like the ongoing *Star Trek* paperbacks, a practice that minimizes the risks, costs, and unpleasantness of having to deal with "name" writers. (Editors know better than anyone that authors at this level of production are not irreplaceable. Indeed, for a hack writer it is a liability to have too identifiable a voice.) Finally, as part of a recent innovation, the most marketable of the older name writers, Asimov and Clarke, have been persuaded to become generic labels, by expanding classic short stories or undertaking "sequels" to the work they wrote before this high-rolling era. The actual work is subcontracted to "co-authors," including such onetime aspirants to menu-A status as Robert Silverberg and Gregory Benford (both of whom have undertaken collaborations with writers of still lesser clout).

These market forces have had a predictable effect on writers, who have had to adapt or die. Few veterans have succeeded at adapting. Silverberg wrote a gargantuan heroic fantasy, *Lord Valentine's Castle*, by way of atoning for the elitist sins of his New Wave days, but it was not quite enough; somehow his audience could hear a Galilean murmur, beneath his formal recantation, of "e pur se muove." With his *Book of the New Sun* tetralogy, Gene Wolfe succeeded at the seemingly impossible task of making literature of the mongrel subgenre of science fantasy, but the work's very excellences told against it in the current sf market. Brian Aldiss experienced a similarly disillusioning *succès d'estime* with his "Helliconia" trilogy.

Conventional publishing wisdom has it that the midlist title is doomed to extinction at most trade publishers, and with it that middle rank of novelists who scrape along by selling fifteen thousand to twenty thousand hardcover copies. Publishing houses, under the dominion of their accountants, no more have a compelling incentive to subsidize the middle rank's scraping along than General Motors has to sustain the existence of Flint, Michigan.

Just as the wiser residents of that city abandoned their homes before they were evicted from them, so a goodly number of the more sensible and prescient science fiction writers have departed the field for other genres or for the traditional haven of the literary writer, academia. Samuel Delany now heads the department of comparative literature at the University of Massachusetts at Amherst and devotes most of his writing energies to criticism and other forms of nonfiction. J. G. Ballard made his entry into the big time with a memoir of his adolescence as a POW in China, *Empire of the Sun*, a work that became a Steven Spielberg epic. John Sladek, whose novels about robots were so long without a U.S. publisher, has become an executive in a firm that designs real robots.

Hollywood and television have proved more eager to assimilate sf ideas into film and video than the writers originating those ideas. It may well be that a different degree of professionalism is required, or (if this is not a tautology) of cynicism. Would Philip K. Dick's two posthumous hits, *Blade Runner* and *Total Recall*, have succeeded at the box office if they had not been dumbed down by show-biz pros? At least in Dick's case, as in that of Arthur Clarke, some credit is given to the original. The great majority of the sf movies that have been hits in recent years—the *Star Wars* series, *E.T.*, *Alien* and *Aliens*, *Back to the Future* parts 1, 2, and 3, and so forth—have been written by director-writer-producer teams who have dealt with sf as a pool of imagery, tropes, and plots in the public domain, which can be cobbled together as well by one creative team as by another. The success of these movies, and dozens of others, has proved them right, and the unhappy consequence for sf writers is that success within the genre is seldom a stepping-stone to any larger success generated by adaptation to film. The significant exceptions in the past decade have been writers of horror fiction, since in that field there is not that disjunction, characteristic of sf, between what readers will read and what audiences will buy tickets to see.

Market forces, though they are powerful, don't explain everything. Sf writers of diverse generations have maintained a steady creative pace throughout their careers with no thought of the main chance or ordinary prudence. Increasingly, as he grew older, Robert Heinlein wrote books that defied the conventions of pulp fiction (and almost every other kind), and they became bestsellers. Dick followed his instincts just as single-mindedly though he was legendarily ill fated and undervalued (admittedly, much of the legend was created by the author, who was an ace self-mythologizer). Frederik Pohl has been producing novels with clockwork diligence for half a century, and enjoying a modest prosperity without ever producing a "crossover" novel. But such continuous, career-long productivity is unusual.

More often there is a gradual tapering-off or a complete cessation, as with Theodore Sturgeon, Ray Bradbury, Judith Merrill, Walter Miller Jr., Alfred Bester, John Wyndham, Algis Budrys, Damon Knight, James Blish, Robert Sheckley, Joanna Russ, and Harlan Ellison (to mention only those considered of the first rank). Diverse as their gifts were, graphs of their creative-energy expenditure would have roughly the same shape, and in few instances, to my knowledge, can these writers offer extrinsic reasons for their diminished production (extrinsic, that is, to the life of the imagination). A happy few continued to produce memorable work, though at a slower rate; others ground out ever more dismal hackwork; a few retired from the field at the height of their powers, sometimes mumbling of a magnum opus in the desk drawer.

Doubtless all the arts have a high attrition rate. If one were to divide all the art in the world, in whatever medium, into that created by those under thirty-five and that by those over thirty-five, the former, I would wager, would be the richer lode. Advance the dividing line to age forty (which is the Yale Younger Poets criterion), and there is little doubt. Work produced before age forty includes everything by Byron, Shelley, Keats, most of Shakespeare, the best of Wordsworth; all of Raphael, Van Gogh, Mozart, Bellini. Even where death or mid-life burnout did not close accounts, even where the highest talents continued in spate into old age, the *defining* work was usually done by age forty, especially in those arts where innovation is at a premium. Cubism, Impressionism, Jugendstil, the modernist movement in poetry—these were all creations of people in their twenties and early thirties.

The same has been true of science fiction. Indeed, the New Wave of the sixties represents the first generational opposition in science fiction. I remember how at a 1969 sf convention I spoke dismissively of the "dinosaurs" then impeding the proper appreciation of young mammals like myself. Twenty-three years later all but a couple of the dinosaurs I had in mind remain the commanding presences in the field, at least from a marketing perspective, and some of my fellow mammals now look more and more like dinosaurs themselves, even those who have not retired to the pastures of the backlist.

Like the elder dinosaurs—Clarke, Asimov, Bradbury—these newly old writers tend to recycle the same imaginative raw material. Ballard is Ballard still, and even in the act of renouncing her earlier fiction Ursula LeGuin perpetuates it. In terms of an individual artist's career track such continuity may be inescapable and even advantageous. But it has been the tacit mandate of science fiction that its writers should create a kind of consensual future, a map of both what we've agreed to wish for and what we collectively dread. The vision of the Asimov-Heinlein generation was the cheery Buck Rogers universe of space travel and infinite economic expansion, an imaginative landscape that mirrored the socioeconomic ideals of America from 1948 through 1962.

The next consensual future, that of the New Wave, sprayed graffiti on the edifices it inherited. Norman Spinrad, in *The Iron Dream*, re-imagined Heinlein's oeuvre through the eyes of Adolf Hitler. Fear of the bomb and distrust of the System were the order of the day. At the essential task of creating a period vision or style—defining images like the rocket ship, the robot, the Gotham City of art deco skyscrapers—the New Wave scored near zero. The magazine *New Worlds* under Michael Moorcock promoted a brand of pop art that montaged Carnaby Street with affirmations of existing pop icons like highway signs and consumer packaging, but pop art celebrated images that were already retro in their day; the "future" in the sixties existed only in quotation marks, as a form of camp and an abandoned faith. This antiquarian quality of the "future" was epitomized by the cover of the 1979 *Science Fiction Encyclopedia*, on which, beneath a giant cantaloupe that, at second glance, may be the moon, an ocean liner is washed up against a tumbling Empire State Building. For the New Wave writer of the sixties, the characteristic future landscape was the ruins of what the thirties and forties had dreamed of.

The next generation in sf is that of the Cyberpunks, whose works are still in progress and so not yet within hindsight's advantaged purview. One thing that can already be said of the Cyberpunks, however, is that they have created a distinctive consensual future with a look all its own, a look consciously adapted from Hollywood set designs, notably those for *Blade Runner*, and from computer graphics. It is a funky look that might be seen as an affirmation of the graffiti the New Wave writers scrawled on the city of the future they inherited, as though to say, "Well, yes, the future is a mess, and a lot of it is in terrible repair, and the rest is mostly an electronic illusion, but you might as well enjoy it while it lasts."

That sense that the future may not last for long is often assumed to be a prerogative of youth, the dialectical complement of another misconception the young are noted for—the conviction that they are immortal. The punk component of the Cyberpunk aesthetic celebrates the fecklessness of youth and its preferred risks: drugs, sex, and macho aggression. But how could it do otherwise in our culture? I think it is more significant that today's older generations share the Cyberpunk vision of a disposable future of diminishing options, to which the logical response is hedonism and the idea that problems can be solved by denying that they exist. Is there a hole in the ozone layer? Does the federal deficit relate to anything real? Just say no.

My sense of the moral dimensions of Cyberpunk was confirmed by an op-ed piece by Lewis Shiner, himself a sometime Cyberpunk, in the *New York Times* of January 7, 1991. In the course of turning in his official resignation from the movement, Shiner delivered this summing-up: Cyberpunk "offers power fantasies, the same dead-end thrills we get from video games and blockbuster movies like *Rambo* and *Aliens*. It gives Nature up for dead, accepts violence and greed as inevitable and promotes the cult of the loner." Shiner began that piece with a simple but telling observation: "I'm 39 years old."

Of course, it is not inevitable that one's aesthetic becomes tender as one's arteries harden. William Burroughs, a patron saint of punk in all its varieties, cyber included, is an author whose prophetic vision has altered scarcely a whit since *Naked Lunch*, of 1959 (when Burroughs had reached the astonishing age, for someone in his actuarial class, of forty-five). He's still going, each new novel as dependably like the last as those of Terry Brooks and Anne McCaffrey, and he has been the most popular bad boy of his era, the discovery of each countercultural generation since the Beats, never more popular than among the Cyberpunks. The secret of Burroughs's appeal is that he is consummately yucky, a living gross-out than whom there is none grosser. His novels wearily recapitulate the same doubtless sincere masturbatory images of young men achieving orgasm at the moment of strangulation while old creeps, dazed with opium, look on. There is also a lot of playful surgery that calls to mind those dental instruments that rolled out of Egaeus's little box. And by way of avant-garde authentication, a portion of Burroughs's oeuvre is given over to verbal montage produced by intercutting existing texts in a random fashion, a method of composition that anyone can emulate (but that no one except the terminally stoned will be likely to read in any quantity). Finally, there is the testimony of the man: a long-term heroin addict, a pederast of sepulchral uncomeliness, a wife-killer, and an unfailing source of trendy paranoid delusions. Surely the man was not of woman born but rather formed from ashes and cerements plundered from the tomb of Edgar Allan Poe.

I exaggerate, but only with regard to the matter of his birth, for Burroughs was, like many of Poe's heroes, a scion of wealth; indeed, the family business has evolved into Unisys, a multinational defense contractor of the kind that rules the Cyberpunk universe. Perhaps there is a hidden blessing in the fact that Burroughs's vocation was for heroin and literature rather than the family business: he might have been just as successful in putting his vision to work for Unisys.

Youth, Too Often Callow

Between them, Poe and Burroughs represent a paradigm of what is most gauche, most deeply and painfully embarrassing, in science fiction, including that of the New Wave. I speak here of youth, not childhood— for childhood, from an adult vantage, is not an embarrassment, and that part of science fiction that recommends itself to the tastes of pre-teens is charming or, at least, harmless. Once such a taste has been acquired, it may be exercised long afterward, as teddy bears may live long secret lives hiding in closets or behind pillows. I came to understand this recently when a student in a writing class passionately protested his readerly loyalty to one of my *bêtes noires*, Piers Anthony. A sophomore, intelligent and socially couth, he could not find any *principle* on which to base his liking. The author's sense of humor was the student's last bulwark, but there was no single joke or whimsy in the text which he could point to as being actually amusing. I realize now that we were fighting over a teddy bear, which he, quite rightly, refused to surrender or renounce, though he could offer no rationale for his loyalty. What can one say in such cases but "He's my teddy, and I love him!" Piers Anthony's work accomplishes its purpose exactly to the degree that an adult taste *can't* tolerate it: his silly puns and patchwork plots stand like toy soldiers forbidding all grownups entry into his never-never land.

In youth the most awkward age—the one that gives us the most to blush for—is the one we have just quitted. College students have a horror of being mistaken for high-schoolers; those in their mid-twenties wince at the gaucheries of college years. Thereafter, embarrassment is not so much a matter of maturity as of social class. Those who write embarrassingly may do so in ignorance of, or despite, generally understood rules of decorum. Usually naivete combines with rashness, as when suburban teenagers write sad tales of the deaths of inner-city hookers, or Bret Easton Ellis imagines what it would be like to be an amoral and well-dressed sex maniac. The new candor that came to science fiction in the seventies (and to the culture at large, for the New Wave was only part of a larger confluence of forces), the liberty to speak of sexual matters in barracks language, has yielded a richness of embarrassments, from Heinlein's first-person pronouncements on female sexual fulfillment to Ballard's solemn but equally hypothetical pontifications in the New Wave mini-classic *The Summer Cannibals*. I quote a typical unit of his prose:

A Krafft-Ebing of Geometry and Posture. He remembered these pleasures: the conjunction of her exposed pubis with the polished contours of the bidet; the white cube of the bathroom quantifying her left breast as she bent over the handbasin; the mysterious eroticism of the multistorey car park, a Krafft-Ebing of geometry and posture; her flattened thighs on the tiles of the swimming pool below; her right hand osculating the finger-smeared panel of the elevator control. Looking at her from the bed, he re-created these situations, conceptualizations of exquisite games.

That passage does elicit some of science fiction's traditional sense of wonder, but after the fashion of one white teenager solemnly misinforming another about the sexual peculiarities of Asian women. Take two mental steps back from "a Krafft-Ebing of geometry and posture," and the author's portentousness just looks silly and self-important, a failed effort to pump significance and glamour into vacation snapshots of the Spanish coast near Alicante, where, Ballard later wrote in a footnote to *The Summer Cannibals*:

I once pushed my tank-like Armstrong-Siddeley to 100 mph on the beach road, and where my wife died in 1964. The curious atmosphere of the Mediterranean beach resorts still awaits its chronicler. . . . It has a unique ambience—nothing, in my brief experience, like Venice, California, or Malibu. At present it is Europe's Florida, an endless parade of hotels, marinas and apartment houses, haunted by criminals running hash from North Africa, stealing antiquities or on the lam from Scotland Yard.

There is nothing wrong with helping the tourist industry glamorize its wares. Writers of all sorts and every degree of sophistication are constantly about such business. What gives Ballard's testimony its ring of callow youth is the arrogance of his assumption that he is the first person ever to see his favorite stretch of beach the way it really is—that *he* is the chronicler Alicante has been waiting for.

Self-importance is commonly the armor of the insecure. Poe wrote "Berenice" in the meanest of circumstances, unemployed, living in the garret where his brother had died, supported by the charity of an indigent aunt who went round to relatives to beg for groceries. And this is how his narrator describes *his* circumstances:

> My baptismal name is Egaeus; that of my family I will not mention. Yet there are no towers in the land more rime-honored than my gloomy, gray, hereditary halls. Our line has been called a race of visionaries; and in many striking particulars—in the character of the family mansion—in the frescos of the chief saloon—in the tapestries of the dormitories—in the chiselling of some buttresses in the armory—but more especially in the gallery of antique paintings—in the fashion of the library chamber—and, lastly, in the very peculiar nature of the library's contents—there is more than sufficient evidence to warrant the belief.

Again, the impulse to compensate for the indignities of poverty by fantasizing about the lifestyles of the rich and famous is a universal trait. What is characteristically youthful in Poe's performance is his ingenuous confidence that he's taking us in.

I feel a particularly keen twinge of embarrassment for Poe at such moments because I can read in all too many passages of my own work exactly the same threadbare pretensions. Recently I learned that an Italian publisher intends to reprint "5 Eggs," a story I wrote at age twenty-three, when I was living in decidedly mean circumstances. The story is a string of embarrassments large and small, but I think this paragraph best captures its tone:

> Standing in the dining room where appetizers, salads, and sauces were spread on the great mahogany table amid the plunder of his mother's cupboard—the gilt-edged china, the heavy silver, the crystal—he stared out the French windows at the bleak, moonlit autumn hills that lay beyond his watered lawn.

And there is this picture of high society a page later:

Mrs. Shreve with her husband was the next to arrive. Shreve was his publisher. Mrs. Shreve received the news of [his fiancée's] desertion politely, as she might have received the news of a friend's bankruptcy, with an invitation to dinner, with the understanding that as long as the friend's evening clothes and composure were intact the invitation stood. Mrs. Shreve had brought along galleys of his latest book, and they talked business and drank.

Nothing in my own prose can match the glory of "the chiselling of some buttresses in the armory," but clearly the same compensatory mechanism is at work. Perhaps it is no accident that the plot of my tale, like Poe's, features a tragic romance of a sort that only young men of pristine inexperience and perfected amour propre have ever imagined. And who should their readership be but other such young men, for whom the authors' inauthenticities are more solacing than a lifetime subscription to *Connoisseur*, from which they would learn only the true dimensions of their exclusion from the frescoed saloons and tapestried dormitories of the rich.

The final and most excruciating callowness of youth is what sf readers particularly prize: Big Ideas. Now, there are some ideas that genuinely are big, which is to say, full of implication and repercussion. Copernicus's remodeled universe is such an idea. But an idea need not even be valid to be big: Spengler's *Decline of the West* is as big as all history, and its central thesis is pure twaddle. But when I was twenty-five, I revered Spengler, and I was willing to accept any amount of twaddle on faith for the sake of his system, the wonderfully lucid pattern that provided a pigeonhole for every datum of history.

There is nothing that so militates against the sense of one's own vast ignorance as adopting some such Big Idea, and the young, whose ignorance is largest and rawest and most exasperating, have a natural predilection for Big Ideas. Marxists, Ayn Randers, Scientologists, and deconstructionists have one thing in common: they tend to have been recruited young. Once in the fold, they may remain there indefinitely and turn into fossils, but twigs are bent in the teens and twenties.

To a certain degree sf provides a natural playground for the harmless exercise of Big Ideas, even those that are radically unsound. Utopias that could never be implemented in the real world are fun to explore in simulation. Witness the utopian sf novels by writers of such diverse temperaments as LeGuin, Suzy McKee Charnas, Heinlein, Larry Niven, and Jerry Pournelle. The Gaia hypothesis is also a natural for science-fictionalization. Indeed, sf anticipated it, in many stories, including Richard

McKenna's 1963 work "Hunter, Come Home." However, not all writers approach Big Ideas in a spirit of intellectual playfulness. Some come to believe in their privileged wisdom and become intolerant of contradiction, and this can happen at various levels of sophistication. The most gullible can simply report to the local Scientology recruiting office. Others dope their sf hobbyhorses with an ideological fix. Ursula LeGuin promotes a return to the wisdom of a Native American never-never land. Michael Moorcock has become an advocate of Andrea Dworkin. The tendency is always to venture toward the current ideological limit as an inherently more dramatic situation, which is also, however, inherently silly.

Ideological silliness is an affliction more tolerable in the young, and, for reasons I've tried to lay out, exactly the same may be said of a taste for science fiction. This is not meant to be my way of abjuring the field or declaring that I am not now nor have I ever been a science fiction writer. I have been and I continue to be. I will even go on reading and reviewing the stuff, as long as some small portion of what is published continues to suit my taste. But I won't act as a booster for the genre as a whole, which has become, as a publishing phenomenon, one of the major symptoms of, if not a causal agent in, the dumbing-down of the younger generation and the lowering of the lowest common denominator.

PART TWO ON SF Forefathers

Poe's Appalling Life

Poor Poe. No other American writer of equivalent fame led such a consistently miserable life as he. Abandoned by his father in infancy; orphaned at age three and entrusted to the care of a rich Richmond merchant, John Allan, whose love and/or money was ever in short supply; renounced by Allan and cut out of his will; perpetually impoverished and obliged often to sell his best work for a pittance; saddled with a wife and mother-in-law as poor as he (who were, as well, his first cousin and aunt) in a marriage that was probably unconsummated; an alcoholic with a penchant for disgracing himself at those rare intervals when a glimmer of sunlight appeared through the clouds of his consistently wretched life; thwarted in virtually all his ambitions. There can have been little happiness for Poe except such times as he was in the embrace of his Muse, and she was fickle, frowsy, and not always *compos mentis*. Little wonder that the last year of his life seems a headlong, hell-bent rush to suicide.

Poor Poe, but poor Kenneth Silverman, too. For to explore Poe's life and lack of character as extensively as a biographer must is to invite certain disenchantment with both the man and his work. Poverty rarely ennobles. Stifled ambition breeds envy and vindictiveness. Practiced liars are liable to become self-deceivers. To these rules Poe was no exception. Even when he was good (i.e., writing well) he was rather pathetic; but when he was bad he almost out-Heroded the libels written about him by his first biographer, mortal enemy, and (by his own request) literary executor, Rufus Griswold, who printed his calumnies as an appendix to the first full-scale edition of Poe's works, thereby securing for Poe the eminence he has enjoyed ever since as Americans' premier *poète maudit*—a wastrel, drunkard, opium addict, and all-round demoniac. Poe was undoubtedly indulging his own Imp of the Perverse in putting Griswold in charge of his posthumous reputation, but he was also exercising his usual instinct for self-promotion. Subsequent biographers have exposed Griswold's lies and forgeries, but none have been able to make Poe look quite human. He remains the object of our baleful fascination, a semi-

---

Review of *Edgar A. Poe: Mournful and Never-Ending Remembrance*, by Kenneth Silverman.

charlatan whose florid poems and lurid tales we can't keep from reading, re-reading, and remembering.

Silverman's is in every respect, including its relative brevity, the best biography of Poe yet written, a position held heretofore by Hervey Allen's *Israfel* of 1934. Allen is much more inclined than Silverman to take Poe at his word, to extenuate his faults, and simply to like him. He is also inclined to gush, and his critical perceptions rarely exceed forty watts. A representative judgment by Allen: "Poe's own mysticism was purely personal, and the subliminal landscapes which he created . . . were the refuges and spiritual lands of his own darkened soul. It was for this reason that his poetry was more original than that of any other American poet of the age." Silverman casts a much colder eye. He is willing to dismiss most of Poe's criticism as bombast and pedantry, his hatchet-jobs inspired by envy and his raves by sycophancy. He would accuse other writers—especially his nemesis, Longfellow—of plagiarisms visible to no eye but his own, while he was an unconscionable plagiarist himself. Silverman quotes a letter in which Poe praises himself for "an inveterate habit of speaking the truth," and comments, "Actually he had fallen into a routine of easy lies and half truths since at least his adolescence."

Nothing in Poe's life so disgraced him as the leaving of it, and the last quarter of Silverman's book is devoted to the period from the summer of 1848 to his death in October of 1849. His child-bride, Virginia, had died of tuberculosis the year before, and Poe, his creative energies seemingly exhausted, turned fortune hunter, wooing several prospective brides simultaneously. The extensive correspondence that has survived shows Poe at his most oleaginous. To a wealthy widow in Providence he wrote, after their first meeting:

> I saw that you were Helen—my Helen—the Helen of a thousand dreams—she whose visionary lips had so often lingered upon my own in the divine trance of passion—she whom the great Giver of all Goods had preordained to be mine—mine only.

This is excerpted from a letter twelve pages long.

When his drunkenness caused his first engagement to be broken off, he returned to his hometown of Richmond, where he had a second widow in reserve. Evidently he had a way with the ladies. Indeed, in drawing room mode, Poe could come across as the beau ideal of gothic romances then and now—a dark, brooding, Byronic figure doomed to wander the earth in torment until he found the Helen of his dreams. His problem was rather in moving from the drawing room to the nuptial chamber, for his horror of conjugal relations and (gasp) physical intimacy was so great that when there seemed no way to escape marriage to his second betrothed he absconded to Baltimore and drank himself to death.

Silverman's most considerable achievement is that despite the man's manifold faults he manages to paint a sympathetic portrait. His Poe is more sinned against than sinning, a victim of an age when only those with private incomes could aspire to careers in the arts. Few American writers (excepting those born into slavery) have accomplished their work in circumstances of such desperate poverty. As to his duplicities, they can be seen as complementary to the trickster side of his character and his art, the first of a long American tradition of scapegrace artists that continues in our time with writers like Henry Miller, Raymond Carver, and Charles Bukowski.

Finally, of course, it is the work, and not the life, that makes us bother with the man at all, and if Silverman's biography has a single flaw it is in the perfunctory nature of his examination of the major tales. For a just critical estimate of Poe's work, for an explanation of why he actually matters, the best book is still Daniel Hoffman's study of 1972, *Poe Poe Poe Poe Poe Poe Poe*. But so little is known of Poe's circumstances in the years when he was accomplishing his best work that a biographer cannot hope to offer much direct critical illumination in any case.

All in all, an appalling life and one that I imagine Mr. Silverman must be happy to have departed.

Luncheon in the Sepulcher: Poe in the Gothic Tradition

"There is no exquisite beauty," says Bacon, Lord Verulan, speaking truly of all the forms and *genera* of beauty, "without some *strangeness* in the proportion."

It is easy enough to assent to this proposition, which comes upon us at the beginning of Poe's "Ligeia." The exquisite beauty of that tale certainly has more than a little strangeness in the proportion, as do the stories collected in this volume. So, if your preference is all for the practice of storytelling, and if its theory has no lure for you, let us make an amicable parting here. You have my assurance that your taste for strangeness will be gratified abundantly, diversely, and perhaps, in one or two instances, to excess. What can an introduction do, finally, but offer that assurance?

Now, for the rest of us left in the study, a rhetorical question: Is it true, as Poe insists, that *all* the forms and *genera* of beauty are endowed with Strangeness? Is it not rather the specific virtue of classic art that it smooths away all traces of the "grotesque and arabesque" to reveal some irreducible wholeness, to offer us the no less exquisite (if not always so immediately arresting) beauty of the Ideal? I don't mean only the classic art of Homer and Praxiteles or of Raphael and Palladio. In this normative sense, the cool architecture of a Cubist still life, or a movie such as *The African Queen*, in which admirable people perform noble deeds in Hollywood's most stately style, can be said to be classical.

With Poe, the Ideal is experienced as oppressive (as in "The Domain of Arnheim"), the normative as ridiculous ("The Devil in the Belfry"). Indeed, without too great of a distortion to his aesthetic, one could reverse Bacon's formula and say that there is, in Poe, no strangeness without some beauty of proportion; no horror that lacks an underlying loveliness.

Bear with me, readers. There is a reason why, though there is not a single story by Poe in this volume, he is the subject of this introduction. It is not so straightforward a reason as cause-and-effect: I don't think all the writers represented here are in a direct line of descent from Poe (though I'd be surprised if there were any who were not on familiar terms with his

Introduction to *Strangeness: A Collection of Curious Tales*, edited by Thomas M. Disch and Charles Naylor.

best work). In fact, such fantasists as Bierce, Lovecraft, and Bradbury, who are too visibly his inheritors, have been deliberately excluded from the contents page. Likewise, there are no stories by writers of the "Southern Gothic" school, since their kinship with Poe is at least of the degree of cousinship. And again, on the grounds that few readers need to be pointed the way to such golden oldies, none of the celebrated progeny of C. Auguste Dupin, Poe's primordial detective, will be met with here. These have been the acknowledged heirs. I believe that Poe's real accomplishment and influence have been greater than this list of legatees would suggest.

His significance is a touchstone, as the first perfected form of a distinctively modern kind of sensibility. This is not the Poe known to his own countrymen, but the Poe celebrated by Baudelaire: Poe considered as a contemporary of Kierkegaard. Americans have always had difficulty viewing Poe in this light, for we are likely to encounter him first at too tender an age and to continue to think of him, in our later years, as a writer for children. That used to be my own case, certainly. I loved to terrify my younger brothers, and myself, reading aloud "The Tell-Tale Heart" by the light of a flashlight. My brothers have since assured me that these were vivid renderings, and I know they were sincere, so it can't be said that I was entirely missing the point—or that Americans do, in general. And part of the point (which Baudelaire misses, as surely as we miss his) is that Poe is as much a charlatan and barnstormer as he is a mystic and modernist. Since an adequate account of his entire artistry is beyond the scope of anything less than a book, and since that book already exists, I will limit myself to recommending it (*Poe Poe Poe Poe Poe Poe Poe*, by Daniel Hoffman) and continue trying to make my single, if elusive, point about him—which is that his work embodies everything in the gothic tradition that can command serious, adult attention; and further, that this tradition is much broader than has usually been reckoned.

Before setting forth a general theory of either Poe or the gothic sensibility, I'd like to consider some of the specific ingredients to be found in his stories. Not the obsessive themes, such as incest or inhumation, for these, besides having received ample attention elsewhere, are idiosyncratic and limiting; nor yet the ornamental, fustian style, of which the same can be said. I mean such specifics as the landscapes he evokes, which are at once so nebulous and so minutely observed, or the peculiar humor of his "grotesque" tales, or the maniacal voices of so many of his narrators. The voice, for instance, of the murderous lunatic who tells "The Tell-Tale Heart": "Now this is the point. You fancy me mad. Madmen know nothing. But you should have seen *me*." This is at once a dry burlesque of the high paranoid style and a lyric to delight the soul of R. D. Laing. For, of course, besides being absurd, it is true: madmen do possess a knowledge that is denied to others. As the same narrator observes: "the disease had sharpened my senses—not destroyed—not dulled them. Above all was the sense of hearing acute. I heard all things in the Heaven and in the earth. I heard many things in hell. How then am I mad?"

Since those words were written the possibility that madness may be— at least for fictional purposes—a higher form of wisdom has become a staple of generations of writers, some of whom one would not readily class with Poe. The stories of Joyce Carol Oates and Virginia Woolf are both prime examples of this vein of psychological horror, or Naturalized Gothic. Oates's affinities with the gothic have occasionally been noted, but . . . Virginia Woolf? Yet her tale "Solid Objects" cannot be considered a fluke, for the same theme of madness as a form of visionary experience is even more intensely rendered in what I believe to be her most representative novel, *Mrs. Dalloway*. Other stories in the present anthology inhabit this same intriguing, prenumbral zone between dementia and poetry, but to say which ones would be to spoil the unfolding of more than one ingenious plot. Another entire volume might be filled with tales in this vein that have acquired the status of the classics, like *The Turn of the Screw*, *The Yellow Wallpaper*, and "Silent Snow, Secret Snow," as well as novels like *The Sound and the Fury* or *Some of Your Blood*. It is very nearly a genre in its own right.

Poe's humorous tales are not as widely read as his exercises in the macabre, but they have not been without their influence. Poe's is a humor of utter alienation. The workaday world involved in its business and domestic affairs becomes a kind of clockwork nightmare, in which ridiculous catastrophes overtake grotesque human automatons, like the unfortunate Psyche Zenobia, who is beheaded by the minute hand of a giant clock and describes the entire process in the first person: "I was not sorry to see the head which had occasioned me so much embarrassment at length make final separation from my body. It first rolled down the side of the steeple, then lodged, for a few seconds, in the gutter, and then made its way, with a plunge, into the middle of the street."

What underlies this humor is the realization that stories, being no more than words on paper, do not have to follow the rules that govern the day-to-day workings of the universe. The writer is free to fabricate . . . anything at all! The freedom is a dangerous one, but like all other freedoms, once it has been set loose upon the world, it becomes impossible to suppress. Samuel Beckett, Harry Matthews, and Michael Moorcock have each written a trilogy of masterful and magnifi-cently funny novels that may be said to spring from the same tradition.

The relevance of landscape to the craft of fiction is a harder matter to expound, yet in Poe's case it is crucial. Often it is all there is. His two longest fictions, "Narrative of A. Gordon Pym" and "The Unparalleled Adventures of One Hans Pfaal," are little more than extended travel-ogues, in which the only significant interactions are between the protagonists and their environments. These landscapes, whether on the monumental scale of the whirlpool in "The Descent into the Maelstrom" or reduced to the claustrophobic dimensions of a coffin, as in "The Premature Burial," are always inimical in a manner identifiably Poe's. The single most succinct rendering of his typical milieu occurs in "The Fall of the House of Usher," when the narrator describes one of the "pure abstractions" painted by Roderick Usher:

> A small picture presented the interior of an immensely long and rectangular vault or tunnel, with low walls, smooth, white, and without interruption or device. Certain accessory points of the design served well to convey the idea that this excavation lay at an exceeding depth below the surface of the earth. No outlet was observed in any portion of its vast extent, and no torch or other artificial source of light was discernible; yet a flood of intense rays rolled throughout, and bathed the whole in a ghastly and inappropriate splendor.

It would be a century before artists like de Chirico, Dalí, and Tanguy would create canvases in the stripped-bare style of Roderick Usher, and they were followed by a generation of French writers who pursued a very similar aesthetic. In practice I find the English practitioners of the roman nouveau—particularly J. G. Ballard and Brian Aldiss—more compellingly readable than Robbe-Grillet and others like him. Readers unfamiliar with this genre could not do better than to turn to Aldiss's novella "Where the Lines Converge," which is an epitome of this kind of infernal geometrizing.

A landscape need not be reduced to diagrammatic plainness for a family resemblance to this kind of avant-garde gothicism to be observable. Much of the fascination of "hard-core" science fiction lies in its creation of environments as spare and enigmatic, as full of strangeness, as any roman nouveau. Arthur Clarke's Rendezvous with Rama is the very apotheosis of this kind of science fiction, being an account of the systematic (and not very dramatic) exploration of an alien artifact, which its explorers never really come to understand. The novel ends, like Poe's "Pym," with a question mark the size of an iceberg. It's altogether maddening, as of course it's meant to be.

In "The Black Cat," another of Poe's mad narrators declares, "My immediate purpose is to place before the world, plainly, succinctly, and without comment, a series of mere household events." That statement might well stand as an epigraph before many of the tales that follow. Poe was one of the first gothic artists to have understood that terror likes to warm its feet at the domestic hearth, that it has no need for exotic paraphernalia. Shirley Jackson's "The Beautiful Stranger" is an excellent example of such curdled coziness, as is her classic story "The Lottery." (For a further consideration of why this should be, may I recommend Freud's brief "Essay on the Uncanny"? Beginning with the simple observation that the German word for "uncanny," *unheimlich*, is often used as an equivalent to its opposite, *heimlich*, or "homelike," Freud deduces a series of consequences as baroque as any of the ratiocinations of C. Auguste Dupin.)

Readers of Poe soon come to the conclusion that the ultimate source of strangeness lies even closer to home than the hearth; it is to be found in the blood-dark depths of the heart, or even deeper, in the soul. All Poe's landscapes, from the arctic desolations at the end of "Pym" to the tatty eclecticism of the "Venice" described in "The Assignation," and most notably the House of Usher and its environs, are externalizations of what is forever unwitnessable within. Poe is not a dramatist; he speaks in a single voice to which even Echo does not reply. His secondary characters, when they exist, are mere wraiths, names without substance. Invariably, they are on hand to serve as victims: Fortunato in "The Cask of Amontillado," Madeleine in "Usher," the wife in "The Black Cat," the nameless old man in "The Tell-Tale Heart." But the isolation of Poe's protagonists is greater still, for even when their contest is between themselves and their environment, that environment is really but the flimsiest of tissues, a screen on which the protagonist (who is Poe) projects his inner conflicts; he inhabits, so to speak, his own dreams.

This may sound like a criticism, and indeed I don't think it's a method that would serve a novelist very well, but for short stories it has proven a highly effective formula. Stories as diverse as Greene's "Under the Garden," Zoline's "The Holland of the Mind," and Mann's "The Wardrobe" all employ this same procedure.

I stated earlier that Poe can profitably be considered a contemporary of

Kierkegaard. What they may be said to have in common is an expertise in the etiology of hidden disorders of the soul, specifically that condition known as "alienation." However, for both writers the traditional term "damnation" is more to the point.

Poe secularized the idea of damnation. For all his gothic paraphernalia, he seldom has recourse to supernatural explanations. In this he is following the Devil's own advice, as it has been presented through such able interpreters as Goethe and Baudelaire, who observes in one of his prose poems that "the Devil's cleverest wile is to convince us that he does not exist."

Whether or not the Devil exists is a matter of opinion, Baudelaire notwithstanding. The existence of the damned, however, is a matter of observable fact, and Poe was one of the fact's best observers. All the specific qualities of his art referred to earlier become, when viewed in this light, facets of a single torment. The heightened awareness of his madness is not different from the unholy knowledge ascribed to such earlier gothic protagonists as Faust, Manfred, or Melmoth. To the damned soul, sealed within its selfhood, the world can appear only as ridiculous or threatening. From this fact proceeds the peculiar, skewed character of Poe's humor, the insubstantiality of his dramatis personae and of his landscapes, as well. The damned are all, all alone: the other is invisible to them in all its forms—in nature, in personal relations—except insofar as these forms have been corrupted by evil, and the vision of the damned is most acute.

I say this not in disparagement of Poe, but by way of homage. Damnation—or, if you prefer, alienation—is the central theme of Romantic literature. It ties together such works as Wordsworth's "Immortality Ode," Blake's "Songs of Experience," Coleridge's "Ancient Mariner," and de Quincey's *Confessions*. And these represent simply the first sounding of the theme, which swelled, by the latter part of the century, into a pandemonium. Within the chorus, Poe's voice remains, even today, one of the most distinct.

Put it another way. Say that the problem is how we are to understand our human destiny, in all its complexity and ambiguity, without the support provided by the theoretical apparatus of religion; especially, how we are to face the problems of evil, of death, of despair, in a world deserted by the friendly gods of springtime. Simply to look the other way, denying the problem's existence, is (as Kierkegaard argues in *The Concept of Dread*) to consign oneself to damnation in its darkest (if also its most common) form. But to face the problem is a treacherous business, as well, and the *safest* way to do so is vicariously, through the agency of art.

An interest in diseases is necessarily a morbid interest, and this is—let us admit it—the nature of our interest in Poe, and in the gothic tradition, in general. That does not make it an unhealthy interest. Dualities must be studied in pairs. Health and disease are phases of a single process. The road to heaven, as mapped out by Dante and many other expert cartographers, proceeds through the central avenues of hell.

BRAVE NEW WORLD Revisited Once Again

Just fifty years ago, at the dawn of the new era that dates from the death of Henry Ford, a young, half-blind, upper-class Englishman published a novel destined to become—along with Orwell's 1984—one of the two most enduring prophetic visions of the future ever to clatter from the typewriter of man. The novel was Brave New World, its author Aldous Huxley, and the vision was of the Jazz Age gone to heaven. Anything goes in A.F. (After Ford) 632, but what goes particularly well are those two pillars of the affluent society, sex and drugs. What has been eliminated from that society as being subversive and destabilizing is: family life, passionate love, social nobility, and any art but the "feelies," fashion design, and dance music. Here's a sample of the song lyrics and the lifestyle of A.F. 632:

Orgy-porgy, Ford and fun,
Kiss the girls and make them One.
Boys at one with girls at peace;
Orgy-porgy gives release.

What was most shocking to the first readers of Brave New World (and probably still is, for the book has always been a favorite target for censors) wasn't so much the way Huxley turns conventional values upside-down but the verve and logic with which his villain, Mustapha Mond, the Resident Controller for Western Europe, justifies a social order based unashamedly on the beehive and the iceberg—with "eight-ninths of the population below the waterline, one ninth above." Mond sums up the lives of the majority of lower-caste Gammas and Epsilons this way: "Seven and a half hours of mild, unexhausting labor, and then the soma ration and games and unrestricted copulation and the feelies. What more can they ask for?" Indeed, even the privileged one-ninth of Alphas above the waterline had better not ask for more than that if they don't want to be shipped to Iceland, where rebels and skeptics are kept in permanent quarantine.

In 1952, when Brave New World was twenty years old and I was twelve, it seemed to me the height of all that was wicked, sophisticated, and far-fetched. (So wicked, indeed, that I had to glue the cover of another thirty-five-cent paperback over the [wonderfully lurid but quite inaccurate] cover art of a couple dressed in nothing but wisps of cloud.)

By the book's twenty-fifth birthday and my seventeenth I still gave it high points for wickedness and sophistication, but rather than thinking it far-fetched I now believed that the world of A.F. 632 was, except for some minor details, already upon us. Those were the years, as you might remember or may have heard, of the Organization Man, of a nationwide conformity enforced not by a 1984-style Big Brother but by the rewards of an affluent consumer society. The first tender shoots of the sexual revolution were up, and even soma—in the form of tranquilizers—had appeared as an "ethical drug." As for Huxley's system of social indoctrination by hypnopaedia, or sleep-teaching, television was already having a fair success instilling such *Brave-New-Worldly* slogans as "Ending is better than mending," and "I love new clothes," and "A gram is better than a damn."

Now, a round half-century after it came out, I was curious to return to Huxley's novel and see if his batting average as a social prophet had grown or shrunk since my last visit. In some obvious ways the book is now more on target than ever—especially if one hearkens to the dire warnings of those who regard "Secular Humanism" as Public Enemy #1. Mustapha Mond, with his cavalier dismissal of family life, freedom, and God and his championing of promiscuity and drugs, is just the antichrist the Moral Majority yearns to combat. If only (they must often wish) Jerry Brown would be as up-front about things.

From a strictly technological point of view Huxley himself, in 1950, admitted: "One vast and obvious failure of foresight is immediately apparent. *Brave New World* contains no reference to nuclear fission." And none, one might add, to television, or space travel, or computer technology, or even to genetic engineering. However, it's only the last subject that's actually relevant to the book's themes. Yet even without breaking the DNA code in advance of Watson and Crick, Huxley's blueprint for a "hatchery" for human infants remains an impressive feat of technological imagining. Less convincing is his rationale for producing people on assembly lines, like Model Ts. Present methods achieve the same results more efficiently at less expense, though no doubt there are some radical feminists who would welcome the experiment.

Where our own world most differs from Huxley's is in the matter of contention and instability. Huxley wrote at a time when it was still possible to believe that the League of Nations might evolve into a world state, that war might be rendered obsolete by sound management, and that antagonistic class divisions might be transformed into a frictionless caste system, in which the lower classes were bred and brainwashed to be happy, dutiful morons. Nowadays world government seems about as likely a prospect as the Second Coming. 1984 has cast a long shadow across the pages of *Brave New World*. In his own book-length reappraisal, *Brave New World Revisited*, written in 1958, Huxley took a grimmer view of the global situation and predicted: "it is a pretty safe bet that, twenty years from now (i.e., in 1978) all the world's overpopulated and underdeveloped countries will be under some form of totalitarian rule—probably by the Communist party." Not a bull's eye, but pretty close.

Brave New World goes widest from the mark, I think, in its picture of a trouble-free, beehive-style caste system. Huxley grew up in an upper-class family in Edwardian England and shared much of the myopia and some of the arrogance of his "class-mates" when he wrote about those who hadn't shared his privileges. Quite simply, he could not conceive that anyone of working-class background could possess more than a rudimentary intelligence or spiritual dignity. (At least in none of his novels did he bother to imagine such a possibility.) In this regard, *Brave New World* is not so much a prophetic vision of the future as nostalgia for a mythical Golden Age before there was a servant problem.

My final quarrel with the book is one of emphasis from my first reading. I've always had a sneaking fondness for the world Huxley invented. I know I'm supposed to disapprove. But I would like to try soma just once, and I wouldn't say no to a night at the Westminster Abbey Cabaret dancing to the music of Calvin Stopes and his Sixteen Sexophonists. The lyrics of the songs may be sappy, but I'll bet they've got a good beat. As for the feelies, I suppose the plots are pretty simpleminded, but any more so than *Raiders of the Lost Ark?*

This is not to endorse all the sinister theories of Mustapha Mond, only to suggest that fun's fun, and that some of the targets of Huxley's satire are mean-spirited, insofar as he is making a case against pop culture, sexual candor, and the consumption of alcoholic beverages.

Relax, Huxley. You worry too much. Have a gram of Tylenol. Things could be worse. This might be 1984.

A Tableful of Twinkies

Ray Bradbury is America's Official Science Fiction Writer, the one most likely to be trotted out on state occasions to give a salute to, as he puts it, "our wild future in space." In 1964 he was hired to "conceptualize" the area of the U.S. World's Fair Pavilion devoted to the Future. From there he went on "to help plan the dreams that went into Spaceship Earth," the latest Disney fairground now under construction. Recently a film clip of the author was the delegate for science fiction at the first TABA Awards ceremony.

To those familiar with the field Bradbury's figurehead status may seem hard to account for, if only because, as he himself notes, so small a part of his output may be called science fiction. If the flagbearer's role were to be assigned to the Oldest Veteran, then by rights Jack Williamson should lead the parade. If a poll of sf readers were to be taken, top honors would probably go to Robert Heinlein. Even the art of self-promotion cannot account for Bradbury's eminence, for Isaac Asimov has been beating the drum of his own reputation with more vigor and persistence for decades. Yet for brand-name recognition Bradbury has them all licked.

Could the answer be sheer literary excellence? No. Only readers who would profess Rod McKuen to be America's greatest poet, or Kahlil Gibran its noblest philosopher, could commend unblushingly Bradbury's stories as literature. If there is any difference between art and kitsch, between steak and baloney, into which category would you place the following prose specimen?

> There are a million small towns like this all over the world. Each as dark, as lonely, each as removed, as full of shuddering and wonder. The reedy playing of minor key violins is the small towns' music, with no lights but many shadows. Oh the vast swelling loneliness of them. The secret damp ravines of them. Life is a horror lived in them at night, when at all sides sanity, marriage, children, happiness, is threatened by an ogre called Death.

That comes from "The Night," the first of one hundred tales collected in *The Stories of Ray Bradbury.* Though published early in his career (1946),

Review of *The Stories of Ray Bradbury: 100 of His Most Celebrated Tales.*

the vein of schmaltz evident in "The Night" recurs in Bradbury's work as regularly as he reaches for the unattainable or addresses Eternity on a one-to-one basis—i.e., in at least half his stories. Early and late are meaningless distinctions in his output. Indeed, the secret of his success may well be that, like Peter Pan, he won't grow up. What's more, he knows it:

> I was *not* embarrassed at circuses. Some people are. Circuses are loud, vulgar, and smell in the sun. By the time many people are fourteen or fifteen, they have been divested of their loves, their ancient and intuitive tastes, one by one, until when they reach maturity there is no fun left, no zest, no gusto, no flavor. Others have criticized, and they have criticized themselves, into embarrassment.

There's the choice—love Ray Bradbury, out there beyond embarrassment, or be enrolled among these loveless, zestless critics who never go to the circus. My own experience suggests other possibilities. I've been to the circus from time to time, invariably enjoyed the show, gasped, applauded, and my ancient and intuitive taste tells me that Ray Bradbury's stories are meretricious more often than not. Because he's risked being loud, vulgar, and smelly? No, because his imagination so regularly gets mired in genteel gush and self-pity, because environing clichés have made him nearly oblivious to new data from any source, and because as a writer he's a slop.

Consider this description (from "The Night"): "You smell lilacs in blossom; fallen apples lying crushed and odorous in the deep grass." Ordinarily apples don't fall when lilacs blossom, but in Bradbury's stories it's always Anymonth in Everywhereville. His dry-ice machine covers the bare stage of his story with a fog of breathy approximations. He means to be evocative and incantatory; he achieves vagueness and prolixity.

Perhaps it is elitist, these days, to discuss the prose style of any very popular writer. A readership in the millions proves that some sort of message is getting through. At a symposium of secondary school teachers I was assured that no sf writer is so teachable as Bradbury: even the least skilled readers are able to turn his sentences into pictures in their heads. Inattentive, artless, and very young readers are probably better able to construct agreeable daydreams out of Bradbury's approximative prose than if they were required to exercise their reading muscles more strenuously.

The Defense might argue that broad outlines, bright colors, and stereotypical characters don't preclude the Possibility of art, or at least of well-engineered amusement. Walt Disney and Norman Rockwell have endeared themselves to large audiences by such means. Indeed, there are other points of comparison even more pertinent. Like Disney, Bradbury has a knack for taming and sanitizing fairy tales and myths so that even fauns and centaurs may be welcomed into the nursery. Like Rockwell, Bradbury celebrates the virtues and flavors of an idyllic, small-town American Way of Life, the myth on which a thousand suburbs have been founded. Myths can serve various purposes: they can be decorative, a kind of literary Fourth of July bunting (as in Bradbury's "A Scent of Sasparilla" [sic]); they can be obfuscatory, a stop-gap lie to tell children before they're ready for the truth (Bradbury's tales of life in funny, old, warmhearted Mexico achieve this purpose); or they can order complex emotional experience in the manner so well described by Bruno Bettelheim in his study of fairy tales, *The Uses of Enchantment*. Some of Bradbury's most memorable tales achieve this last and largest purpose of mythmaking—simple fictional analogues of matters usually not referred to—fear of death or of one's own infantile rage—offering symbolically effective ways of thinking about the unthinkable.

Even as mythmaker, however, Bradbury's failures outnumber his successes. He summons spirits from the vasty deep, but they don't come. "The Black Ferris," one of only six stories collected for the first time in this volume, is Bradbury at his worst, at once portentous and trivializing, overwrought and twee. (The author himself thought so much of it that it became the basis of his novel *Something Wicked This Way Comes*.)

"The Black Ferris" begins with a great gust from the fog machine— "The carnival had come to town like an October wind, like a dark bat flying over the cold lake, bones rattling in the night, mourning, sighing, whispering up the tents in the dark rain"—and goes on to recount how two small boys, Peter and Hank, discover that Mr. Cooger, the thirty-five-year-old manager of the visiting carnival, has transformed himself into the "li'l orphan boy" who has been taken into the household of poor rich Mrs. Foley. He does this by riding the black Ferris of the title twenty-five times in reverse. The two boys immediately apprehend the purpose of this imposture and go to Mrs. Foley to warn her:

> "He's from the carnival, and he ain't a boy, he's a man, and he's planning on living with you until he finds where your money is and then run off with it some night, and people will look for him but because they'll be looking for a little ten-year-old boy they won't recognize him when he walks by a thirty-five-year-old man, named Mr. Cooger!"

Mrs. Foley refuses to heed this word to the wise, and there's nothing our little heroes can do but chase the false orphan back to the carnival. Too late to prevent him from getting back into the time-defying Ferris, they assault the blind hunchback at the controls. The Ferris spins, unchecked, until . . . what do you think?

"Look," everybody said.

The policeman turned and the carnival people turned and the fisher-men turned and they all looked at the occupant in the black-painted seat at the bottom of the ride. The wind touched and moved the black wooden seat in a gentle rocking rhythm, crooning over the occupant in the dim carnival light.

A skeleton sat there, a paper bag of money in its hands, a brown derby hat on its head.

If that tickles your sense of wonder, then there are ninety-nine other stories in the book just as good or even better. (To my mind, any halfway bright eleven-year-old could do as well, given twenty years to practice.) There can be charm in art of such systematically false naivete, and some few writers have managed to have it both ways, writing stories that are equally amusing to grown-ups and exciting for children: Hans Christian Andersen, A. A. Milne, Maurice Sendak. But Bradbury is not in their league. His sense of humor doesn't operate on both sides of the generation gap; his horrors are redolent of Halloween costumery; his sentimentality cloys; his sermons are intrusive and schoolmarmish; he is uninformed and undisciplined. He is an artist only in the sense that he is not a hydraulic engineer.

The fact remains that for many adults these stories can serve as a direct link back to their prematurely buried eleven-year-old selves and that kids will respond (as I did, back when) to their appeal quite as though they were the genuine articles, a whole buffet of Hostess Twinkies, candy corn, and strawberry Kool-Aid, all gleaming, like Mars itself, with the eerie glow of Red Dye Number 2.

Sic, Sic, Sic

There can be few more alarming examples of the decline of scholarly standards in American universities during the recent decades of rapid growth than this collection of essays about Arthur C. Clarke, edited—as part of a series—by Drs. Joseph D. Olander, an associate professor of anthropology at Florida International University, and Martin Harry Greenberg, director of graduate studies at the University of Wisconsin–Green Bay. Academic critics are traditionally forgiven for flat prose and laborings of the obvious, but the infelicity, imprecision, and leadenheadedness of the introduction to which these learned gentlemen have signed their names are not up to the level of literacy one may demand of an undergraduate paper.

A sample:

> One of the major images which emerges about Arthur C. Clarke is that of "hard science fiction" writer. When all is said and done, Clarke's authentic commitment seems to be to the universe and, like Asimov, to the underlying sets of laws of behavior by which the mystery inherent in it will probably be explained.
>
> How is it, then, that he is associated with mysticism, mythology, theological speculation, and "cosmic" loneliness? Hard science fiction, if nothing else, usually needs to come to closure, in its qualities of validity and consistency, with specific explanations and scientific justifications. Yet much of Clarke's fiction pushes the mind outward and ever open. If this is accomplished by an explication of assumed or searched-for universal laws, it is understandable and consistent with science-based extrapolation.

Not all the contributors achieve the same heady combination of slow-think and academic duckspeak, but only two of the nine essays evidence any amplitude of argument or close attention to a text. Many offer no more than descriptive catalogues of Clarke's stories and novels without

Review of *Arthur C. Clarke*, by Joseph D. Olander and Martin Harry Greenberg; and *The Best of Arthur C. Clarke*, Volume 1 (1937–1955), Volume 2 (1956–1972), edited by Angus Wells.

any effort at seeking other meanings than those the author himself has underlined. In "The Cosmic Loneliness of Arthur C. Clarke," Thomas Clareson explicitly denies a psychological dimension to his fiction, maintaining that Clarke's "loneliness" can be understood as a relation solely between mankind and the cosmos. It is disingenuous in a critic, not to say evasive, to discuss Clarke's loneliness without ever noting such salient associated features of his fiction as the virtual absence of interpersonal conflict (commonly called drama), the exclusion of women from his dramatis personae, and an affective landscape as arid as the moon's.

By his refusal to interpret Clarke's work, Clareson at least avoids the pitfalls that Betty Harfat and Robert Plank fall into as they try, in the tradition of The Pooh Perplex, to fit Clarke into Jungian and Freudian schemas. Of the two, Harfat's essay is the more awesomely malapropos. She devotes entire pages to explaining the spiritual truths of yoga, and when she finally gets round to relating these to Clarke, the result is such butchery as Cinderella's sisters experienced trying to squeeze into her slipper. None of the contributors, however, surpasses Robert Plank in his ability to write passages that can evoke a proverbial sense of wonder. Here he is discussing the fortuitous resemblance he has observed between the extraterrestrial slabs in 2001, "a heavy block of black granite" in St. Exupery's Citadelle, and a 1962 painting by an Austrian artist:

> How can such a convergence of view be explained? . . . Do we have here a manifestation of a universal, genetically transmitted and unconsciously understood symbol, that postulated psychic structure which plays a rather small role in Freud's theory but which Jung makes a cornerstone of his? Very little has been done so far to confirm or refute the hypothesis through empirical studies. The thought rarely strikes laymen that this might be needed. It is unlikely for instance that Gilliatt (a reviewer of the film) made any survey to find out whether to "atheists" (by which term she probably, though erroneously, means to designate people without religious feeling) the slabs do or do not look like girders. The newer discipline of semiotics might claim the problem as within its jurisdiction, but does not seem to have gotten round to it. It would be preposterous to think that we could solve it here. As an indication of the emotional significance of the slabs, though, it is highly telling.

Of course, quoting out of context is always unfair. One must read Plank's entire essay to appreciate the degree of muddle he is able, in only twenty-eight pages, to achieve.

The two essays in the book that are not major intellectual embarrassments (those by David N. Samuelson and John Huntington) first appeared in *Science Fiction Studies*, a Canadian journal that has proven, along with the English *Foundation*, that one may accord academic attention to sf without becoming an accomplice in the decline of the West. However, with the scholastic fortune of science fiction entrusted to the likes of Olander, Greenberg, & Co., I have little hope of the field's escaping a ghettoization within academe parallel to its ghettoization without.

Poor Clarke—he has been as ill-served by his publisher as by his critics. In 1973, Sidgwick and Jackson brought out *The Best of Arthur C. Clarke* at £2.50; four years later they have reissued it in two paperback-sized volumes, shoddily produced, for £3.95 each. Inflation alone can't account for a price rise of 316 percent. Clarke is a popular writer, and when early editions of his books wear out, libraries automatically restock them. I can think of no other explanation for such pricing policy. Surely for £7.90 one might expect *The Complete Short Stories* rather than this haphazard selection. There are no criteria by which these eighteen stories can be considered their author's best work. The first four are the rawest juvenilia. (The earliest of these dates from 1937, not 1932, as the title on the book jacket of volume 1 mistakenly declares—a fair sample of Sidgwick and Jackson's production standards.) No stories have been included from *Tales from the White Hart*, and only a single vignette from *Reach for Tomorrow*, collections that represent Clarke's maturity. Further, too many of the stories chosen have obsolesced badly and can only be read as period pieces.

On the whole, however, Clarke suffers less than most equally prolific writers would by having such a random sample served up as his best. Aside from the few undeniable classics, such as "The Star" and "A Meeting with Medusa" (both included), his work is more notable for its reliable evenness than for peaks of excellence and troughs of failed ambition. He writes to a formula—but the pleasure of reading his shorter fictions is like that afforded by watching good billiard players. Clarke is an expert at inventing scenarios that illustrate Newton's laws of motion, of deploying vector quantities with human names in the ideal frictionless environment, not of green baize, but of outer space.

A Bus Trip to Heaven

There was a double valence in Arthur C. Clarke's earlier novels that made them congenial to two distinct audiences on either side of the two-cultures gap. Technocrats could respond to his blueprints of zero-souled engineers at war against nature, while his visions of a trans-human future, hinted at in the conclusions of his two best-known novels, *Childhood's End* and *2001*, have become icons of the counterculture. Only the cis-transcendental sector of his audience will be likely to endorse Clarke's assertion (in the jacket copy of the book) that *The Fountains of Paradise* is his best novel. Never before has Clarke concentrated the entire interest of a long narrative on the fabrication of a Wonderful Invention to the exclusion not only of ordinary human interest (never his strong suit) but as well of that earlier sustaining tension between a universe in which Meccano sets reign supreme and one in which God, in one of his latter-day disguises, can come down from outer space and help humanity slip loose from mortal coils. In *Fountains*, a philosophy of pure mechanism triumphs over an entire mountaintop of Buddhist monks and succeeds at raising a genuine Tower of Babel going all the way to heaven.

Clarke's vision of the monastic life is summed up by one of the novel's many apt epigraphs: "Religion is a byproduct of malnutrition." As antagonists to the builder of the tower (a twenty-second-century Isambard Brunel) the monks never get off the ground. Their single act of opposition is not of their own doing but the work of that old pulp standby, a Mad Scientist. Sane or mad, only Science gets results. To cinch the triumph of rationality an extra-terrestrial visitor appears in part II to announce, like some anti-Paraclete, that God is an unnecessary hypothesis that the more intelligent races of the universe do not entertain. Earth's religions dutifully expire at this news.

Though such a resolute stacking of the deck is not conducive to dramatic tension, *Fountains* maintains the narrative momentum of a well-developed and surprising axiom in geometry. No sf writer understands better than Clarke how to craft viable tales from no other material than the construction and operation of gigantic machineries. The big machine

---

Review of *The Fountains of Paradise*, by Arthur C. Clarke.

in this case is a satellite-supported lift from earth to outer space. By the time Clarke has got done documenting his hyper-elevator only those readers who never believed in the possibility of rocket ships will have been able to resist suspending disbelief. As to the significance of such a feat of engineering, Clarke is quite explicit: it portends the democritization and banalization of space flight. Mankind rides "in comfort and safety to the stars." Some apotheosis. *Childhood's End*, therefore, it's not. Yet *Fountains* does represent Clarke's own maturity as a consistent materialist content to live, and die, without illusions. It also represents his maturity as an artist. With a palette limited to shades of high-tech gray, Clarke achieves a consistent texture of elegy. One suspects that even he, the high priest of Technocracy, has doubts as to whether his tale is a working model of the future or instead a comforting fairy tale for the last days. In the limited category of novels about machinery *The Fountains of Paradise* must stand at the top of the list.

The Doldrums of Space

In the last few years, science fiction has come of age. Not as an art form; since at least the time of Wells a small portion has merited passing grades aesthetically. Rather, it's come of age financially. Intermittently since Clarke and Kubrick's 2001 and quite regularly since *Star Wars*, sf titles have been appearing on both hardcover and paperback national bestseller lists. In just the last few months, Frank Herbert, Anne McCaffrey, Stephen Donaldson, and Robert Heinlein have jostled for position with the likes of Ludlum, King, and McCullough—and if that doesn't sound like a list of Nobel nominees that's because these days books are not judged by canons of Serlit, but by those of Sacprac, or Sound Accounting Practices. In terms strictly of Sacprac there could hardly be two more marketable commodities than the latest books (to call them "novels" would smack too much of Serlit, and anyhow they really aren't) by those major brand names of science fiction, Isaac Asimov and Arthur C. Clarke.

Now though Asimov and Clarke are as close to household words as any writers in the field, a name alone is not enough if a book is to be bankrolled to the tune of a million-plus dollars, the publicized advances received by both Asimov's *Foundation's Edge* and Clarke's *2010: Odyssey Two*. The name must also represent continuation of already established success—in Asimov's case his *Foundation* trilogy, with five million copies in print and the retroactive Hugo Award as "Best All-Time SF Series"; in Clarke's case the antecedent work is 2001, the movie of which was still on *Variety*'s list of the ten best-grossing movies the last time I looked. Furthermore—and caveat emptor to all mere readers—both books trail off with a sense of many golden eggs still to be gathered. "The End (for now)" is how Asimov puts it on page 366. Clarke is not so succinct in his promise of the vast read ahead: "only one of them can inherit the solar system. Which it will be, not even the Gods know yet."

Far be it from me to fly in the face of Sacprac and suggest that the lack of either a beginning or an end ought to be accounted a liability in a fictional commodity. Let's be fair and judge each slice of these two con-

Review of *2010: Odyssey Two*, by Arthur C. Clarke; and *Foundation's Edge*, by Isaac Asimov.

tinua on its own merits. Was it fun to read? Did the pages turn effortlessly, or at least voluntarily? These are questions that a responsible accountant ought to ask of sequels that are to be followed by sequels of their own, since even the most loyal name-brand consumer may grow bored and stop consuming if a certain bare minimum of drama hasn't been provided.

My sense of the matter is that 2010 delivers the goods—not abundantly but better than one might expect, given the act it had to follow—while *Foundation's Edge* proves after only a few pages' testing to be unpickupable. I did read every chapter, from a reverence for the Protestant Work Ethic, but it may well have been the dullest book of its length I've ever read all the way through.

However, before I get into an anatomy of that debacle, it would be well to speak of the merits of 2010, since they are quite representative of the merits of the genre as a whole at its meat-and-potatoes mid-range (and therefore of what Asimov omits to provide). Clarke's recipe for fiction stew can be as bland as those blenderized dinners the astronauts grimaced at in the movie of 2001, but even so there is always something engineered to be tasty, or at least mind-filling, in every chapter. His best moments are intensely pictorial. Those who've seen 2001 will be able to recycle its props and characters as they read 2010, and if they can splice these memories with the stunning NASA photos of the *Voyager* fly-by of Jupiter, the result will be as close to a theatrical premiere unreeling in the imagination as the unassisted printed page can offer.

The story enacted against this Jovian backdrop does not afford dramatic satisfactions on a par with the scenic pleasures. Plot—in the sense of characters interacting—has never been Clarke's strong suit, and in 2010 he is weighted down by the expository problem of all sequels, how to rehash the story-to-now while getting a new show on the read. He accomplishes the task with professional economy, if not magical ease (an accomplishment I didn't appreciate till I was halfway done with the Asimov book, for Asimov is never done reciting his trilogy's antecedent plot). Clarke's expository problem is compounded by the fact that the characters of 2010, a joint Russian-American exploratory team, are sent to find out what happened to the spaceship *Discovery* and dear old HAL the computer, a mystery to which viewers of 2001 already know the solution. Worst of all, Clarke is obliged to reintroduce the metamorphosed hero of 2001, David Bowman, into the cast of 2010, and Clarke's imagination doesn't function well at transcendental temperatures. Bowman flits about the solar system like a faster-than-light ghost in search of someone to haunt, and the ease of his flitting tends to set at naught all the slower-moving hardware the author has been at such pains to build.

Clarke labors against these difficulties with stoic cheer (and the confidence, no doubt, that at the end of his long trek through this familiar territory there will be a gold mine as his reward), and if the results are neither stirring nor mind-bending, there is a sense of intellectual cohesion. Some of the logical lacunae of 2001 are puttied up (such as, Why was that big black brick parked way out by Jupiter?), and the stage is set for 20,001: *Odyssey Three*, which is almost certain to be more fun than the book in hand, now that the stage has been so carefully set.

In the face of *Foundation's Edge* having fun and reading a book begin to seem like incompatible activities. Asimov attempts so little and achieves so much less that a critic shrinks before the task of describing emptiness so vast. To say that Asimov's characters are wooden and his dialogue cliché-ridden is only to point out what even his boosters willingly concede. In any case, wood may well be the best construction material to use when aiming at a mass audience. But there should then be—as all kinds of popular literature know how to provide—compensatory pleasures, such as pacing, derring-do, and grand-manner melodrama. As to pace, *Foundation's Edge* is so slow that its entire gist can be condensed into a small novelette (and so it was: you can read it in the October *Omni*). There is virtually no action but the movement of puppets' jaws. The dramatic impact of the story falls short of a Senate filibuster. Nothing happens but a succession of stilted arguments about vague threats to the galactic order among characters who have no existence apart from their conference tables. There ensues a slow game of Spaceship A following Spaceship B through hyperspace, with Spaceship C trailing along at a leisurely pace, all as thrilling as an evening of Parchesi. This leads up to a showdown at which all concerned are deceived into thinking they've reached a negotiated agreement, a deception accomplished by beings of virtually omnipotent "mentalic" powers, which, had they been exercised at the start of the long tale, would have obviated all debate.

Even this summary doesn't begin to express the *tameness* of the book. Just as there is no action, there is nothing that can pass muster as an idea. Ideas are supposed to be science fiction's forte, and the realm of ideas staked out by the *Foundation* series is nothing less than (literally) universal history. But history, for Asimov, is a seventh-grade pageant conducted before the PTA. There is no account of daily life, no consideration as to how political control is exerted or maintained. Two social classes are in view—orators at conference tables and (briefly) farmers who speak in

Amish accents (and are called Hamish). No thought has been given to such potentially interesting, and historically momentous, considerations as logistics, trade, or communications, as these would be modified by galactic distance. Perhaps in 1950, when the trilogy was finished in its magazine version and Asimov and the world were both so much younger, that degree of fine-tuning might have been asking for the moon, but there has simply been too much water under the sf bridge since 1950—the work of Delany, LeGuin, and Aldiss, to mention only three galactically minded future historians—for such pabulum to be promoted as food for thought.

What then of the *scientific* razzmatazz that Clarke can fill a chapter with when all else fails? Asimov, after all, is a first-rate expositor of science to the lay audience. No one is more capable of explaining neutrinos and black holes so that they seem to make sense.

In *Foundation's Edge*, alas, there's scarcely a glimmer of that capability. In order, perhaps, to keep the book consistent with the original trilogy, all scientific imaginings are conducted at Captain Video level. Spaceships and thought-controlling "mentalic" rays zip through hyperspace as nimbly as fingers can type. At journey's end there is one (count it, one) new idea; new, that is, to this series. It's an idea that's been around sf long enough to have earned chestnut status, and readers who would like to encounter the idea with some of its first gloss still on it should track down Richard McKenna's fine novella "Hunter, Come Home."

Whether, despite all this, the book will enjoy the success of its antecedent trilogy would seem to lie in the hands of the ten-to-twelve-year-old segment of the reading public. My own advice to them is to save their quarters for the video games at their shopping malls. They'll have more fun—and learn a marketable skill at the same time.

Isaac Asimov (1920–1992)

Isaac Asimov was a lot like the sci-fi magazines he wrote for as a boy genius—astonishing, astounding, and amazing. Astonishing for an output that allowed him to publish, in 1984, his *Opus 300*, with selections from his first three hundred books. Astounding for both the range and the lucidity of his scientific learning. He could produce, off the top of his head, guidebooks to any scientific subject as up-to-date and well-organized as a textbook vetted by a committee of specialists, and so yes-of-course comprehensible that even quantum mechanics could be coped with in the Asimov version.

He was amazing, most of all, for his co-invention, with Arthur C. Clarke and Robert Heinlein, of modern science fiction. "Nightfall," the story he wrote at age twenty-one, has repeatedly been hailed as the greatest sf tale of all time. It tells the story of a panic that overwhelms a planet when there is a total eclipse of its six suns and for the first time in its history the stars become visible—and the size of the universe imaginable.

That gasp of wonder was the Asimovian grail, and it is evoked most powerfully in the early novels of the *Foundation* series, and in the books mandating the Three Laws of Robotics, especially *The Caves of Steel* (1954). That book is also Asimov's first cautionary tale about the dangers of overpopulation. Unlike most other technophile sci-fi writers who have acted as NASA's unpaid cheerleaders, Asimov was a political liberal throughout his life, and became the president of the American Humanist Association.

He was also a lifelong teenager, and his persona, whenever he was far enough away from the typewriter to wear one, was that of a typical high school, slide-rule-toting science nerd. But in Asimov's case, the nerd was triumphant. Every month his face could be seen, with its bushy white muttonchops, on the cover of the science fiction magazine named in his honor. Often he'd be costumed as an astronaut by way of reminding us that it's not the jocks but brains like Asimov who are the real architects of our futures.

Asimov's New Guide to Science, rev. ed. (1984). The best single one-volume science reference book for home libraries.

The Foundation Trilogy. A space opera version of the decline and fall of the Roman Empire and probably the mostly widely read sf work of all time.

The Robot Novels. Sci-fi whodunits featuring the team of Baley (human) and Olivaw (robot), the Nick and Nora of Time and Space.

The End of Eternity (1955). By merely literary standards, this tale of time travel from the ninety-fifth century is generally rated Asimov's best.

Jokes across the Generation Gap

Writers, and especially novelists, have become the saints of our secular culture, not so much in the sense that they are thought to be morally superior, but because they have by their own efforts (unlike royalty, whose advantages are inherited) found a way to transcend the job market. They enjoy the same existential happiness as movie stars, who are paid money simply for being, or "expressing" themselves. That, at least, is the ideal, and if many writers (like Kurt Vonnegut's shadow-self, the sf hack Kilgore Trout) fail to achieve that ideal, such failure is simply the darkness that lends success a brighter luster.

As the luster grows and the reputation swells, the writer gains an interest independent of his work. With each new novel the question is asked, "Has success spoiled X?" That is, Is the new book equal to those before? Has age withered or custom staled the known persona? To answer that question at once vis-à-vis *Galapagos:* no, Vonnegut is as good as ever and better than usual, and he is still, exactly, Kurt Vonnegut, still the same droll, disingenuous, utterly middle-American, if now high-middle-aged, Huck Finn, telling a plain tale in the same trademarked style that combines the homespun and the streetwise in a patchwork of one-liners, catchphrases, and tangential anecdotes that yields a sum wonderfully larger than its parts. His is an artlessness that seems so sincere that it takes in not only his popular audience, who love him all the more for being their Everyman and ombudsman to the court of Literature, but as well the literary establishment, who can, on this account, comfortably dismiss Vonnegut as a naif with a knack for low comedy, but not "serious," not an artist, not canonical.

Yet Vonnegut, despite his consistent popular success, is an artist surely destined for canonization, with an oeuvre that will someday support as much scholarship as any novelist's alive and a Life that promises juicy biographies to come. If he is not "serious" in the establishment sense, that is because seriousness is, by definition, the domain of fuddy-duddies, a territory in which a foxy novelist will never let himself be apprehended by the hounds of criticism.

Review of *Galapagos*, by Kurt Vonnegut.

Consider, for instance, the matter of style. Sentence by sentence, no one, not even Hemingway, the new Horace of today's monoglot schools of creative writing, can be sparer, simpler, easier to parse, but Hemingway's spareness was at the service of refining away an auctorial voice that would tell instead of—as a perfected naturalism commands—show and letting the reader work out for herself the larger meanings that may loom behind a plain unvarnished tale. Vonnegut, by contrast, is always explicating his own text, often before he's written it. Consider the following paragraph (which comes early in *Galapagos*) of manic self-interpretation:

> If Selena was Nature's experiment with blindness, then her father was Nature's experiment with heartlessness. Yes, and Jesus Ortiz was Nature's experiment with admiration for the rich, and I was Nature's experiment with insatiable voyeurism, and my father was Nature's experiment with cynicism, and my mother was Nature's experiment with optimism, and the Captain of the *Bahia de Darwin* was Nature's experiment with ill-founded self-confidence, and James Wait was Nature's experiment with purposeless greed, and Hisako Hirogochi was Nature's experiment with depression, and Akiko was Nature's experiment with furriness, and on and on.

The Hemingway style flatters its readers by pretending not to manipulate them; the Vonnegut style teases its audience, as a testy parent might tease a child, but then a moment later (being a kind parent at heart) Vonnegut renews the enchantment of his story, which, like any good Hausmärchen, is full of wonders and whimsies not allowed to a writer addressing "serious," grown-up readers. Here it is the literal-minded popular audience that is likely to grow restive, for those readers whose hungers are normally satisfied by the lumpen-realism of Arthur Hailey or James Michener must be seduced into a more playful and imaginative frame of mind, and this Vonnegut does in two ways: by the plausive strategies of science fiction (in which genre Vonnegut served much of his literary apprenticeship) and by humor, the broader the better. As he remarks of the new human race that is to evolve in the Galapagos Islands over the next million years:

> People still laugh about as much as they ever did, despite their shrunken brains. If a bunch of them are lying around on a beach, and one of them farts, everybody else laughs and laughs, just as people would have done a million years ago.

Laughter, whether at farts or more complex behavior, is Vonnegut's forte, in support of which proposition I must quote at length a passage I think is irresistibly funny, though the humor is once again at the expense of digestive processes. This is his account of the marine iguana, a reptile that has been selected as the "totemic animal of the cruise" of the *Bahia de Darwin*, the ship of fools whose voyage to, and shipwreck on, the Galapagos Islands is the focus of the novel:

> The creature could be more than a metre long, and look as fearsome as a Chinese dragon. Actually, though, it was no more dangerous to life forms of any sort, with the exception of seaweed, than a liverwurst. Here is what its life is like in the present day, which is exactly what life was like a million years ago.
>
> It has no enemies, so it sits in one place, staring into the middle of the distance at nothing, wanting nothing, worried about nothing until it is hungry. It then waddles down to the ocean and swims slowly and not all that ably until it is a few metres from shore. Then it dives, like a submarine, and stuffs itself with seaweed, which is at that time ingestible. The seaweed is going to have to be cooked before it is digestible.
>
> So the marine iguana pops to the surface, swims ashore, and sits on the lava in the sunshine again. It is using itself for a covered stewpot, getting hotter and hotter while the sunshine cooks the seaweed. It continues to stare into the middle distance at nothing, as before, but with this difference: It now spits up increasingly hot salt water from time to time.
>
> During the million years I have spent in these islands, the Law of Natural Selection has found no way to improve, or, for that matter, to worsen this particular survival scheme.

The comic premise of *Galapagos* is that the survivors of the voyage devolve, by Darwinian logic, to the condition of that marine iguana, and a more unlikely lot of survivors Nature could not easily have selected: a single fertile male who refuses to breed, and nine females, one of whom is infertile, one of whom is congenitally blind and also refuses to breed, one of whom is pregnant with a male child with genes mutated by the Hiroshima bomb, while the remaining six are cannibal foundlings of the near-extinct tribe of the Kanka-bonos, whose horror of the fertile male precludes any possibility of sex. How this ill-assorted set of Adam and Eves produces a new human race, while the rest of the species suffers extinction, provides the social comedy of the novel, and it is black enough, but Vonnegut's genius is for satire on the broadest Voltairean lines. His targets are not the foibles of social behavior but (as befits an American of the post-war era) targets as broad as the pax Americana: war, genocide, economic imperialism, ecological catastrophe, nuclear extinction, and the madness and futility of all religions and idiologies. The difficulty of aiming at such broad targets is not in scoring bullseyes but in avoiding the preaching-to-the-converted complacence of such cosy jeremiads as Lessing's *Canopus* fantasies, and this Vonnegut achieves by irony. Like Samuel Butler in *Erewhon* (where illness is treated as criminal behavior and crime as a disease), Vonnegut contends with poker-faced consistency that the problem of the human race has been its *excessive* intelligence and imagination, and that a devolution to the condition of seals and walruses represents the race's only hope for survival.

In designing the tale that supports this thesis Vonnegut commands almost the full spectrum of comedic possibility. He is a masterful debunker, a superb monologuist, an ingenious farceur, and has a quick and wicked tongue. Like Chaplin he can switch from farce to sentiment by the batting of a lash. All that he lacks to be a decathlon champion of comedy is the mimetic genius of a Dickens, but though Vonnegut is a shrewd observer of character, his dramatic strategy would militate against ventriloquism, even if he had the knack.

Vonnegut writes in a single voice, the one his readers know to be the voice of Kurt Vonnegut. In *Galapagos* he assumes the alias of Leon Trotsky Trout, the son of Kilgore Trout, the sf writer Vonnegut fears he might have been but for the grace of God and the reading public, but the tropes and elisions of this Leon Trout all bear the Vonnegut trademark: the moving-right-along diffidence of paragraphs that commence "Yes, and" and end "and so on and so on"; the same claims to ease and evanescence of composition (Leon writes, "I have written these words in air—with the tip of the index finger of my left hand, which is also air") so that we seem to hear the story rather than to read it as prose on a page; the same beery glee in appropriating clichés that any self-respecting novelist would shrink from ("We were certainly no spring chickens," Vonnegut wrote in his own voice in the prologue to *Slapstick*, and Leon uses the same low locution in *Galapagos*, where he writes, of Captain von Kleist: "He did not know shit from Shinola about navigation").

To cavil at these monogrammed tics, as critics regularly do, is to fall into the trap of supposing that Vonnegut is being a lazy writer or that he is pretending to be a klutz in order to ingratiate himself to a world of klutzes. Neither is the case. The Vonnegut audience is in large part a generation younger than himself (he is now sixty-three) and college-educated. His catchphrases are not those his readers would use but belong to their parents' generation, and are *meant* to annoy them in just the way they annoy the critics and also to establish an imaginary generation gap between the writer and his readers, the better to get on with the avuncular purpose of his comedy, which is moral instruction.

Indeed, the interest of the Vonnegut voice is not in what it reveals of the author but in the audience that it hypothesizes, an audience that must have the most basic facts of Life explained in the simplest terms, an audience that will crack up at the sound of a fart, an audience that has the best of intentions even as it paves the road to hell, an audience of children who know they need to be scolded. Vonnegut is unusual among novelists who dramatize the conflict (ever recurring in his work) between fathers and sons in that his sympathies always lie on the sadder-but-wiser side of the generation gap. In an era that has institutionalized adolescent rebellion, here is a father for foundlings of all ages. Small wonder he is so popular.

Time, Space, the Limitlessness of the Imagination—and Abs to Die for

Superannuated visions of the future—the covers and illustrations for old sci-fi pulps and paperbacks—are a prime American collectible, more plentiful than scrimshaw or old quilts, quaint as cigar boxes, full of anecdotal and associational interest, and priced to be competitive with comic books and baseball trading cards. Those who cannot afford the original art can at least amass cartons of old pulp magazines and paperbacks for which the Old Masters—Chesley Bonestell (1888–1986), Earle J. Bergey (1901–1952), Frank R. Paul (1884–1963), et al.—produced their cover paintings and interior line drawings.

The technical quality of this work ranges from sincere and primitive (Earle Bergey's babes-in-brass-bras covers for *Startling Stories* in the forties), to the chaste astronomical landscapes of Chesley Bonestell, to the lowbrow, high-definition erotic cheesecake of contemporary artists like Boris Vallejo and Frank Frazetta. As collectibles, the better work of Bergey, Bonestell, and Vallejo occupies the same general range—$7,000 to $15,000. A Frazetta—the most popular and priciest sci-fi artist—can command $30,000 and upward (his cover art for a *Vampirella* comic book was auctioned for $70,000 in 1990), but sci-fi art rarely carries price tags comparable to those found at even mid-level galleries.

In some artists this has provoked a simple and understandable chip-on-the-shoulder resentment. The more confident, like Di Fate himself, the author of *Infinite Worlds*, usually shrug off the chip, but a few develop a kind of compensatory megalomania similar to that of those sf writers who dismiss all other writing but sf as "mundane" and lacking the transcendental value of space opera. Ray Bradbury's foreword to *Infinite Worlds* is a prime specimen of this form of denial, as Bradbury, the Eternal American Boy, recounts his reaction to a Jasper Johns retrospective at the Museum of Modern Art:

> I left with fewer brains than when I arrived. How an artist can be born
> to live in one of the great centuries of electric-visual-audiosensual

---

Review of *Infinite Worlds: The Fantastic Visions of Science Fiction Art*, by Vincent Di Fate.

metaphor and have not even one two-cent stamp of optical surprise stick to his retina flabbers one's gast. I felt as if I had made a lunatic turn into a time alley where the graffiti never knew that Freud, Apple Computer or Carl Sagan were ever born. . . . Suffering bends from lack of some fresh-air image, I fled MOMA and hurled myself into the nearest poster gallery to refill on rockets, marshmallow-suited astronauts, and Mélès's Moon. . . .

Such confident philistinism has become increasingly rare fun in our era of universal college education, but Bradbury is probably correct in supposing that he speaks (or sees) for the majority, who admire any picture in proportion as it is a magic window offering a high-resolution view of something for which they feel fondness, curiosity, or reverence. The sense of wonder is what sf fandom claims as the genre's special territory, and this corresponds in the visual arts to the Sublime, for which in painting there have been two main channels, eye-popping landscapes and heroic nudes. These continue to be the wares offered by the artists whom Di Fate celebrates.

However, judging by his brief account of the history of sf art, Di Fate is as innocent of earlier versions of the Sublime—indeed, of anything painted before 1930—as any American third-grader. He's heard rumors of da Vinci, seen some reproductions of Bosch, and that's about it for the past, until the premiere of Rocketship X-M in 1950. In his own way, he (and most of the artists whose work his book reproduces) seems as authentic a primitive as Grandma Moses or the Siennese of the thirteenth century.

Like those artists, the sf illustrators were perpetuating traditions of imagery and craftsmanship they had inherited from a vanished civilization. Behind the fantastic landscapes of artists like James Gurney (of Dinotopia fame) or the outer-space panoramas of John Berkey loom the Babylonian dioramas of John Martin (1789–1854), whose work probably did not impinge on American illustrators except through Martin's influence on Gustave Doré and the set designer of Griffith's Intolerance. Time and again, sf artists (and writers) have reinvented the wheel (or cannily infringed on the patent), and an interesting book might be written on that subject. This is not that book.

Like most coffee table books, this is simply a picture album, showing a sampling of the work of a goodly number of sf artists, presented in alphabetical order. There is no information as to the size, medium, date, or present provenance of the works reproduced, and the brief bios of the artists read like the flattest PR boilerplate, as in this numb appreciation of James E. Bama:

Bama's commercial art career encompassed a variety of subjects, and he is regarded as a major figure in the illustration mainstream. His extraordinary ability to paint figures and to render textures influenced dozens of other artists, and the impact of his work is still felt today, many years after his retirement from the field.

Di Fate makes no odious comparisons and creates no invidious distinctions. Everyone on view is like Howard V. Brown (1878–?): "a versatile, highly skilled artist," who emerged as one of the most talented and popular artists in the genre, though from the six *Astounding* covers reproduced, Brown would seem to be a hack of minimal technical competence, derivative ideas, and zero flair.

Despite Di Fate's intransigent blandness, it is possible to winkle out some interesting data from the assembled bios—how the more foresightful artists of the genre, like Jim Burns and David Mattingly, were regularly co-opted by Hollywood and thereby ceased to produce collectible art, since the studios owned all they produced; how often, today as in the Renaissance, careers in illustration are a family business carried on by fathers and sons, husbands and wives. But of the dollars-and-cents realities of these artists' lives Di Fate has almost nothing to say.

It might have been interesting to see what the artists themselves look like, but that is a pleasure we are allowed only in the case of Boris Vallejo. The text glosses a Vallejo painting of a lucite figure with Schwarzenegger biceps and torso as the artist himself, posed as a robotic deity for a painting that speaks of time, space, and the limitlessness of the imagination. Well, why not? Things quite as grandiose and no less silly have often been said of Vallejo's great-great-role-model Michelangelo. Painters are not the best spokesmen for their own art, which is why poets and other underemployed writers are hired to hype them in places like *ArtNews*.

An honest appraisal of the pleasures and embarrassments to be obtained from the non-lunar-rock side of sf art would have to take into account the degree to which the artist equivocates or luxuriates in the pornographic element of his art. Frazetta and Vallejo have been commendably up-front in this regard, and their prices among collectors reflect that. But the most audacious and successful of sf illustrators is represented in *Infinite Worlds* only by one postcard-sized reproduction depicting a monster with a head more blatantly phallic than that of Joe Camel. This is the work of an artist not given exhibition space in the book, and one of the few artists about whom Di Fate is snide, the Swiss H. R. Giger. Giger did not illustrate other people's stories, but was the inventor of his own nightmarish fancies, a designer of aliens (including the *Alien* of cinematic fame) whose every bone and internal organ is a pornographic pun. Giger's vagina-dentata monsters of the 1970s and 1980s are unveilings of the id meaning of the bug-eyed monster of the earlier pulp magazines, and a book of sf art without a selection of Giger's images is like a book about Dutch art with no mention of Rembrandt.

Giger's absence may well be his own choice and not Di Fate's. It's not as though there were an argument being pursued in this book or a historical overview being advanced. There are simply a lot of pictures, clearly reproduced, many on the same scale as when they first served as covers for *Astounding Stories* or illustrations in *Omni*. There are enough prime specimens and ho-hum hackwork in all categories—ancient camp, lunar landscapes, gruesome monsters, soft-core porn, gaga gore, and lyric whimsy—to make me wish that someday someone might write the text that should have been part of the package.

PART THREE ON SF The Bully Pulpit

The King and His Minions: Thoughts of a TWILIGHT ZONE Reviewer

"The time has been," Macbeth reminisces in Act V, "my senses would have cool'd to hear a night-shriek, and my fell of hair would at a dismal treatise rouse and stir as life were in it." Read a few too many dismal treatises, however, and you may find, along with Macbeth, that: "I have supp'd full with horrors; direness, familiar to my slaughterous thoughts, cannot once start me."

It may be, however, that this disclaimer, coming just before his "tomorrow and tomorrow and tomorrow" speech, is the theatrical equivalent to the obligatory false alarm in every horror movie when the cat leaps out from behind the curtains and we all shriek, and then have to laugh to reassure ourselves that "It's only the cat!"—though we know quite well that there is enough direness ahead of us to cool our senses to freezing. Not only such basic physical direness as death, disease, the frailty and corruption of the flesh, the hunger of various predators, and the dangers posed by psychopaths at loose after dark, but the further, horrible suspicion that the social system we are necessarily a part of, which is supposed to keep these dangers at bay, may instead have formed some kind of unholy alliance with them—the suspicion, to put it another way, that Macbeth may be the person who's answering the phone when we dial 911.

Those would seem to be enough different varieties of direness to guarantee some degree of timeliness and universality to the genre of the horror story. This plentitude explains why the range of the horror story, in terms of literary sophistication, should be wider than that of any other literary genre, running the gamut from the elemental night-shrieking nastiness of EC Comics to the highbrow *frissons* of James's *The Turn of the Screw* or Kafka's *Metamorphosis*. Horror, like his brother Death, is an equal opportunity employer.

To the degree that a theme is universal, it is in proportion exploitable, and the proliferation of schlock horror novels in the wake of such box office successes as *The Omen* series, et al., is hardly to be wondered at. So long as there are rustics to buy ballad-sheets there will be balladeers to supply them, though as the mean reading speed of the audience and the technology of printing have both greatly advanced in recent centuries, it's not ballad-sheets that are hawked nowadays but paperback originals.

Without dwelling on the easy irony of the word "original," let's take a quick peek inside a recent 329-page ballad-sheet brought out by Pocket Books, *The Deathstone*, by Ken Eulo, author of *The Bloodstone* and *The Brownstone* (and doubtless, if the market holds up, of *The Headstone*, *The Whetstone*, and *The Rhinestone*). There is nothing intrinsically unworkable in the book's premise of a small town keeping up the pagan tradition of human sacrifice: it's done yeoman service for Shirley Jackson's story "The Lottery," and the movie *The Wicker Man*. Horror stories are usually reenactments of favorite myths. What sinks Eulo's book to the rock-bottom of the sophistication spectrum (from savvy to sappy) is the style of his reenactment, a style that is equal parts soap-opera mawkish and button-pushing portentous, graduating to dithering hysteria for the big moments:

> They were circling the fire now, dancing in a madman's frenzy, delirium, their huge animal heads weaving in and out of shadows. The fire blazed up with a roar, sending a column of red flames soaring. They moaned and wailed and shouted. Even though the words were unintelligible, Ron felt that their hideous shrieks were like a hand held toward him, a handshake with death.

Don't worry though, kids. Ron doesn't die. He saves Chandal and little Kristy from the Widow Wheatley and the other wicked Satanists and returns to his talent agency in Hollywood.

If there is one key to prejudging books and consigning them, half-read, to the holocaust, it must be Style, and "Style" is the single word most likely to provoke hack writers and hack readers to postures of defense. Storytelling and yarn-spinning are simple, wholesome crafts, they would aver, to which questions of Style are irrelevant. Style is to be left to stylists, like Hemingway or Faulkner or Joyce, the writers you have to read in school.

Nonsense. Style is simply a way of handling yourself in prose so as to signal to an attentive reader that she is in the presence of someone possessed of honesty, wit, sophistication, irony, compassion, or whatever other attributes one looks for in a person to whom one is about to give over n-many hours of one's mental life. People who insist otherwise usually have mental halitosis.

Which is why I think it's fair for reviewers to indicate which books they have found unreadable. Otherwise the longest, dullest, worst books would only be reviewed by people able to read them, i.e., unable or unwilling to recognize their gross defects. Only creative writing teachers would review John Gardner. Only Scientologists and veterans of the Golden Age of science fiction would review *Battlefield Earth*. Only authors' friends would review, say, such a book as John Shirley's *Cellars*. And publishers would come to think that no one ever actually noticed what they were doing.

I might suggest burning *Cellars*, though, as it's a paperback, it will yield at most only enough heat to roast some marshmallows. The tell-tale elements are a willingness to fill a blank space with any cliché that comes to mind ("like a thundering symphony"), an urge to dress up the text with portentous guff ("And the sage remembers"), a merciless determination to recycle said guff, and an emotional sympathy lavished exclusively upon the first-person singular. To these attractions the novel proper adds a couple wheelbarrowfuls of standard-issue splatter-movie grue ("A woman spread-eagled on her back. Her blouse had been torn away. . . . Her breasts had been symmetrically quartered like fruit sections in salad"), and a misogynistic regard for the fair sex to a degree that makes Mickey Spillane look like a radical feminist—all smoothed over with mystic mummeries so false they're probably intended as comic relief, as when our hero explains to the Keystone Kops the killing style associated with the mayhem quoted above: "The lettering on the circle looks like ancient Persian to me, and I suspect the ritual has something to do with the demon Ahriman." Ah so!

So *Cellars* goes, the grue alternating with the hokum for 295 pages of prose that is 85 percent pulp padding and 15 percent amplified scream (under another hat Shirley is the head of a punk rock group called Obsession). There is, I admit, an aesthetic to screaming, and Shirley's shriller screams can get to your crystal ware, but screaming is, as a general rule, less effective on the printed page than in rock music, where the silly lyrics are blessedly incomprehensible and the beat goes on. Novels, alas, don't have a rhythm section to keep them moving—so when the pages refuse to turn: burn, baby, burn.

Let me state clearly here that I am not disparaging "escapist reading" in order to promote "serious literature." I have a keen appetite for entertainment novels of all kinds. For some readers, it may be, the very unnaturalness and ineptitude of the lower grade of occult novels are welcome distancing devices from what might otherwise be too scary, too close for comfort. For them, mustache-twirling villainy and dime-store Halloween masks serve the same sanitizing function that the code of genteel taste serves for readers of more middlebrow spinemasseurs (tinglers they're not), such as Jonathan Carroll's *Voice of Our Shadow*, a preppy ghost story as decorously conventional and capably tailored as a Brooks Brothers suit. Carroll just doesn't believe in ghosts, and his disbelief is contagious. But does anyone believe in ghosts, after all?

Spiritualism flourished in the nineteenth century and lingered into the early decades of the twentieth. Since it was the chief tenet of spiritualist faith that there *are* ghosts, many writers of ghost stories in those years expropriated for their own use much of the spiritualists' genteel intellectual baggage. This new breed of ghosts were not specters of the damned, like Hamlet's father, nor bleedin' 'orrors, beloved by readers of the penny dreadfuls. They were, instead, Lost Souls—most in transit to the Other Side, confused about but not necessarily ill-disposed toward creatures of the flesh.

Under this new dispensation, ghosts were domesticated and made to conform to the decorous tastes of a middle-class, middlebrow audience. In the American pulps there was still full-frontal ghastliness, but British ghosts were expected to comport themselves like ordinary people. When an ex-wife wished to haunt her faithless husband (as in Mary Treadgold's "The Telephone"), her reproaches were conveyed over the phone, in what we must imagine to be a subdued tone. The theory is that ghosts are credible in proportion to the gentility of their manners. The brush of a sleeve, a stifled sigh—these are to be the stuff of horror, and in the hands of a good writer they serve very well. The greatest of all ghost stories, James's *The Turn of the Screw*, doesn't bother with horrid shrieks and rattled chains.

Yet if they were on their oaths, I'm sure most of the best ghost-story writers would admit that their ghosts are symbols of Something Else. Which is a roundabout way of saying that, finally, Eulo and Shirley and Carroll (and unnumbered others) fail for this reason—a reluctance to make eye contact with their fears. Instead of real horrors to sup upon, with meat and maggots on their bones, they offer plastic skeletons.

Stephen King is another matter. He has enjoyed his success precisely because he's remained true to his own clearest sense of what is fearful, fearfuler, fearfulest. What King fears is his own and other people's capacity for cruelty and brutality, madness, loneliness, disease, pain, and death: men, women, most forms of animal life, and the weather. When King introduces supernatural or paranormal elements into his tales it is as a stand-in for one of the above-mentioned "natural" fears. Thus, Carrie's telekinetic powers in his first novel are emblematic of the force of a long-stifled anger erupting into rage, and the horror of *Salem's Lot* is that of witnessing the archetypal Our Town of Rockwell, Wilder, and Bradbury electing Dracula as mayor and appointing his wives to the Board of Education.

King's *Different Seasons* is a collection of four quite separate tales, only one of which (and that, thankfully, the shortest) failed to shiver my timbers perceptibly—though King has throughout *Different Seasons* kept to the hither side of the natural/supernatural divide. The other three, in ascending order of both length and personal preference, are: "Rita Hayworth and Shawshank Redemption," a quietly paranoid curtain-raiser that persuaded me *never* to be framed for murder and sentenced to life imprisonment; "The Body," a vivid if sometimes self-consciously "serious" account of the rites of passage practiced by the aboriginal teenagers of Maine's lower-middle class (and a telling pendant to the novel *Salem's Lot*); finally, the hands-down winner of the four and, I think, King's most accomplished piece of fiction at any length, "Apt Pupil." (In his book's afterword, King complains about the difficulty of publishing novellas of twenty-five thousand to thirty-five thousand words. Yet "The Body" and "Apt Pupil" are, respectively, double those lengths, and even the shorter tale would have made a weightier book than Carroll's *Voice of Our Shadow*. I don't mean to look a gift horse in the mouth, only to point out that *Different Seasons* is more nearly a collection of novels than of stories.)

The premise for "Apt Pupil" could scarcely be simpler. A bright, all-American thirteen-year-old discovers that one of his suburban neighbors is the infamous Kurt Dussander, commandant of a Nazi death camp. Instead of reporting Dussander to the police, this paragon of the eighth grade begins to blackmail him—not for money but just "to hear about it":

"'*Hear* about it?'" Dussander echoed. He looked utterly perplexed.

Todd leaned forward, tanned elbows on bluejeaned knees. "Sure. The firing squads. The gas chambers. The ovens. The guys who had to dig their own graves and then stand on the ends so they'd fall into them. The . . ." His tongue came out and wetted his lips. "The examinations. The experiments. Everything. All the gooshy stuff."

Dussander stared at him with a certain amazed detachment, the way a veterinarian might stare at a cat who was giving birth to a succession of two-headed kittens. "You are a monster," he said softly.

To tell more of how this oddest of all couples leapfrog down the road to damnation would be a disservice to anyone who hasn't yet read the book. I'm told by those who have a hand on the pulse of sf and fantasy fandom that "Apt Pupil" has not been exactly taken to the hearts of King's usually quite faithful subjects. I can only suppose that this is a tribute to how closely it cuts to the bone. Surely, in terms simply of generating suspense and keeping the plot twisting, "Apt Pupil" cannot be faulted. I hope Losey gets to make the movie, or that Hitchcock could return from the grave for just one more production. Not since *Strangers on a Train* has there been a plot so perfectly suited to his passion for ethical symmetries.

As I write this, Stephen King's *Pet Sematary* has already been on the *New York Times* bestseller list for ten weeks. The considerable interest (and ultimate failure) of *Pet Sematary* is directly related to the themes I've been dealing with above. The story concerns a doctor disordered by his grief for a loved child, and who succumbs to the temptation of "resurrecting" the child by interring its corpse in an Indian burial ground that has the spectral property of reanimating the dead. King does his usual skillful job of seducing us into accepting his unlikely story, and at the same time creates an atmosphere drenched in the fear of death. One would have to be a very guileless reader indeed not to foresee that the author has doomed his hero's child to an early death. The real element of suspense is how the child will behave in its resurrected state, and King's answer is to have the little zombie go on a rampage of homicide and dirty talk that is like watching a cassette of *The Exorcist* on fast-forward. My objection to this denouement is neither to its strain on credibility nor to its mayhem, but to the way it fails to carry forward, still less to resolve, the novel's so powerfully stated themes—the human need to believe, at any cost, in an afterlife, a need that can drive those who lack the safety valve of a religious faith to such bizarre excesses as spiritualism.

King's opting for a conventional splatter-movie resolution to the question "What if the dead were to live again?" is all the more regrettable, since in the figure of Church, a zombified cat, he has prefigured a possibility that is both more harrowing and more pertinent to the central themes of loss and grief, though in Church's case it is the loss of those vital energies that together constitute the soul. From having been the beau ideal of cattiness, Church degenerates into a sluggish, surly scavenger; not at all a demonic cat, just spoiled meat. If the dead child had returned from the grave similarly disensouled, the horror would have been infinitely greater, because that loss would be a vivid correlative to a parental fear of a fate truly worse than death, the fear that one's child may be severely mentally impaired.

It's doubtful, of course, whether the public wants to be harrowed. The blustering denouement King does provide is reassuring to readers precisely to the degree that it's conventional; it's King's way of telling us not to be upset: it was only a ghost story, after all.

Part of the problem is simply that ghost stories are by their nature short, since the psychology of most literary ghosts is simple in the extreme: they want to getcha. "Dark fantasy" (Charles L. Grant's high-toned euphemism for "horror stories"; thus undertakers become "grief counselors" and garbagemen "sanitary engineers") is a traditional rather than an experimental or innovative art form, as much a ritual as a form of literature, and its "devotees" bring to bear criteria of judgment that have less to do with criticism than with incantation and magic. The old ways must not be departed from, nor any traditional rite omitted.

There are undeniable advantages to playing the game by the rules. Geniuses may fly in the face of tradition, but when their epigones attempt to follow them, the result is likely to lack both the strength of conventional post-and-lintel construction and the energy of first defiance. Traditional values in fiction (a strong plot, believable characters, flowing prose) are a safeguard against major debacle in much the way that wearing evening clothes protects one against sartorial solecisms. They offer, as do the sonnet and the sonata form, the aesthetic satisfaction of tight closure. But the chief virtue of a traditional narrative, for most readers, is surely that it is *comfortable*, like a couch one has lived with many years and that has learned the shape of one's head. Since horror stories must deal with subjects that are inherently disquieting, this observance of aesthetic decorums ("Once upon a time") helps defuse—or at least distance—feelings that could be genuinely dangerous, if given a less circumscribed expression.

At his best, Stephen King has shown himself capable of combining the *frissons* of the supernatural thriller with the weightier stuff of tragedy, but in the present instance he has decided to sidestep that harder task and just lay on the special effects till he's spent his budget of potential victims. I hope it doesn't represent a long-term decision.

In the two-and-a-fraction years that I reviewed for *Twilight Zone* magazine, I was able to divide my column inches about equally between the genres of science fiction and horror, with occasional forays outside those adjoining ghettos, but I confess that I found less and less of it that I could read with pleasure, interest, or vigorous dissent. In the case of horror fiction, this is probably not to be wondered at. Being by definition limited to the evocation of a single emotion, and by hoary convention to a few traditional narrative themes, a steady diet of the stuff is calculated to produce an eventual toxic reaction. As well give all one's musical attention to oboe concerti.

Even in science fiction, while its potential may be undiminished, the actual stuff that sees print has been (with some honorable exceptions) more tepid, more formulaic, and more ill-written than at any time since its last cyclic nadir in the late fifties and early sixties. In part it's the publishers who are to be blamed; they manufacture a product suitable for the most reliable part of their market, the proverbial Lowest Common Denominator, who are, not to put too fine a point on it, dopes, or if that seems too harsh, let us say they suffer from reading dysfunctions.

There has been increasingly louder lamentation in the publishing industry during the last few years over the fate of what is euphemistically called midlist fiction, by which is meant novels not likely to become bestsellers. Most fiction of any quality nowadays falls into this midlist category, as witness the now virtually total disparity between the books the *New York Times Book Review* commends to our attention and those that fill its hardcover and paperback bestseller lists. Consider the sf titles on the *Times* list for the week of, say, January 9, 1983. There is *The E.T. Storybook*, titles by Clarke and Asimov (I won't rehash my dissatisfaction with *Foundation's Edge* and *2010* except to say I found the plots of both books numbingly predictable and the wattage of the prose varying between sixty and fifteen), a prehistoric bodice-ripper, and a new potpourri of toothless whimsies by Douglas Adams. A sorry lot, but no sorrier, in literary terms, than the rest of the list, which contained not a single title remotely conceivable as a candidate for the major literary awards.

Why does dreck so often rise to the top of the bestseller list? Is there some merit in these books that their prose disfigures, as acne can disfigure a structurally handsome face? Or is it (I will propose) precisely their faults that endear them to an audience who recognizes in these novels a true mirror image of their own lame brains?

Meanwhile, in the realm of Something Lower, where books are but numbers in a series, the hacks grind out and the presses print the sf and horror equivalent of Silhouette Romances, the sheer mass of which is awesome in much the same way that Niagara Falls is awesome: there is so much of it and it never stops. The metaphor needn't stop there: it is, similarly, not very potable, and most of it courses through the paperback racks without ever being reviewed. Why should it be, after all? Are sneakers or soft drinks or matchbooks reviewed? Commodities are made to be consumed, and surely it is an unkindness for those favored by fortune with steak in plenty to be disdainful of the "taste" of people who must make do with Hamburger Helper.

This is not the proper occasion to speculate how this situation has come about; whether the publishers by their greed, the writers by laziness or native incapacity, or the audience by its hunger for the swill are most culpable. Yet I can't resist stepping down from the platform without relating one final anecdote that bears on these matters. Recently at an sf gathering where fans and writers were mingling, a younger writer from Texas insisted on explaining to me, at great length, the secret of his success. (His first tetralogy has been through several printings; his second, he assured me, was destined for still bigger bucks.) His secret was that he'd found out the name and address of every sales rep who worked for his publisher and had programmed his computer to write each one of them a warm and personal letter thanking them for the efforts he was sure they were making on his behalf. He said it was especially important to get the sales reps to stock your title at airport book stalls; he knew this because he'd been in the distribution end of the business before he'd turned to writing. He assured me that the quality of a book was quite beside the point and that what mattered most of all was the writer's relationship with the reps. When I was in high school we had a name for that relationship.

Well, it's a good anecdote, but I don't think it explains the smell of the world in general. Some lousy writers—and those usually the most successful—are doing their level best. Other lousy writers kvetch about market forces but are happy for the excuse to produce slipshod work. In many cases, the problem is engine failure.

My tenure of office as *Twilight Zone's* book critic from the issue of May 1982 until February 1985 was not all as discouraging as those last dire reflections may sound. I may be disgruntled by some of the poorer books that came under review, but not driven to despair by them. Indeed, rereading assorted columns, I am reminded not only of the original pleasure of combat, but also of the simpler, gregarious pleasures of working with TZ's then-editor T. E. D. Klein, who offered a reviewer all he could ask for: *carte blanche* in the choice of what I reviewed, decent wages, a sufficiency of applause, and hours of good talk about writers and what they write. Since leaving my post at TZ, it is those visits with Ted that I've most missed.

Though I had *carte blanche* at TZ, it was nevertheless imperative that I should deal with any new Stephen King book that appeared. He was not only the King of the genre but already, even then, of bestsellerdom as a whole. Ordinarily I would have shied away from reviewing a writer in that position. As someone who tills in the same genres—but for vastly lower wages—enthusiasm for his work can easily look like one is sucking up to the man and his success, while to give him any critical lumps at all can easily be interpreted as sour grapes. In the context of *Twilight Zone*, such reservations seemed to loom less large.

Furthermore the kind of criticism that King's work most lacks is the kind that deals with more than theme and that awards merits or demerits for "originality" or "style"—that is, a kind of criticism that goes beyond reviewing. But that kind of criticism is hard work, and I doubt whether King's oeuvre really requires such attention. For that reason, and also because the latest additions to the oeuvre have not seemed especially tempting (I've read *Thinner* and thought it thin; I've contemplated the horrid bulk of *IT*, read its reviews, and shuddered), I have not taken advantage of this opportunity to double my two-cents-worth on the subject, except to note, in as neutral a tone as I can command, that the interest of King's work stems at least as much from its success as a commodity as from its aesthetic merits. King is more than a writer, he is a publishing phenomenon and as such transcends criticism.

His most salient virtue, as a commodity, is the consistency and reliability with which the Product is produced. Fame hasn't made King slack off or aspire greatly. The result is a fictional Levittown, acres of decent housing all at exactly the same middling level of accomplishment and ambition. It doesn't give a critic much to consider.

It's the personality and the situation that are interesting. King has been very successful in creating a public image of himself as a Big Kid who's just having fun and goofing off and filling nickel tablets with million-dollar novels, the latest of which, *IT*, concerns a novelist in just that happy situation. Self-referentiality is supposedly a hallmark of postmodern writing, and there's King being as self-referential as can be. But why? Because the Stephen King Story cries out to be told? Or because he has a canny sense of the market and knows that every fannish (i.e., addicted) Reader entertains daydreams of becoming a Writer like King, rich and famous and triumphant over all those insensitive souls who laughed when he sat down to play?

Talking with Jesus

A week ago, as I first sat down to write this column, Jesus appeared to me in a burst of glory and said, "Wait a minute, Thomas. You've got a new assignment."

I was not a little taken aback, being unused to divine visitations. The occasional epiphany is about my limit—hints, portents, glows, tremblings—but never before a direct one-to-One communication.

After He'd dimmed His radiance enough for me to look at Him without blinking, I began rather defensively to explain the idea for the column I'd already begun. It was to have been about five books just on or well outside the border between sf and the mainstream, but all, nevertheless, possessing a distinct appeal to the sensibility of the Ideal Reader of the genre.

"Yes, I know what you intended," said Jesus, "and some other time you can write that column. But now I want you to write about these books." He reached under his robe and took out five books, which He placed on my desk. "You see," He said, with a look no reviewer could have resisted, "these are about Me."

"Oh," said I.

"So obviously," He went on, "they should take precedence over other books. The role I'm assigned varies in its meatiness from book to book, but that I should appear onstage, as it were, in five so different works must be accounted a trend. And isn't that what reviewers are always trying to spot—'trends'?"

I looked at the spines of the books He'd given me and discovered they were the same books I'd already started to review. No miracle could have come more welcomely, for I'm a slow reader and my deadline was upon me.

"May I ask which of the five is Your favorite?"

He shook His head and smiled. "On the Day of Judgment I'll reveal who My favorites are—not till then."

Review of *Jesus Tales*, by Romulus Linney; *Valis*, by Philip K. Dick; *Scripts for the Pageant*, by James Merrill; *White Light*, by Rudy Rucker; and *Their Immortal Hearts*, edited by Bruce McAllister.

"Then could You say something about the possible significance of the trend? Could it be a sign that we're entering a new Age of Faith?"

"No, almost the contrary, I fear. It indicates, to Me, that all too many writers regard my gospels as little more than fabrications on a par with their own trashy novels, and regard Me as a character, like Santa Claus or Sherlock Holmes, no longer safeguarded by copyright laws and fallen into the public domain."

"It seems to me, Jesus, that You fell into the public domain when You were born."

"Very funny."

"Seriously. Have you read Elaine Pagels's *The Gnostic Gospels?* Some of those Gnostic scrolls are as old as any of the synoptic gospels. The trend goes back two thousand years."

"Apocryphal tales!" He snorted. "Jokebooks!"

"But aren't jokes, in a sense, the primal form of Wisdom? Didn't You speak in parables by preference? For example. There's a story in here"—I opened Romulus Linney's *Jesus Tales*—"in which You and St. Peter spend the night drinking with a couple of Basque hillbillies called Jacques and Jeannette. They fall to telling all sorts of wild tales, including some lulus about Jesus Himself, which He enjoys so much that when He leaves the next morning He performs a miracle for His hosts. He tells them, 'What this morning you first begin will not stop until tonight.'"

"And then what happens?" Jesus asked, pulling up a chair to the desk and helping himself to coffee from the pot on the warmer.

"Well, Jeannette takes in washing for a living, so she starts in on that, and more and more clothes keep coming out of the tub, as though it were bottomless. But that isn't the end of the story. The rich farmers down in the valley get wind of what happened, and when Jesus and St. Peter are passing through their town five years later they put on a spectacular party for them, expecting to reap a similar reward. But instead—here, let me read it from the book:

> The farmers hardly waited until Jesus and Saint Peter were off down the road before they all gathered around the richest farmer.
>
> "You all know what to do," he said. "Everybody has his purse. You start right now, counting money out of your purses. The money, like those clothes, will keep coming out, all day long. Everybody ready?"
>
> They all were. But the farmer stopped a minute, and thought.
>
> "Wait," he said. "We should all go into the woods and relieve ourselves first. That way we won't have to stop later, or waste any time counting money."

So the farmers take his advice—and you can guess how they spend the rest of the day."

Jesus guffawed.

It turned out that Jesus hadn't read Linney's book, so I went on to retell more of the *Jesus Tales*, and threw in a couple of jokes I'd just heard from my brother in Minnesota about Jesus and St. Peter golfing.

"Well, I hope the book as a whole is as good as that sample," said Jesus, in His mellowest humor.

"It's a delight. I intend to give it a rave review. And if You'd like to add a little testimonial of Your own . . ." I hinted.

"Oh, I couldn't possibly do that. This visit has to be unofficial. That's why I came to you. As a fiction writer, and an sf writer at that, people will assume, if you mention any of this, that you're just making it up. Or"— He smiled slyly—"that you've gone off your rocker. Like our friend here"—He tapped His finger on the cover of *Valis*—"Mr. Philip K. Dick."

"Not to change the subject, but do You know the poem by Jacopone da Todi called (I can't remember the Italian) 'It Is the Highest Wisdom to Be Considered Crazy for the Love of Christ'?"

Jesus nodded, and quoted the first line in a rich Tuscan accent: "Senno me pare e cortesia, empazir per lo bel Messia." Then, for my benefit, He translated: "It's plain good sense and common courtesy to drive yourself crazy for Christ's dear sake."

"Thus spake da Todi, and likewise William Blake," I put in, unable to resist an easy rhyme. "I mentioned that poem because it seems to me that Dick is carrying on in that tradition. Also, like La Todi, and like Blake too, he's aware of the paradoxes involved, he knows he sounds nuts, and the situation fascinates him. There's a passage I underlined on page 26; let me read it to You:

> You cannot say that an encounter with God is to mental illness what death is to cancer: the logical outcome of a deteriorating illness process. The technical term—theological technical term, not psychiatric—is theophany. A theophany consists of a self-disclosure by the divine. It does not consist of something the percipient does; it consists of something the divine—the God or gods, the high power—does.

At that point Dick goes on to speculate how to distinguish between a genuine theophany and a hallucination. And of course there is no certain way to distinguish, unless God discloses some information that one couldn't possibly know by any other means. Which is rarely, if ever, the case."

Jesus nodded. "Yes, that's the basic theory We work on. What would become of human freedom if everyone knew for a fact that heaven is always, as it were, on patrol? The Age of Miracles is over."

"Except in novels. In novels (as in the Scriptures) miracles are easy to arrange. The peculiar fascination of Valis is that for much of its length it's not exactly a novel. Dick did have his own honest-to-God theophany back in 1974, and on the one occasion I met him, some time afterward, he gave me an account of that experience that follows the 'plot' of Valis fairly closely."

"And did you believe him?" Jesus asked.

"I believed that he believed that he'd been in touch with something supernatural. Indeed, I was a bit envious, having never had a theophany of my own. Until," I thought to add, "this afternoon."

Jesus smiled enigmatically.

"I hope Dick won't think I'm betraying his confidence mentioning that; he's discussed the same experience in his interview in Charles Platt's Dream Makers, and in Valis itself the hero is called 'Philip K. Dick,' though he also appears in the form of an alter ego called 'Horselover Fat' (which is his own name, rendered from Greek and German). The fascination of the book, what's most artful and confounding about it, is the way the line between Dick and Fat shifts and wavers, Dick representing the professional novelist who understands that all these mystic revelations are his own novelistic imaginings, while Fat is the part of him that receives, for a while, and believes, a little longer, messages from . . . You, Lord."

"Oh, I'm not the half of it in Valis. Wagner, Ikhnaton, UFOs, the Roman Empire, Richard Nixon—they all are conflated into one thick Jungian stew. When I do appear in person, so to speak, I've been transmogrified into a two-year-old girl."

"Mm, that was a good scene."

"And the book as a whole? Do you honestly think Dick has made a novel of that mish-mash of theology and psuedo-science? You, the esthete, the skeptic, the Doubting Thomas?"

"I'll admit that as a novel, as a whole novel, I thought it went off the rails sometimes. But the first half holds together wonderfully, considering how much there is to be held together. If you read it as a realistic, confessional novel, in the sad-mad-glad vein of Plath's The Bell Jar or (better) Pirsig's Zen and the Art of Motorcycle Maintenance, Valis scores, oh let's say 8.416 on a scale of 10. Even its wilder flights of fancy fall into place, not as a system of belief to be considered on its merits, but as components of the self being confessed. Dick has always had the most hyperkinetic imagination in science fiction. His plots have often played elaborate games with the mechanics of suspended disbelief. In those ways *Valis* is the new logical aesthetic step. Where it went wrong, for me, is when Dick, Fat, and their friends go off to see a movie called *Valis*. *Valis*-the-movie is a bore, and it is also, significantly, the moment when the book shifts from a confessional, psychological mode into sf. That is, the world of the novel ceases to be the world of everyday common consensus and begins to conform to Horselover Fat's imaginings. Suddenly the dialectic tightrope goes slack, and Dick almost falls into the net. But not quite. In fact, his recovery is masterful."

"From your description of *Valis*, Thomas, I don't think its own author would recognize it. I think Dick is more than half-persuaded that his syncretistic ruminations—that long appendix he calls *Tractates Cryptica Scriptura*—are the God's truth. I think, in short, that he's a heretic!"

"And James Merrill?"

"Another heretic."

"*Scripts for the Pageant* is the last book in a trilogy, as You know. Have you read the two preceding, *Divine Comedies* and *Mirabell*?

"To be perfectly frank, Thomas, I don't have the patience for most poetry. A little Milton, long ago, and some Dante before that. Merrill's book seems to aim at enlightenment more than entertainment, and being a major source of enlightenment myself . . ."

"You're not alone in feeling that way, but I don't think it's a valid antithesis. Why can't Truth be amusing? Think of Castaneda, or Pirsig, or *Valis*, for that matter. If novels can aspire to the condition of Holy Writ (and still be fun), why not poetry?"

"In theory I agree. But modern poetry has become so abstract. Dante, by contrast, was first and foremost a marvelous storyteller."

"So is Merrill, though the story he tells is admittedly rather sedentary. Merrill and his friend David Jackson begin to receive messages on a ouija board from an otherworldly figure called Ephraim, who puts them in touch with the hierarchy of elemental spirits and with many of their own lately deceased friends and culture heroes. It's like Dante without the geography, but *with* all the great cameo performances."

"Including a libelous twelve-line role for Yours Truly."

"You don't figure very largely in Merrill's scheme of the afterlife, that's so, but in a pluralistic society and a secular age . . ."

"I should be happy to receive so much as a footnote? Mohammed, by contrast, rates a full scene of his own, and his verses are much more vividly written. What's more, he's introduced, by the Master of Ceremonies, as 'the one still very much alive force in that crowd.' The crowd, namely, of Buddha, myself, Mohammed, and Mercury. Do you really think Christianity deserves being relegated to the status of Roman mythology?"

"Of course not, Jesus. Merrill is referring only to the *demographic* strength of Islam, to the fanatic loyalty it can still command. I do think this is a side issue. Poets are entitled to some poetic license, and—"

"We'll see what Merrill is entitled to on the Day of Judgment, shall we? (And it won't be another Pulitzer or NBA, I can assure you.) Meanwhile, tell me this—do you think science fiction *readers* will want to read three volumes of ouija messages in heroic couplets?"

"Not all sf readers, no. But those who aren't shy of a bit of intellectual exercise can enjoy his poem in exactly the way they'd enjoy Dick—as an imaginative experience of the first order.

'Enjoy' is such a tame word for it, though. The trilogy as a whole may well be the finest large-scale poem any American has ever written—lots of knowledgable critics are already saying so—and it's certainly more polished, more integrated, and just plain more fun than any of the contenders. *The Cantos*, say, or *Paterson*. But its specific appeal for sf readers is the way Merrill turns the dry straw of science textbooks into poetry of pure spun gold. Everyone is always saying that that's what modern poetry *should* be doing, but most poets today are scientific illiterates. Merrill is—"

"The Messiah, by the sound of it!"

"We're never going to agree about this, Jesus. Tell me, what did you think of *White Light*?"

"From a strictly Christian point of view, it seemed the least libelous. I'm represented quite orthodoxly as contesting with Satan for the soul of a departed spirit. That scene, however, is almost the only part of the book that offers a traditional view of the afterlife. Most of the action takes place in a kind of non-Euclidian Heaven called Cimön, where everything, even single blades of grass, is infinite. Being infinite Myself in many ways, I can appreciate the difficulty of the task Mr. Rucker set himself. By and large I thought he carried it off rather well."

"Sounds almost like a Judgment to me."

Jesus smiled. "Well, after all, it's only a story, so I feel I can be charitable. *White Light* doesn't make any claims, as Dick's book does, or Merrill's, on a reader's literal Faith. Besides, I like a story with an orderly plot and characters who get their just desserts. Call Me old-fashioned, but I thought it was a damned good read. You can quote Me if you like."

"Mm. I don't know if Rucker—or, indeed, most readers—would consider *White Light* 'old-fashioned.' There haven't been many sf novels that use pure mathematics as the basis for constructing an alien world. *Flat-*

land, a couple short stories by Norman Kagan, and . . . what else? And the tone of the book is as singular as its conceptual framework, a sort of cross between Raymond Chandler and Lewis Carroll (another mathematicizing fabulist) with a tip of the hat along the way to Franz Kafka, who appears, in beetle form, as Virgil to the narrator's Dante. Old-fashioned?"

"Your perspective on Time naturally differs from Mine. I think too much is made of whether things are new or old. Good and bad, intelligent and dumb, powerful and weak—those are surely more relevant standards of Judgment than pure novelty and timeliness."

"I'd have to agree, and I'd add that *White Light* is a good, intelligent, powerful novel, and the most auspicious debut in the sf field since . . . Well, considering it's his first novel, since I don't know when."

"I hope you won't, when you review it," said Jesus, "give away too much of the plot. There's a special circle in hell for reviewers who spoil a story's best surprises. And with that word to the wise, I'd really best be on My way. This has been an awfully long theophany."

"Wait, wait—there's one more book."

I took out *Their Immortal Hearts* from the bottom of the pile. It was an anthology in three parts: "Cold War Orphans," a novelette by Michael Bishop; the title novella of eighty pages, by Bruce McAllister (who is also the book's publisher); and a novella of forty pages by Barry Malzberg, "La Croix." It is the Malzberg story that includes Jesus among its dramatis personae. Of the five treatments of Christ, Malzberg's is in some ways the most reverent—or, at least, the most anguished—but also the most skeptical. Like Ingmar Bergman, like Graham Greene, like a lot of us, Malzberg seems hungry for his own theophany, and yet one can't escape the feeling that even if God spoke to him directly from a burning bush he'd immediately suspect someone else of having set the fire. I was anxious, therefore, to know Jesus's opinion of so representative a modern instance.

Jesus rifled the pages of *Their Immortal Hearts.* "Oh yes. Mm—hm. Well." He closed the book with a sigh. "The Bishop story was rather strong, I thought. Who would expect a writer his age to capture so vividly the atmosphere of an Air Force base in Turkey in the 1950s? I wouldn't call it sf, but there's no sin in that. As for the McAllister novella, dear Me, what can I say? I thought it was dull, and certainly much too long. Writers who need editors shouldn't publish their own work. But I daresay many sf readers will enjoy it more than any of the other books we've been speaking of. Doesn't it say somewhere in the Bible, 'If you can't say something nice, don't say anything at all'?"

"That's from *Bambi*."

"It's still a good maxim."

"Jesus," I insisted, even as He started to fade away, "what did you think of Barry Malzberg's story?"

"Oh yes, 'La Croix.'" His voice faded to a whisper, thence to a hollowed silence. I thought I could see tears forming in His eyes. Just before he disappeared altogether He took a pencil from the breast pocket of His robe, flipped open James Merrill's *Scripts for the Pageant,* and drew a line beside the following passage. (I still have the copy He marked for anyone who may doubt the veridical truth of this narrative.) This is the passage Jesus scored:

But, after all, we bookish people live
In bondage to those reigning narrative
Conventions whereby the past two or three
Hundred years have seen a superhuman
All-shaping Father dwindle (as in Newman)
To ghostly, disputable essence, or
Some shaggy-browed, morality-play bore
(As in the Prologue to *Faust*). Today the line
Is drawn esthetic. One allows divine
Discourse, if at all, in paraphrase.
Why should God speak? How humdrum what he *says*
Next to his works: out of a black sleeve, lo!
Sun, Earth and Stars in eloquent dumb show.
Our human words are weakest, I would urge,
When He resorts to them. Here on the verge
Of these objections, one does well to keep
One's mouth shut.

The Labor Day Group

The annuals are out, and here, if we can trust the amalgamated wisdom of our four editors, are the thirty best stories of 1979. It is in the nature of annual reports to pose the question, *Was it a good year?* and it pains me, as both a shareholder and a consumer, to answer that for science fiction, as for so many other sectors of the economy, 1979 was not a good year.

Against such a sweeping judgment it may be countered that sf is not a unitary phenomenon nor one easily comparable to the tomato harvest. Sf is a congeries of individual writers, each producing stories of distinct and varying merit. A year of stories is as arbitrary a measure as mileage in painting. Nevertheless, that is how the matter is arranged, not only by anthologists but by those who organize the two prize-giving systems, SFWA, which awards the Nebulas, and Fandom, which gathers once a year to hand out Hugos. The overlap between the contents of the annuals and the short-lists for the prizes is so great that one may fairly surmise that something like cause-and-effect is at work. As the SFWA nominating procedures are conducted in plain view, it seems certain that the editors will keep their eyes open for the likeliest contenders, since the annual that most successfully second-guesses the awards nominees has a clear advantage over its rivals.

All this preamble as a caveat to those seeking a buyers' guide to the supremely best of the three annuals. Each one has its unique excellences (as well as excellences shared with a rival); each, sad to say, includes stories that would be more at home in a workshop than an anthology. What I mean to do is to lump the three annuals together and review the year 1979 in all its annualness, including the awards for short fiction.

First, some raw data. Not counting overlapping choices, there are thirty stories, by twenty-nine writers, in the three annuals. These include all but one of the short story nominees for the Hugo and the Nebula (the omitted writer is represented by another story) and five of the ten nominees for novelette.

Review of *The Best Science Fiction of the Year #9*, edited by Terry Carr; *Best Science Fiction Stories of the Year*, edited by Gardner Dozois; *The 1980 Annual World's Best SF*, edited by Donald A. Wollheim and Arthur W. Saha; and *Timescape*, by Gregory Benford.

A significant proportion of the authors of the nominated stories constitute a generation unto themselves. George R. R. Martin, Vonda McIntyre, Tanith Lee, Jack Dann, Ed Bryant, Michael Bishop, and John Varley were all born between 1945 and 1948 and first began publishing within two years, either way, of 1971. *The Science Fiction Encyclopedia* doesn't have an entry for Orson Scott Card, a multiple nominee, so presumably he came to prominence somewhat later, but my guess, based on internal evidence, is that he would belong to this group. These eight, from a total of twenty-nine writers, wrote something better than 40 percent of the total fiction wordage in the three annuals, and they have to their communal credit seventeen Hugo and Nebula nominations this year. All of them (except Tanith Lee, who is English) are listed as members of SFWA. Most of them were at Noreascon Two in Boston on Labor Day this year, where I met some of them and didn't meet others.

I don't mean to suggest that anything like a cabal is at work, only that a coherent generational grouping exists, such as the groupings Malcolm Cowley speaks of in his essay "And Jesse Begat." Further, I'd suggest that these writers have more in common than those (myself among them) who were lumped together under the rubric "New Wave," that they possess something approaching solidarity, as the Futurians did in their day. The relative strength of their showing at award time may be accounted for innocently enough by the natural fecundity of writers in their early thirties, as well as by the ordinary mechanics of literary careers. Older writers of established reputation tend to devote more of their time and talent to novels. Younger writers are often best able to claim their place in the sun by devoting their best energies to shorter forms and then crossing their fingers at award time.

The awards are a serious business. If there were any doubt of that, one need only listen to the testimony of the winners, one of whom, George Martin, in accepting his award this year, spoke of how he'd lusted after a Hugo when first he'd attended a world convention in the early days of his career. Another, Orson Scott Card, wrote eloquently in a fanzine of his own high regard for the significance of both awards.

Man is a political animal and inclined to pursue self-interest, so it should not be wondered at that in the past, some writers have politicked for these awards with varying degrees of high-mindedness and high-handedness. My reason for noting so much that is common knowledge is not to deplore human nature but to suggest that the work of this latest generation of sf writers—the Labor Day Group, I'd like to call them, since that is when they are most likely to be found all together—has been unduly and unnecessarily influenced by the clubhouse atmosphere of the sf world and its awards systems. A sense of personal vision is rare in their stories, while a sense of writing to please a particular audience, Fandom, is sometimes obtrusively present—as it was, for me, in last year's double award-winner, "The Persistence of Vision," by John Varley.

There are solid behaviorist reasons why this might be so. Having served their literary apprenticeships in the sf magazines during the seventies (a decade otherwise notable for disillusionment and retrenchment), they were witness to the failure of the "New Wave" both as an aesthetic program (art can't be brought into existence by manifestos) and commercially. To a reasonably levelheaded apprentice writer it became increasingly clear through the seventies that art was a problematical commodity and that most of what went by that name was claptrap anyhow. By contrast a competent entertainment engineer who could guarantee production of n-many pages of fictionware might do very well for himself. Look what happened to Star Wars. What the market rewards are simple problems clearly solved by wholesome, likeable characters; ideally, the interest of the work should be telegraphable in one sentence: "What if there were a world as big as its orbit round its sun?" "What if snakes were beneficent instead of poisonous?" "What if there were Giant Insects?" It was good enough for Grandpa, it was good enough for Grandma, and it's good enough for the Labor Day Group. If art's to be part of it, it must be the kind that conceals art, and conceals it well; on the whole, it isn't worth troubling about. Art, these days, is a branch of the welfare department, and worth maybe five thousand dollars in an NEA grant. A Hugo can bring in fifty thousand dollars on the next paperback contract.

Some cases in point, from this year's crop of Labor Day Group stories: Ed Bryant's (or bryANT's) "giANTS" (in the Dozois annual) is about giant ants, like in the movie Them, only different. There are these ants in South America, see, that are really scary and they're heading this way, and here's bryANT's twist—we defeat the ant invasion by inducing immoderate growth, since beyond a certain size exoskeletons are dysfunctional. I remember encountering the same observation some years ago in a book of essays by Arthur Clarke, and I'm sure the idea wasn't original to him. Bryant dramatizes this common knowledge by having someone unaware of it informed of it, after much cajoling, by someone in the know—generally, and in this case, a poor sort of drama, since by a simple shift of point of view the story is reduced to the bare notion one already knows. Inexplicably, "giANTS" won a Nebula. Congratulations.

The winner of the Hugo for short story, George R. R. Martin's "The Way of Cross and Dragon," appears in both the Dozois and Wollheim/Saha annuals. Though full of a good deal of incidental sf invention (droll aliens, pretty planets), the dramatic structure is like that of "giANTS," but the idea being ferreted out by the protagonist is both more original and full of resonance. Martin contends that all supernatural religions are the result of someone's decision to tell a whopping lie, a contention that deserves ampler and more serious treatment than it receives here. Were it set in 100 A.D. instead of in the far future it might have grown teeth at least as effective as those belonging to Martin's other winner this year (capturing both Hugo and Nebula for best novelette), "Sandkings" (in the Carr and Dozois annuals). Like "giANTs," "Sandkings" is an insect-horror story; unlike "giANTS" it fleshes out its premise with ample and well-paced suspense, heaping on grue and ingenuity all the way to the gratifyingly inevitable end. Apart from a couple of sideways glances in the direction of sex, "Sandkings" could have appeared in 1940 in *Astounding* without a ripple of anachronism, and if it had, we'd still be reading it today. I think it's destined to become not only a great movie but a classic board game as well: it's that neat.

There are at least three nominated short stories in the annuals that seem superior to the winning stories by Bryant and Martin. "Vernalfest Morning" (in the Dozois annual) is a relatively minor effort by Michael Bishop, but fiercely imagined within its small compass. (Bishop, I should remark, is probably the least representative figure in the Labor Day Group. Numerous stories and his recent novel *Transfigurations* evidence a degree of extramural literary savvy and ambition that promises still better things to come. His chief point of correspondence with the Group is the way in which all traditional sf ideas comfortably coexist—space wars, telepathy, aliens, catsup, onions, mayonnaise.)

"Unaccompanied Sonata," by Orson Scott Card (in the Wollheim/Saha annual), is a grimly effective futuristic fairy tale, whose pastel colors adorn a heart of purest anthracite. The best story Bradbury's written in years.

My own favorite among the also-rans is Connie Willis's first published story, "Daisy in the Sun" (in the Wollheim/Saha annual). With lyric ellipses, Willis describes a world in the grip of epidemic schizophrenia precipitated by news that the sun is going nova. The heroine is a sexually disturbed adolescent girl in a condition of fugal amnesia. All the way through I thought, "This won't work," but it did. What a great way to begin a career.

So far, I realize, 1979 doesn't look so bad. Indeed, from the thirty stories at hand I'd be able to assemble a selection of at least eleven tales that fizzed agreeably in the mind. That selection would include all the stories mentioned above, except "giANTS," and, from the Carr annual, stories by Philip K. Dick, James P. Girard, and George Turner; from the Dozois annual, a novella by Hilbert Schenck, "The Battle of the Abaco Reefs," that exercises the geopolitical imagination as well as a week of dire headlines. That's nine. Well, put in Rick Gauger's "The Vacuum-Packed Picnic" (in the Carr annual), a piece of good-natured high-tech bawdry, and then let the flip of a coin decide between "Options," by John Varley (in the Carr and Wollheim/Saha annuals), and "Down and Out on Ellfive Prime," by Dean Ing (in the Carr and Dozois annuals). Varley pussyfoots about a ticklish subject and finally avoids it, but his evasions are at least craftsmanlike. The pleasure of Ing's tale is in the engineering problem he's devised for his space colony; superadded to that, however, is a thesis, stated but not to my mind proven, that bums will survive better in outer space because . . . I can't remember why.

Meanwhile, down at the bottom of the barrel, it would be possible to assemble a counter-anthology of the worst of these thirty "best" stories that few readers could read through without dark thoughts about 1979 and what it may bode for the future of sf. No need to castigate those by novices; they are less to blame than their editors for being picked before they're ripe. My pick of the worst by Labor Day Group members flies in the face of received opinion, since one (bryANT's "giANTS") got a Nebula, another was a Hugo nominee (McIntyre's "Fireflood," which I discussed in the July 1980 Book column), and the third, "The Thaw," by Tanith Lee, appears in both the Carr and Wollheim/Saha annuals. "The Thaw" is a conventional sf horror story told in the wisecracking style of a fifties sitcom and set in a woefully underimagined far future.

Finally it isn't worth my time or yours to explain exactly why a particular dumb idea is particularly dumb, especially when the dumb ideas come from pros who probably know better and intend to have the damn thing published anyhow. So without elaboration, and with one loud boo each, I will add to the list of worst stories: "Galatea Galante, the Perfect Popsy," by Alfred Bester, and "Lime Shards," by Gregory Benford (both in the Carr annual); "Bloodsisters," by Joe Haldeman (in the Dozois annual); and "The Locusts," by Larry Niven and Steve Barnes (in the Wollheim/Saha annual).

Enough of trees and back to the forest. It occurs to me that the fault may not lie with the 1979 harvest but with their being too many harvesters in the field. Can sf support three competing anthologies? By way of odious comparison I got down two of Judith Merrill's anthologies, from 1965 and 1966, and yes, by golly, not only were tomatoes juicier in that golden age but there were more of them—thirty-three contributions in Merrill's 1965 volume and thirty-five in 1966. Nor was hers the only annual at the time, for Carr and Wollheim were producing one for Ace. In both years there were more stories of Hall of Fame caliber, stories I still remember vividly at this distance in time, a much larger proportion of work by writers of established reputation within the field, and—the most significant difference—several stories by writers who weren't dues-paying members of the club. In 1979, by contrast, none of the editors has ventured outside the ghetto walls (unless Carr's taking Dick's story from *Rolling Stone College Papers* can be construed that way). In their honorable mention lists at the back of their books neither Carr nor Dozois cites any stories from non-genre magazines or anthologies. (The Wollheim/Saha anthology doesn't trouble to provide a list of runners-up, nor does it offer a survey of the sf year, as the other two annuals do. People who like to talk to the driver of the omnibus will miss such small courtesies.)

It's no longer enough to speak of the walls of the ghetto: now there's a dome, and (on the evidence of most of these stories) communications with the outside have ceased. For a writers' organization to give an award to such a story as "giANTS" is tantamount to erecting a sign at the airlock, saying: "Science Fiction—abandon all taste, ye who enter here." Indeed, I've heard it argued that sf transcends, in its nature, the canons of mundane literary taste. How often, though, what seems like transcendence from one point of view looks like a lack of plumbing from another.

This is not to suggest that sf, in its institutional aspects, should be disbanded. Conventions are fun, and trophies decorate the den like nothing else. But for writers (or readers) to frame a standard of excellence based on purely intramural criteria, and to make it their conscious goal to *win an award*, is to confuse literature with bowling.

Of a book as good as Gregory Benford's *Timescape*, a reviewer can say very little except, take my word, this is superlative, read it. Not only does *Timescape* accomplish the specific task of science fiction (what that task is may be assumed, in these pages, to be self-evident), but it also clears the hurdles of the mainstream novel with strength, grace, and intellectual distinction. Its prose is lucid, flexible, and eloquent without straining after "poetic" effects. Its characterizations have a precision and amplitude of observation rare in even the best sf, since it is difficult to be precise or observant about hypothetical social structures. Contemporary realism necessarily has its edge in that regard, but Benford is able to possess himself of that advantage by setting half his novel in 1962. His scrupulous treatment of the recent past becomes his touchstone for that part of the book set in 1998, a date equidistant (from 1980) in the near future. The year 1962 seems amazingly long ago, an age of Golden Oldies, blithely unaware of the crises pregnant in the womb of time; crises that have become by 1998 an economic and ecological debacle of global proportions.

The plot concerns the efforts of a group of Cambridge physicists in 1998 to get a message back to the scientific establishment of the year 1962 warning them of the world's impending doom. The medium of communication is a beam of tachyons, a particle theoretically symmetrical in relation to time and thus able to ignore the One Way traffic sign that grosser particles (and mortals) must obey. It will give away few turns of the plot to note that the tachyons get through to 1962, since the story's suspense depends rather on how the message is interpreted and whether it is to be believed, a drama that allows full scope to Benford's ability to portray scientists in the round—as politicians, as professional intellectuals, as members of a common culture. As a group portrait of the scientific community *Timescape* compares favorably with the novels of C. P. Snow or even with a nonfiction work like Watson's *The Double Helix*.

As a work of the imagination, comparison becomes more difficult, since sf writers so seldom attempt anything of this magnitude and seriousness. "Seriousness" is usually a term I cringe at, since it implies a kind of moral superiority in a work of art. Nevertheless, I would call this "serious fiction" in the sense that it eschews playfulness and works with the simplest materials on the largest possible scale to create a moral paradigm of great hortatory force. Beside it even such admirable recent works as *The Dispossessed* or *The Fountains of Paradise* (to cite works that share Benford's "seriousness" and his determination to express the imaginative core of scientific thought) seem thin and schematic.

While I can't pretend to judge the physics of the book, I'm willing to defer in such conjectures to the authority of Dr. Benford, who heads the physics department of a major university, and is accounted *the* expert on tachyons. I'll take his word on tachyons. However, when the characters beg to speculate about standard time-travel paradoxes, such as "Was that my grandfather I murdered last night and should I warn him about me?" I feel no such compunction. The only answers to such eternal quandaries are those that art provides, the sense of closure that comes when an engrossing story finds the tellingly right cadences for its finale.

To speak in more detail of the beautiful resolution of the plot would be to spoil the pleasure of a first reading. Avoid, if you can, the inside blurb of the book jacket, which gives away far too much of the story. Indeed, just throw away the book jacket—it's sinfully drab.

Timescape is a superlative novel, i.e., beyond comparison. Read it and proselitize for it. This is one of those rare works of sf, like A Canticle for Leibowitz, that can speak to the unconverted.

1979: Fluff and Fizzles

Few writers consistently give their best energies to short fiction. To judge by internal evidence, many short stories serve to take up the slack between novels or to channel the spillover of manic moments. Sometimes the results merit attention, but—as any magazine reader can bear witness— sometimes they don't. However, if the writer has a name, even his slightest tales are likely to find a publisher unwary or desperate enough to issue them as a collection. Some writers, by the uniformly high quality of their shorter fiction, would seem to defy this cheerless theory, but even in their cases I doubt that editorial discretion has been responsible. Writers seem able to find excuses for reprinting anything they've published (just as the parents of mutants, in all those stories, try to protect their six-fingered, limbless children). These all-worthy collections are either by writers so unvaryingly artful that they never have off-moments or (more likely) by those civil enough to employ their creative troughs in some other way than by cranking out words at three cents each.

Each of the three story collections under review is an honorable exception to the above rule—but only partially. Of the lot, Brian Aldiss's *New Arrivals, Old Encounters* achieves the highest level of wheat to chaff. Of its twelve stories, three are among his most accomplished, another three or four are middling-to-good, a few are only so-so, and one, "Space for Reflection," is godawful—full of lame jokes, woozy philosophizing, slipshod prose, and interpolated fables of smug whimsicality, all thrown into a shapeless picaresque bundle of *Candide* as told to Kurt Vonnegut. Not only is it as bad as all that, but Aldiss knows it is, even as he writes it. Witness this bit of dialogue between Dumb Dragon and the hero, who is touring the universe in search of truth:

> "I really must tell you," says Dumb Dragon, "one of my latest animal stories. Do you mind very much?"
> Jeffris enjoyed the man's company. "Make me like it."
> "That's good. Storytellers are brave men—they always battle with

Review of *New Arrivals, Old Encounters*, by Brian Aldiss; *The Golden Man*, by Philip K. Dick; *Dark Is the Sun*, by Philip Farmer; *The Catalyst*, by Charles Harness; and *Fireflood*, by Vonda McIntyre.

the listeners' wish to dislike what they [sic] hear, for the listener wishes to be ruler of the story, although inwardly he longs to be dominated by it."

Truly, the only way this listener is ever going to like that story is by some greater torture than having to read it (which I did, every word). It isn't as though Aldiss were incapable of high humor, philosphic aplomb, agreeable whimsy, or sheer madcap invention. But sometimes (it seems) he wakes up in the morning with an ashy taste in his mouth and decides that writing is a bum's business and that he'll revenge himself on the fact by writing something fascinatingly abominable. He's capable of writing a whole book under that impetus (e.g., *The Eighty-Minute Hour*), but usually his dyspepsia is dispelled by a single tale.

"Space for Reflection" is perversely (i.e., deliberately) bad. Aldiss also has days when he merely nods, and the result (again, with an interpolated self-criticism) rambles on like this (from "Song of the Silencer"):

> "I recognise that your intentions, and the intentions of government are good. That you have become tainted by power is inescapable. Such is human nature. Power warps imagination."
> "Cut the verbosity!"
> "That is my endeavour. I'm nervous, can't you see?"

If Aldiss can't resist the impulse to conquer his bluer moments by *writing* them away, at least he should be able to recognize, with a year or two of hindsight, that the bottom of his barrel is far inferior to the top of his bent and that the twain should never meet in one collection. With a little more patience, *New Arrivals, Old Encounters* might have been a thoroughly good book—indeed, a classic collection—rather than a miscellany of hits and misses, for Aldiss has that essential virtue of the complete short story writer, Range.

The three best stories in the book exhibit that range at full stretch. "The Small Bones of Tu Fu" is an extended metaphor in the most graceful of chinoiserie frames, the narrative equivalent of a perfectly turned sonnet that yet avoids becoming that hybrid anomaly, a prose poem. "A Spot of Konfrontation" is broad farce, skillfully constructed and richly ornamented, set in a future Tahiti, where— But why spoil good jokes by telegraphing their punch lines? Enough to say that Aldiss here combines the mellow bawdry of his mainstream novels, such as *A Soldier Erect*, with the verbal ingenuities of *Barefoot in the Head*. "Indifference" is sf of classic simplicity in both design and execution. The drama is subdued but heartfelt. It treats of philosophical matters that all too easily (on the evidence of "Song of the Silencer") could lead the author into hollow pontifications, but because the ideas are grounded in characters roundly and ironically imagined, their expression has the timbre of life.

When Aldiss is good, he is very, very good, but when he is bad he longs inwardly to be dominated by an editor. Thus Spake Dumb Dragon.

On some days of the week Philip K. Dick is my favorite science fiction writer, but while I'm in the witness box and under oath I must say that when *he* is bad he, too, is horrid. *The Golden Man* is not without A+ offerings, and no serious reader should flinch from the categorical imperative of buying it: fifteen heretofore uncollected stories spanning the years from 1953 to 1974, with an introduction and notes by the author—a first edition, in fact, for only $2.25. However, a lot of the fowl in this book are turkeys. As such they have a baleful fascination for us loyalists who must ask ourselves how the germs of Dick's greatness can be discerned in, Lord help us, *this*.

An instance of this, from "The Last of the Masters" (1954), a hyperkinetic foray into hairy-chested-style hugger-mugger. Here is the tail-end of its action-packed denouement:

> Tolby was heavier. But he was exhausted. He had crawled hours, beat his way through the mountains, walked endlessly. He was at the end of his strength. The car wreck, the days of walking. Green was in perfect shape. His wiry, agile body twisted away. His hands came up. Fingers dug into Tolby's windpipe; he kicked the youth in the groin. Green staggered back, convulsed and bent over with pain.
>
> "All right," Green gasped, face ugly and dark. His hand fumbled with his pistol. The barrel came up.
>
> Half of Green's head dissolved. His hands opened and his gun fell to the floor.

If that isn't bogus machismo, John Wayne never had a career. But I suppose we all looked silly, we pulp writers of long, long ago, so I shouldn't cast the first stone.

Other stories here resist being liked by virtue of their depressive rather than their manic tendencies. My least favorite, "Precious Artifact" (1964, when Dick was in his novelistic prime), presents the archetypal Dickean situation—the world as a mirage engineered by invading aliens. But the tone is flat and affectless, the supporting detail thin and uninspired, the prose written with a dogged determination to provide a week's groceries.

The story's sixteen pages read like sixty—not because his theme is depressing, but because he is writing with his last three ergs of working energy.

I've written elsewhere, in his praise, that Dick's method relies, more than most writers', on improvisation. Characters spring to life and seem to behave autonomously. Such a method is easier to employ in novels, where there's more room, but Dick's best stories display a similar scatty sense of design and amplitude of invention. It may be that Dick conserves his best inspirations for his novels—or else those ideas just grow, like Topsy, into novels, while lesser inspirations wither on the vine. Whyever, his ratio of success for short stories has not been as high as for novels, and these stories represent a kind of second or third pressing, having been passed over when his earlier (and better) collections were assembled.

Even so, the book includes a couple classics. "The Little Black Box" (1964) is a masterful account of Christian conversion as alien invasion; it strikes a Mozartean balance between irony and sympathy. The title story, from 1954, though a degree less quintessential, is a thoroughly implausible though well-worked-out account of a superman of the Blond Beast variety. One can't read it without wondering what the results would have been if Dick had freaked out in that direction. Jorge Borges goes to Gor!

But he never would or could have. Witness "The King of the Elves" (1953), a fantasy that rivals Wells's "Mr. Skelmerdale in Fairyland" for its blend of the banal and the magical. The hero, Shadrach Jones, a filling-station attendant, is approached one night by a group of indigent, pathetic Elves. They elect him to be their king and ask him to lead them to battle against the Trolls, who are, as we all know, taking over everything. Jones is doubly an underdog, the victim not only of his Trollish employer but of his minion Elves (who represent a kind of Divine Schizophrenia à la R. D. Laing). While many underdogs may turn out to be supermen when their secret identity is revealed, Dick's underdogs are too grounded in an observed humanity for fantasies of ressentiment to come to a van Vogtian fruition.

The jewel of the book is the introduction, a meditation on the nature of sf and a memoir of his career, in which he tells of grocery shopping at the Lucky Dog Pet Store and of writing fan letters to Capitol Records to prophesy that Linda Ronstadt's new record would be "the beginning of a career unparalleled in the record industry." He daydreams of the epitaph to be carved on his gravestone in his alternate existence as a talent scout:

HE DISCOVERED LINDA RONSTADT
AND SIGNED HER UP

It's that beguiling mixture of bravado and humility that gives his best stories and novels their induplicable air of being centered in something more than an alert intelligence; Dick's fiction seems prophetic, not in the trivial sense of predicting events or trends, but in the Old Testament sense, in the sense that Dante, Blake, and Shelley are prophetic, because they speak from the burning bush of an achieved human wisdom. Readers who feel such claims are not too large will not rejoice greatly in *The Golden Man*, but Dick is of that stature where even his failures merit publication.

In a recently published interview, J. G. Ballard remarked that he always gives a favorable review to a book if he hasn't read it. He also professed to find it puzzling that when he'd told this reviewer of his charitable practice I appeared to be shocked. Truly, I am of the puritanical conviction that a reviewer is obliged to read to the bitter end in fair exchange for his pay and the right to crack wise. However, this often leads to a situation where the unworthiest books never receive their just desserts critically because savvy reviewers, dreading to read them, don't undertake to review them. That leaves bad novels in the hands of bad or venal reviewers, not an ideal alternative.

All this by way of excusing myself in advance for being unable to finish Philip Farmer's *Dark Is the Sun*. Its four hundred–plus pages grew stiff beneath my despairing gaze and would not turn. This review became overdue, and still each time I'd read another few pages it would happen again. My problem is I'm unable to read fast enough and carelessly enough to enter the hypnagogic state demanded by this sort of book. *Dark Is the Sun* is meant for speed readers whose high-speed attention will construct from the asphalt of the prose a world of low resolution and high escapist involvement; not a novel but a daydream in remedial-reading English. It doesn't work on me. Like a skeptical visitor to Disneyland, I find my attention straying to all the inauthentic details: the concrete trunks of the palm trees, the threadbare astroturf, the staticky roar of the android lion. After a while only the tourists are of interest—i.e., the question of whether *anyone* can enjoy something so routinely phony and, if so, whether it's the inauthenticity itself that they enjoy, or have they, incredibly, suspended disbelief.

It begins slowly. In chapter 1 the hero, a teenage Tarzan, sets off from his barbarian home to quest for a bride. In chapter 2 he saves his dog Jum from a furry blue crocodile, or athaksum. In the process, Farmer spells out his artistic credo:

"Hang on!" Deyv shouted. Later, he was to think that this had been nonsense advice, since the dog had no hands. But he had to say something; that was the essence of a human being. Say something, even if it means nothing, because as long as one is talking, one is alive.

(For the entire one hundred pages I could get through, Deyv's exploits were frugally padded out with such say-something, say-anything maunderings.)

In chapter 3 Deyv walks along an Old Highway and admires the jungle scenery. In chapter 4 he flees a pack of hungry khratikl:

There were perhaps a hundred of them. They flew swiftly, cutting across the wind, their leathery wings flapping. Deyv staggered across the short grass. His legs felt weak, and his head swam. He drove on, aware that Jum and Aejip were not running in their best form by any means. Nonetheless, they were faster than he. A glance showed him that the khratikl had veered to cut him off. He tried to increase his pace, and he did. But not by much. Whatever had shocked him had taken a great deal out of him.

That paragraph is representative. Without perpetrating any real, and possibly amusing, howlers, the prose clunks and thuds and hobbles from one perfunctory thrill to the next. The imaginative component is of a piece with the prose; one composite animal follows another, but not one is scary or even interestingly odd because Farmer's heart isn't in it. He knows, from his earlier imitations of ERB & Company, what formulas to follow, and he follows them like a train on its tracks.

Why flog a dead horse? First, because Farmer is able to produce much better work, when his imagination is in gear, and it should be made clear to him that no one mistakes this mouthwash for roses. One assumes he manufactures it because he thinks it's what the audience demands. More likely, it's what his editors tell him the audience demands, and that is the second reason for flogging this dead horse: Dark Is the Sun typifies the worst tendencies of commercial publishing to cash in on any established success with any imitation, however brummagem and tawdry. Farmer is no stranger to such trafficking. Indeed, he's sometimes shown genius in finding legal ways to expropriate literary properties as diverse as Edgar Rice Burroughs and Kurt Vonnegut. But he always showed himself to be a merry sort of rogue in those encounters, out-Heroding Herod with X-rated hyper-vulgarity. This time he's eliminated all gleeful traces of his own talent for outrage, and what is left is perfectly represented by Ballantine's klutzy, sanitized-Frazetta cover art. Science fiction offers so many richer varieties of Barsoom-derived opiates that even the twelve-year-olds and the addicts should have a hard time getting off on this one.

Charles Harness's *The Catalyst* is a different sort of sad story, an honest effort to write a good book, which fails through one fatal miscalculation: it shouldn't have been sf. An earlier sf novel, *The Ring of Ritornel*, has been held up as an exemplar of baroque pizzazz by both Damon Knight and Brian Aldiss—sf as choreographed by Busby Berkeley. Unlike that book, *The Catalyst* is set in a gray day-after-tomorrow where not much happens. A team of scientists sets out to find a catalyst that will allow them to synthesize a new drug economically. They do, and then (surprise) Trialine, the drug so synthesized, proves to be effective against novarella, a dread disease Harness has invented for the express purpose of giving Trialine something to do. Along the way, boy meets girl.

On these dry bones there is nevertheless enough meat that even two-thirds of the way through, the story seemed redeemable. However, most even of these meaty bits, which concern office politics in the chemical industry, are spoiled by the blurry focus of the near-future setting. Harness's incidental extrapolations don't hang together: the industrial scenery seems rather contemporary, but there are grown-up clones on hand—in A.D. 2006. If the same tale had been set in 1980, as it easily could have been, Harness would have had the advantage of drawing from live models. Concerning chemical technology he obviously knows whereof he speaks, but when the periodic table intrudes itself it is like a visit from Godzilla. The girl destined for the hero's arms is a clone traumatized by her lack of a navel. Even sillier, by way of supplying an apotheosis with some transcendental wallop, she *gets* a belly button. Shades of *Pinocchio!*

To become a rock musician one need not have mastered counterpoint, and one can begin to publish science fiction with only a rudimentary knowledge of the craft (never mind the art) of writing. Characteristically, sf writers have had public apprenticeships. We start off young and—again, like rock stars—are under a certain pressure to remain, as Dylan has it, "Forever Young," since even today's expanded audience is still predominantly adolescent and college-aged and wants to read stories that speak to the condition of youth. This being so, it isn't hard to understand why so many of sf's brightest stars have attained their stardom by their mid-twenties.

One of the recentest such stars, already with two Nebulas to her credit, is Vonda McIntyre. McIntyre's stories, collected in *Fireflood*, appeal not just to the condition of youth but, more particularly, to the condition of female youth in the seventies—to, in a word, girls. And why not? Most sf till now has taken the form of daydreams for adolescent boys (e.g., *Dark Is the Sun*); why shouldn't girls be allowed the same cheap thrills? (Not a pejorative, mind you, but an allusion to Janis Joplin.)

In assessing *Fireflood*, therefore, I want to distinguish between its strictly literary failings, which may be ascribed to inexperience, and two extraliterary features, which, though I find them off-putting, have undoubtedly contributed to McIntyre's success with her chosen audience. These are: (1) a worldview that divides everyone into an uncaring, imperceptive, closed-minded Them and a loving, hip, holistic, and victimized Us; and (2) a tendency toward tears. In story after story characters are implored to surrender to their stifled need to cry or else are discovered crying as the curtain rises by way of proving they're one of Us. An instance, from the Nebula-winning "Of Mist, and Grass, and Sand":

> "Can any of you cry?" she said. "Can any of you cry for me and my despair, or for them and their guilt, or for small things and their pain?" She felt tears slip down her cheeks.
>
> They did not understand her; they were offended by her crying.

Well yes, they were, rather. Though I can wet a handkerchief with the best of them, I do find such solicitations tasteless, not to say mawkish. If a drama awakens sorrow and pity, well and good, but a writer shouldn't *ask* for tears, not, especially, in a tone of righteousness. But girls will be girls, and vice versa. The fact remains that McIntyre is a talented storyteller and, more commendably, a writer who works at perfecting her craft and extending her range. Rarely is she lazy or slipshod or glib (as all the other books under review are, in part or, in Farmer's case, in whole). Her plots unfold naturally and move at the right, deliberate pace. Her characters, when not being forced into the role of spokespersons for Us, are modeled with conscious art and seem dimensional. Once a story has got off the ground, she can write spare, modulated prose of varying intensity that bears comparison to Christopher Priest's or her mentor's, Ursula LeGuin. Best of all (if the arrangement of the stories in the book can be construed as chronological), she seems to be moving from strength to strength. In the concluding novella, "Aztecs," she is able finally to write "paid" to an emotional theme dealt with obsessively, but never quite successfully, in many of the other stories—the need to renounce a love that

THOMAS M. DISCH

is in conflict with personal growth. In "Aztecs," the science-fictional metaphor is the natural embodiment of this theme, and McIntyre is able to dispense with homilies and lachrymose appeals for sympathy. She just tells her story, and it works.

While *Fireflood* certainly merits an A for effort, it doesn't work. Though McIntyre usually steers clear of formula hugger-mugger, she is capable of sacrificing narrative consistency on the altar of those old heathen idols of the pulps, Suspense and Adventure. In the title story the heroine, a human being mutated into a super armadillo, is fleeing from Them and is slowed in her subterranean progress by tree roots whose "malleable consistency made them harder to penetrate than solid rock." Somehow I doubt that, but if there were no obstacles in her path how would she overcome them? In the matter of extending her range, McIntyre often attempts more than she can handle. On the evidence of the one satirical story, "Recourse, Inc.," I'm convinced she has no sense of humor. She needs lots of room for takeoff: her very short stories lack all pith and crackle. But these are negligible failings and don't weigh much in the balance against the success of a story like "Aztecs." Vonda McIntyre will undoubtedly carry off a lot more Nebulas.

The Feast of St. Bradbury

> Annually at sunset on August 22 (the great man's birthday), editors, book
> reviewers, and workers in related trades celebrate the feast of St. Bradbury. On
> that day they gather up all the books they have been unable, despite their best
> intentions and firmest resolves, to read all the way to the end, tie them in bun-
> dles, and take them to the local book-burning facilities. There, amid cries of
> "Boring!" "Pretentious!" "Trashy!" and "Inept!" they roast weiners and barbecue
> chickens over the offending volumes and experience that sweet tristesse peculiar to
> the Feast of St. Bradbury: that mingling of relief at the onerous task at last
> abandoned—and horror that so many writers have written and publishers pub-
> lished in vain, all in vain.

Battlefield Earth by L. Ron Hubbard is to other, ordinary dumb books what
a Dyson sphere is to an ordinary lampshade—awesomely much bigger,
though not different in kind. Page by page, it's about on a par with the latest ersatz quest-adventure by Philip José Farmer or with most hack writing of the pulp era—the Golden Age, as it is known to those who were
young then (as what age is not?). Which is to say it's about what you'd
expect from the author of Slaves of Sleep if, instead of leading a religion for
the last thirty years, he'd been cryogenically frozen, then resurrected and
given a year to produce the longest dime novel of all time—one that contains, as Hubbard writes in his introduction, "practically every type of
story there is—detective, spy, adventure, western, love, air war, you name
it. All except fantasy; there's none of that."

A book will usually let you know if it's meant for burning within the
first few pages, and Battlefield Earth's seven pages of introduction are a little treasury of self-incriminations. Here's Hubbard on his early career: "I
was what they called a high-production writer, and these fields were just
not big enough to take everything I could write." And: "I had, myself,
somewhat of a science background, had done some pioneer work in

---

Review of Battlefield Earth, by L. Ron Hubbard; No Enemy But Time, by Michael Bishop;
The Transmigration of Timothy Archer, by Philip K. Dick; Friday, by Robert Heinlein; The
Engines of the Night; Citadel of the Autarch, by Gene Wolfe; The Void Captain's Tale, by Nor-
man Spinrad; The Birth of the People's Republic of Antarctica, by John Calvin Batchelor;
White Gold Wielder, by Stephen R. Donaldson; Medusa: A Tiger by the Tale, by Jack L.
Chalker; and Dream Makers, Volume II, by Charles Platt.

rockets and liquid gases, but I was studying the branches of man's past knowledge at that time to see whether he had ever come up with anything valid." Then, a little later, on these same themes of science and intellectual history: "But I do notice every time modern science thinks it is down to the nitty-gritty of it all, it runs into (and sometimes adopts) such things as the Egyptian myths that man came from the mud, or something like that." And finally for sheer reverse verbal bravura, consider the following pronouncement: "man, currently, has sunk into a materialistic binge."

Battlefield Earth is such a cornucopia of boners, groaners, and macro-clichés (such as the ineffably klutzy destruction of the planet of the evil Psychlos by atomic bombs, which turns it into a "radioactive sun") that many readers may be tempted to spare it from the flames of St. Bradbury and place it on that shelf of the immortally goofy anti-classics of the genre, such as Zarlah the Martian and The Bell from Infinity. Despite all this, or maybe because of it, I'll wager that Battlefield Earth will be a strong contender at Hugo time. If not, what are disciples for?

It should be noted that nowhere in the introduction or the press releases for Battlefield Earth is the word "Scientology" used. The nearest Hubbard comes to frankness is this: "Some of my readers may wonder that I did not include my own serious subjects in this book. It was with no thought of dismissal of them. It was just that I put on my professional writer's hat. I also did not want to give anyone the idea I was doing a press relations job for my other serious works." To his credit, those parts of the book I read seemed no more partisan on behalf of Scientology than, say, C. S. Lewis's trilogy is on behalf of the Anglican church. An allegorical interpretation is possible in both cases, but the reader is not being overtly recruited.

There is another way in which the sf and the historical imagination may cross-fertilize, and that is in stories of time travel into the past. Since Mark Twain invented the idea in 1889, it has become almost an sf genre in its own right. The drama of time travel lies in the collision between a historical civilization and a consciousness formed in our own time; between, as well, the sense of history as an inalterable fact and the effort of some Connecticut Yankee to make his mark on it—or not to, if the time traveler observes the decorums of field anthropology. The second possibility gets around the paradoxes involved in introducing microwave mousetraps into the court of Charlemagne, but drama is hard to come by, since the protagonist–time traveler must keep such a low profile.

All of this preamble to explain the particular excellence and originality of Michael Bishop's No Enemy But Time, a time-travel novel that does it the hard way and succeeds. Bishop's hero is born in Seville in 1962, the bastard son of Encarnacion Ocampo, a mute Morisco "whore and black marketeer," and a black enlisted man in the Strategic Air Command. Adopted into the family of another SAC staff sergeant, he becomes John Monegal and grows up in a variety of stateside Air Force bases. The milieu of career servicemen is one that Bishop, an Air Force brat himself, knows like the back of his hand, and his novel shares the virtue of so many of his best stories in portraying that milieu realistically and sympathetically, but without the Alamo psychology of the School of Heinlein.

Through his childhood John Monegal has dream visions of Pleistocene Africa, and as a young man he is recruited as a time traveler to that era and area, when Homo sapiens was only a twinkle in the eye of the ape-like Homo habilis. The core of the story's science-fictional excitement lies in John's life as an assimilated member of a tribe of habilene huntsmen, and in these Pleistocene chapters, which alternate in a strict A-B-A-B pattern with chapters recounting John's growing up, Bishop has created a vicarious treat of three-scoops-and-a-cherry dimensions, a kind of Tarzan for the eighties, based on sound paleontological evidence and shrewd anthropological extrapolation, but no less fun for being well informed.

The remarkable thing about Bishop's book is that the story of John's growing up through the sixties and into the eighties always holds its own dramatically against his adventures among the habilenes. As in LeGuin's The Dispossessed, the alternating time schemes are tightly interlocked so that present and past illuminate and elucidate each other. As in Benford's Timescape, the chapters set in the recent historical past serve as a kind of litmus test of the author's ability to tell home truths about real people. The clarity, sanity, and truthfulness of these essentially "mainstream" chapters give the author's more imaginative flights an authority and verisimilitude all too rare in genre sf. Like both LeGuin and Benford, Bishop is determined to write about human goodness without resorting to the mock heroics of formula adventure stories. There are no villains in the book, even among the habilenes. The central and absorbing drama of the book is the hero's growing love for the pre-Rhematic habilene Helen. (The Rhematic period is, according to the Oxford English Dictionary, the first period of specifically human history, when language came into being.) Looming behind this love story is a larger theme, the formation across the entire span of history of the Family of Man, a phrase that becomes, as the novel ripens to its conclusion, no mere liberal piety but a fully realized dramatic affirmation.

This is not to say the book is flawless. As with most time-travel stories, the rationale for "how it's done" is embarrassingly unconvincing. Better to offer no explanation than one that leaks this badly. But that's a small exception to take to a large achievement. After *No Enemy But Time* it would be an insult to continue to speak of Michael Bishop as one of science fiction's most promising writers. The promise has been fulfilled.

> That this trying out of every possible idea to see if it would fit finally destroyed Tim Archer can't be disputed. He tried out too many ideas, picked them up, examined them . . . some of the ideas, however, as if possessing a life of their own, came back around the far side of the barn and got him. That is history; this is an historical fact. Tim is dead. The ideas did not work. . . . One thing, however could not be obscured. Tim Archer could tell when he was locked in a life and death struggle, and, upon perceiving this, he assumed the posture of grim defense. . . . Fate, to get Tim Archer would have to run him through. Fate had to murder him.

That paragraph, from the twelfth chapter of Philip K. Dick's last novel, *The Transmigration of Timothy Archer*, seems an uncannily well-tailored epitaph for the man who wrote it. No doubt one ought to resist the impulse to mythologize a writer's life as soon as his death has made its shape certain, but Dick's last three novels are singularly difficult to consider apart from their author and his legend. Indeed, the first of the three, *Valis*, is one of the most remarkable, not to say strangest, self-portraits in all literature, and *The Transmigration*, although based on aspects of the career of Dick's friend James Pike, the Episcopal bishop and celebrity author, is (surely not unconsciously) in essential respects another self-portrait, and one that succeeds better at capturing certain characteristics of its author than does *Valis*. Sometimes it helps not to study the mirror too closely.

Before these books are mined for what they may contribute to Dick's myth or the shape of his entire oeuvre, they should be considered on their individual merits. Are they engrossing stories told with intensity, economy, and wit? Do they take us somewhere Dick's earlier novels did not explore? (The better the author and the more prolific he's been, the harder it becomes to "make it new" each time he goes to bat.) Finally, what can be said for their claim to be considered a trilogy: is the whole more than the sum of its parts?

Valis, which Bantam published in 1980, is the unique example of an autobiographical novel in the literature of science fiction. Think about it. Who could, except by writing a novel in the future tense, write a science fiction novel based on the events of his own life? Dick, who has written so many accounts of alternative and subjective realities, managed to do so in

Valis, but at the considerable psychological risk of busting through those thin partitions that proverbially divide madness from great wit. *Valis* is an unsparing account of a period in Dick's life when he underwent what may be described as either visionary experience or psychosis. While the novel differs in many artful particulars from its raw materials (as known from conversations, letters, and even public speeches), the essential drama of a mind divided between a savvy rationality and a grateful and credulous receptivity to otherworldly inputs is soundly based on Dick's experience.

The Divine Invasion, now in paperback, would seem at first glance to have little more in common with the preceding novel of the "trilogy" than a concern for the wilder shores of theological speculation, where the Talmud and the Gnostic Gospels form love knots in the locks of Holy Wisdom. The story is set in that grungy, starveling, astroturfed future common to many Dick novels, wherein a bumbling Unholy Alliance between the Papacy and the Kremlin acts the role of Herod vis-à-vis a new Messiah being smuggled by spaceship to the Bethlehem of Earth. Readers expecting a replay of the traditional gospel tale will be pleasantly surprised (or perhaps dismayed) by the direction the story takes following these Nativity sequences, for Dick's mythmaking is as revisionist as his theology. As in other of his best novels (*The Three Stigmata of Palmer Eldritch*; or, *Do Androids Dream of Electric Sheep?*, which served as suggestion box for the movie *Bladerunner*), the plot is so devious as to defy synopsis. Instead of finding it a page-turner, I tended to set *The Divine Invasion* aside at intervals of twenty pages in order to catch my mental breath. Far from being a liability, I consider this a sign of the book's rare excellence. True originality shouldn't come across as popcorn. When Jacob encountered the angel, they had to wrestle. By the end of the book I had no doubt that it was one of Dick's finest accomplishments.

The Transmigration of Timothy Archer strikes a fine synthetic balance between the "case history" tone of *Valis* and the phantasmagorical high jinks of *The Divine Invasion*. It can also claim the dubious distinction of being the first unequivocally mainstream novel to be published under an sf imprint. Dick wrote many mainstream novels, most of which lie cryogenically frozen in a California university library. One earlier mainstream novel was published in 1975 by Entwhistle Books, *Confessions of a Crap Artist*. While it compelled my interest, *Confessions* struck me as lacking both the force and the flair of Dick's best sf. By contrast, *The Transmigration* I found to be the most vividly engaging of the three last novels—perhaps in part because it is also, aesthetically speaking, the least adventuresome *and* the surest-footed.

Like the historical Bishop Pike, the book's hero allows his better judgment to founder in grief and guilt for a son's suicide; he becomes involved with spirit mediums and writes a book in defense of spiritualism. Later, realizing he's been led into error by his overactive imagination (see the first paragraph above), Archer tries to resist the whirlpool of self-destructive impulse impelling him to a quasi-suicide in the Dead Sea Desert—but his resistance is too late and too little. Note the similarity between this plot and Dick's ambivalent feelings about his own visionary experiences, as chronicled in *Valis*. Here, however, art is more firmly in command, and the plot is resolved with a *coup de théâtre* that has the explosive power of his best sf without compromising the book's grounding in a Balzacean realism. The unwritten moral at the end of the trilogy (or "trinity," as I would rather term the nonlinear unity the three books achieve) is an affirmation of the vision received with a chagrined appreciation of the folly inherent in too hot pursuit of any grail; with maybe, one step beyond this quixotic polarity, a sheer unqualified love for any fool who has the courage of such folly.

If there is a silver lining to be found in the unalterable, sorrowful fact of Philip Dick's death at the age of fifty-two, it is surely that his last three books do such honor to his genius. Fate at least allowed him to exit in style.

Robert Heinlein's new novel, *Friday*, offers a similar though by no means sorrowful cause for rejoicing, for *Friday* is quite the best novel he's written in years (sixteen, if you liked *The Moon Is a Harsh Mistress* greatly; twenty-one, if *Stranger in a Strange Land* is your touchstone). His last three novels went from bad to worse and developed elephantiasis in the process. Even his most faithful admirers found themselves hard put to exonerate, much less praise, *The Number of the Beast*, and readers who'd never taken oaths of fealty simply looked the other way in polite dismay (knowing quite well that their attention would not be missed by the author, whose books prospered in the marketplace in almost inverse proportion to their merits).

How cheering, then, to be able to root once again for an old master at the height of his form. *Friday* is probably not Heinlein's best novel, but it can lay claim to lesser superlatives: oddest, drollest, most comfortable, and (in some ways) most original. Its oddity derives from the paradox that while the story seems to zip right along, page by quick-turning page, it never (in terms of simple narrative) goes anywhere in particular.

This supersonic meander opens with a narrative hook big enough to land a Spielberg shark:

As I left the Kenya Beanstalk capsule he was right on my heels. He followed me through the door leading to Customs, Health, and Immigration. As the door contracted behind him, I killed him.

(Let us note, in passing, the homage to one of his critics, S. R. Delany, who has cited Heinlein's sentence "The door dilated" as the *locus classicus* of all science fiction.) The narrator, Miss Friday, proceeds to stuff the resulting corpse and a pesky Public Eye into a luggage locker, then uses its credit cards to cover her tracks electronically. One might suppose from such a beginning that *Friday* is to be a futuristic James Bond adventure. It's not, though the *action* is often of that ilk. However, the action is rarely anything but icing on the cake and rarely serves to advance the plot.

There is a plot, though the author contrives with great grace to let it all take place in the reader's peripheral vision. Thus, a great many chapters are spent following the heroine as, having just knocked off a cop who'd been wanting in good manners, she tries to get back to home base during an international crisis that has sealed the borders of a balkanized North America. She caroms about the map without reaching her goal; we never do learn what the crisis was really about, or whose side she would have been on had she got home, since the organization she serves is so security-conscious that it never discusses its ends, only its means, of which Friday herself is one of the best. Observe how neatly, by this method, Heinlein finesses those critics who are disposed to argue about his politics on the macroscopic level of history and headlines. Miss Friday is as innocent of politics as Lassie, another heroine whose overriding concern is to find her way home.

So it is too with the politics of sex, which is (as one may surmise from the delightful dedication page, with its harem of thirty-one dedicatees, including, among others, Betsy, Bubbles, Judy-Lynn, Pepper, Rebel, Ursula, Vonda, and Yumiko) the theme about which Heinlein's subtext is organized. In many ways *Friday* fulfills the demands of many feminist critics for a macho heroine and beyond that for a world in which macho heroines may rumble with other macho heroines, then take a quick tumble in the hay, and proceed on their way to fresh adventures in the spirit of picaresque daydreaming that boys of all ages have so long enjoyed. Heinlein, who can be as fair-minded as he is cantankerous, readily acknowledges the right of women to equal wages and equal fun, and some of the book's drollest moments are a result of casting women in traditionally male roles, as when Miss Friday is recruited into a mercenary army by one Sergeant Mary Gumm, who is as tough as they come, and who, when she makes a pass at Miss Friday . . . ah, but that would spoil the fun.

This is not to say that the feminist contingent, and others, won't be driven up various walls by one or another aspect of the book—its wry denouement in particular—but that Heinlein has exercised all his novelistic wiles to embody his argument in a story as devious as an eel—so that even if one disagrees there can be great sport in doing so. This, by contrast to the hectoring and bloated monologues of recent memory, is a good reason to get the book and to pass it along. It's one of those that will sustain hours of arguing as to what the man is actually getting at. Such postmortems can be, with books as with parties, half the entertainment.

The Engines of the Night so candidly asks to be censured that any reviewer is put into the position of the sadist in the classic joke, who, from a more refined cruelty, refuses to grant the masochist the beating he begs for. Rarely does a book appear that is at once so self-loathing (one of the author's favorite characterizations of himself) and so self-serving (a subject on which he is more reticent). The publisher abets its author's desire to make his name anathema by publishing blurbs from two colleagues who evidently disliked the book as much as I did, and the following equivocal praise from Algis Budrys: "Destined to be misunderstood and misused, this cry from the heart will prove once more that honesty is suicidal."

I think, on the contrary, that it's destined to be understood by anyone who bothers to read it and used as a cautionary example of how the practice of hack writing, too long indulged, can sap the character, wilt the judgment, and turn to jelly the prose of writers who can't resist a fast buck. The author (who, as a special, Dantean torment, shall remain nameless in this review) would seem in his own darker moments to endorse even the harshest of these judgments, but he also suffers fits of megalomania when he insists that his career has been peculiarly congruent with the history of all science fiction, and that he embodies a kind of tragic fate that dooms him (and all science fiction) to mediocrity, oblivion, and a pauper's grave. He loves to cover himself with ashes and tell sad tales of the deaths of writers, such times as his word processor isn't on automatic pilot and churning out such portentous piffle as this passage, which is the book's only gloss on its title:

Ah but still. Still, oh still. Still Kazin, Broyard, Epstein, Podhoretz and Howe; grinding away slowly in the center of all purpose, taking us to the millennium: the engines of the night.

(Those names are the critics the author feels particularly neglected by, but as to what the rest of that trans-syntactical paragraph may mean, only the author knows—and he's not saying.)

Does this seem a mite draconian? Well, judge for yourself. Here's a less inchoate example of the author in his kvetching vein, with pique in control and self-pity momentarily in abeyance:

> The writer—the experienced writer in any event—knows that most editors acquire and publish not in an effort to be successful so much as to avoid failure. Defensive driving. They seek, then, that which they consider safe, and the writers who are at the mercy of those editors function from the same motivation. (It can be presumed that those who feel or function differently find it almost impossible to get their work into the mass market.) . . . Science fiction, like all commercial fiction (and quality lit too although in a slightly different way), can perhaps be best understood in terms of what is *not* written rather than what is. Self-censorship controls. Any writer who understands this at all will know what not to try. As good a definition of professionalism as any other.

If that's professional, how would you define craven? Such preemptive surrender to the "demands of the market" is all the more reprehensible when one realizes that the author is a man who presently makes his living by selling his own professional expertise, pseudonymously, to fledgling writers.

If the book were only a "personal bitch" (as Alexei Panshin describes it on the back cover), it would not be worth even this much notice, but it lays claim in its subtitle, *Science Fiction in the Eighties*, to have a larger subject. The claim is specious. As a critic, the author is careless, ungenerous, and fainthearted. He praises the work of his friends out of proportion to their merits, especially that of Robert Silverberg, which so often echoes the author's lamentations on the futility of writing sf. There is scarcely one generalization about sf in the book to which some significant exception cannot be made, either because the author practices defensive reading or because he writes faster than he thinks. And for all his constant insistence on the essential inescapable second-rateness of all sf, he never has the guts to come out and say that any particular book by any particular writer is bad. Indeed, there is scarcely a senior member of the sf establishment that isn't kowtowed to at some point and scarcely a junior member that gets mentioned.

All in all, a shameful performance. And you can quote that on the cover of the paperback.

At the present moment, the most reliable butcher shop (or florist), science-fictionally speaking, is Timescape Books, which has published Gene Wolfe's *Citadel of the Autarch*. *Citadel* is the fourth (though not quite conclusive) volume in Wolfe's paperback tetralogy, *The Book of the New Sun*, whose popular success has confounded all conventional wisdom, both the Industry's and my own. *The Shadow of the Torturer* won a World Fantasy Award, *The Claw of the Conciliator* a Nebula, and last year's *The Sword of the Lictor* is the likeliest mammalian contender in a field liable to be dominated by four dinosaurs—Clarke, Asimov, Heinlein, and Hubbard. Now we have *Citadel*, and it is possible to take a deep breath and try, if not to achieve closure, at least to figure out what really happens and what it all *means*.

For rarely has there been a work of genre fiction in which the import of the story is so elusive, to say nothing of the bare facts. Such was its appeal to the literary detective in me that halfway through this last volume I could resist no longer and phoned up my old friend and fellow Wolfe-enthusiast, John Clute, to suggest that we not wait the dozen or so years that even a masterpiece is supposed to age in the cask but set about at once to edit a volume of interpretive essays, supplemented with a glossary and other suitable rites of scholarship. John said, "Good idea," and immediately began to jot down some questions that remained moot after his first reading of the four volumes, but still seemed answerable. As a sample of the fascination of *The Book of the New Sun*, I can't resist quoting (with his permission) from John's list of conundrums:

"—Who is the woman lying bleeding beneath the Matachin Towel whom Severian almost forgets?

—Just how is an Autarch actually chosen? And who is Paeon?

—Are all the khaibits in the novel identified as such? And just how do exultants prolong their lives?

—Is Cyriaca S's mother?"

(After more reflection, John concluded that Cyriaca was not Severian's mother, and he developed an ingenious theory of who, amazingly, his mother might be, which I'm sworn not to hint at here, as John's entitled to dibs for his discovery.)

Do you begin to sense what very odd books these must be that they can leave such questions in the air and still generate such applause and loyalty? Of the four volumes *Citadel* is surely the oddest, for it is almost perversely anticlimactic in its denial of those pleasures usually associated with finishing a long epic narrative; there are no confrontation scenes between Severian and the many major characters from the earlier volumes (no accounting, indeed, for many of them), no poetic justice for the villains, no coronal ceremonies for the triumphant hero. The last eight chapters, which show Severian as Autarch, are one long dying fall, as though no music would suit the rites of passage to ethical maturity (for this is what the allegory is allegorizing; that much at least is clear) save the muffled drumbeats of a funeral march.

I realize this is not the stuff that blurb writers' dreams are made of, but most sf readers by now will already have begun to read *The Book of the New Sun* and will know their own taste in the matter. Nor can I imagine that any reader of the first three volumes could be *prevented* from continuing to the end. At this moment the whole tetralogy seems simply too large for ordinary critical epithets to apply; one might as well scrawl "pretty damned big!" on the Great Pyramid.

Temperamentally no two authors could be more unlike than Gene Wolfe and Norman Spinrad, and few novels could be more disparate in their achievement than *The Book of the New Sun* and *The Void Captain's Tale*. Wolfe is decorous, devious, sacerdotal; one suspects that, like T. S. Eliot, he is an Anglican in his religion, a monarchist in his politics. Spinrad is brash, forthright, profane; his intellectual allegiances hark back not centuries but a mere twenty-five years, to the late fifties, when Spinrad's namesake and role model, Norman Mailer, was in flower.

Mailer's chief significance to writers of my own and Norman's generation can be bounded in the nutshells of two powerful stories from *Advertisements for Myself* (1959), "The Man Who Studied Yoga" and "The Time of Her Time." In those stories Mailer found a new way to turn to account the sexual explicitness that recent court decisions had made possible for American writers. Prior to Mailer, writing about sex tended to fall into two categories—the steamy (a tradition carried on in our time by Judith Krantz, Harold Robbins, et al.) and the risque, a category broad enough to subsume centuries of bawdry, from Rabelais to the joke pages of *Playboy*. Both modes tend to trivialize sex and deny its sometime sublimity. Mailer found a language that was streetwise without being loutish, eloquent without gushing, a language more true to sexual experience than any of his contemporaries.

Norman Spinrad was the first sf writer to apply the lessons of Mailer to the material of science fiction, and he was rewarded for his achievement by having the book in which he did this, *Bug Jack Barron* (1969), banned from England's largest bookstore chain and denounced in the House of

Commons. Spinrad has written seven novels since then, only one of which departs markedly from a Mailerean rhetoric. The lone exception is the delightfully bonkers *The Iron Dream* (1972), which purports to be an sf pulp adventure penned by Adolf Hitler. In the other novels (excepting the latest), Spinrad was up against the same problem that so often baffled Mailer in his later fiction: the voice he'd crafted for his breakthrough work did not always suit later occasions. *A World Between* (1979), an effort to confront the issues raised by feminism, seemed to me as tendentious and off-target as Mailer's *The Prisoner of Sex*, while *Songs from the Stars* (1980) created a postapocalyptic utopia extrapolated from back issues of the *Whole Earth Catalogue* that shared the problem of most utopias: blandness. *The Void Captain's Tale* represents a new synthesis of Spinrad's main strengths. The earnestness of the metasexual theorizer is qualified by the irony and livened by the playfulness that characterizes *The Iron Dream* and his best short fiction.

The central premise could not be simpler: interstellar flight by means of electronically amplified orgasm. Only female orgasm, however, acts as propellant; the male role is the honorific one of pressing the takeoff button—and therein lies *The Void Captain's Tale*. The *reductio ad absurdum* of the old metaphoric equation, Orgasm = Grail, is elaborated in great extrapolative detail, but the central sexual drama would soon come to seem an absurdity plain and simple if Spinrad had not cast his tale into an evolved lingo of his own invention, a kind of Berlitz for Space Travelers that generates an atmosphere of constant, ever-shifting unnaturalness. It is a language as capable of flights of eloquence as of pratfalls of pomposity. The effect of reading much of it, as with the neo-English of *A Clockwork Orange* or *Riddley Walker*, is that as we learn the language we enter the culture of the book, becoming, in effect, its naturalized citizens. The comparison to Burgess's and Hoban's books can be misleading in one way, however, for the effect of the Spinradical *sprach* is not so much to make commonplace speech richer, stranger, and more poetic, but to signify the artifice of social conventions, to be symptomatic of the central thesis of the book—that the sexual grail is something that words, in their nature, cannot express.

The Birth of the People's Republic of Antarctica, by John Calvin Batchelor, is not published as a science fiction novel, but as a "novel of the imminent future." Usually I would argue that any story set in the future is by its nature science fiction, but Batchelor's muse harks back to far older traditions, as far back, indeed, as *Beowulf*, though *Moby Dick* is probably a more apt formal comparison. There is the same potent mix of epic adventure and lofty speculation acted out by larger-than-life figures against a background of global dimensions—in this case, a near-future crisis that has filled the oceans of the world with a multinational diaspora of supremely wretched men and women. (That's a quote from the book jacket, but I don't think it's cheating to repeat it, since it was a quote I wrote.) The book chronicles a Swedish prison break led by the hero's Ahab-large grandfather; a voyage ever-Southwards through an Atlantic as dismal as the oceans of Poe's "Narrative of A. Gordon Pym"; then, with uncanny prescience (for this was written and contracted before the actual British-Argentine war), Batchelor depicts a war in the Falkland Islands, which leads to the book's awesome conclusion in the "ice camps" of Antarctica. Here is a sample of the author's summing-up of the situation in Chapter the Last:

> The wretched in the South, we wretches, we were not all innocent victims of some fabulous conspiracy to disenfranchise lambs. . . . We . . . were the worst possible remnant. The genuine meek, the genuinely wronged . . . they had been left far behind, dead in their hovels, on the beaches, in the sea. We in the ice camps had come through our ordeals because we were tougher, wilder, crueler than our brethren. We were the lucky remnant. We were the most vicious wretched: pirates, killers, thieves, madmen, lost to reason and utterly embittered. As we suffered atrocities, we were atrocious.
> . . . We did drink the blood. We did eat the dead.

Batchelor manages to make good on his promise of the highest and widest drama precisely because he keeps a certain distance from his cast of high-voltage characters and handles their passions, crimes, and ordeals with electrician's gloves. He anatomizes them, as a historian might, rather than presenting them always in cinematically detailed scenes. The danger with this technique is that a certain chill may set in (though it's scarcely a danger in this book) or that the prose may be infected with the language of contemporary psychology, a sorry fate for any novel. Again, that danger never threatens, since Batchelor took his degree at Union Theological Seminary, and the language he uses in his anatomies of the soul is as timeless as the King James Bible's or Dr. Johnson's.

How the time flies. It seems like only yesterday we were celebrating the Feast of St. Bradbury, when, at sunset on August 22, book reviewers gather at great communal bonfires to burn those books they could not bring themselves to read all the way through. But already the year has turned full circle, and it is time to offer new volumes to the purifying flames. A joyful occasion, surely, but a solemn one as well, for often these unreadable books have been more successful in the marketplace than the books favored by the general consensus of reviewers, and we must ask ourselves why. Why does dreck so often rise to the top of the bestseller list? Is there some merit in these books that their prose obscures, as acne can disfigure a structurally handsome face? Or is it (as I will propose) precisely their faults that endear them to an audience who recognizes in these novels a true mirror image of their own lame brains?

I use that pejorative advisedly—as a reminder that it is often the case that a brain, like a limb, can be "lame," and by way of apologizing for some plain speaking ahead. The lamebrained may be no more to blame for their condition than those more literally lamed; their condition may in fact be equivalently pitiable, but they are seldom liable to acknowledge their impediment. Indeed, they will even fight to have lamebrainedness written into the Constitution, as in the creationists' demands for equal time (concerning whom, see below), and to dismiss any evidence of a sound mind as elitism. In their utopia, as in Vonnegut's classic tale "Harrison Bergeron," all brains not naturally lame will be lamed prosthetically, and the Olympics shall be conducted exclusively from wheelchairs. It is to guard against that possibility that it is needful from time to time, even at the risk of hurt feelings, to call a dunce a dunce, instead of politely looking the other way.

Let me state clearly at the outset that I am not disparaging "escapist reading" in order to promote serious literature. I have a keen appetite for entertainment novels of almost all kinds. So it's not because *White Gold Wielder* by Stephen R. Donaldson and *Medusa: A Tiger by the Tale* by Jack L. Chalker are written solely to entertain that I consider them stinkers, but because they set about that task so ineptly. Readers hungry for high fantasy in Donaldson's vein or for old-fashioned space opera can find literate specimens of both genres in such recent first-quality offerings as Jack Vance's *Lyonesse* or Keith Laumer's *Retief* series, books that feature livelier plots, more vivid characters, and infinitely more lucid (and ludic) prose than the stinkers under consideration.

But before I rave on, I must offer examples of what I am inveighing against—the first a descriptive passage by Chalker, the second a crucial confrontation scene from *White Gold Wielder*:

> The drawing, a very good drawing by a very skilled artist, was of a stunningly beautiful woman, perhaps the most stunning vision of womanhood I'd ever seen. Rendered in colored pencils, the drawing showed a

dark-skinned beauty with long mixed blond and light brown hair, two very large and sexy dark green eyes, set in perhaps the most sensual face I could imagine. The body was large, lean, sexy, and sleek, but the sexual organs were very exaggerated. The artist had drawn multiple views, including one of the figure crouching, animal-like, like some perfect primal savage, wearing some sort of spotted animal skin. It was an incredible vision, a bestial sex machine. Even though it was only a cartoon in colored pencils, I felt the intent in the artist's skilled strokes and could only whistle.

He raised one hand like a smear across her sight. In his grasp, the band began to blaze. His shout gathered force until she feared it would shatter the mountain.

"Here at last I hold possession of all life and Time forever! Let my Enemy look to his survival and be daunted! Freed from my gaol and torment, I will rule the cosmos!"

She could not remain upright under the weight of his exaltation. His voice split her hearing, hampered the rhythm of her heart. Kneeling on the tremorous stone, she gritted her teeth, swore to herself that even though she had failed at everything else she would at least breathe no more of this damnable attar. The walls threw argent in carillon from all their facets. The Despiser's power scaled toward apocalypse.

Yet she heard Covenant. Somehow, he kept his feet. He did not shout but every word he said was as distinct as augury.

"Big deal. I could do the same Thing—if I were as crazy as you." His certainty was unmatched. "It doesn't take power. Just delusion. You're out of your mind."

It's hard, with Donaldson, to leave off quoting. The passage continues for pages at the same amazingly high density of pratfalls per paragraph, with the same wonderful swings from school-playground bombast to teenybopper psychobabble. By comparison, Chalker's prose is almost stately, in the manner of a fifth-grade book report. There is even a kind of savage, minimalist beauty in his rudimentary description of "two very large and sexy dark green eyes, set in perhaps the most sensual face I could imagine." Quasimodo couldn't have put it any better.

The appeal of Donaldson's prose is less obvious. The original meaning of "bombast" is instructive in his case: cotton wool used as padding or stuffing for clothes, from which it came to have its figurative meaning of inflated or turgid language. Cotton, that's to say, in its inchoate condition, before it's been spun into cloth; language, therefore, not yet formulated into meaning. Further, those parts of the anatomy liable to be augmented with bombast were usually those associated with mature development. The analogy holds for bombastic prose. Donaldson's evocations of emotional experience are at once shrill and nebulous, the miasmic imagining of an oceanic angst, where any impulse at once elicits an equal and opposite reaction:

> Her senses told her things that appalled her. Though his own perceptions were flatly truncated, he felt the potential for hysteria creep upward in her. But instead of screaming she became scarcely able to move. How virulent would Lord Foul be to nerves as vulnerable as hers. Covenant was at least protected by his numbness.

This is not to suggest that Donaldson's work is "depressing" because its characters—the lachrymose and overwrought heroine in particular—have "vulnerable nerves." Indeed, I suspect his books appeal to young persons who themselves are subject to a chronic, unspecific depression—a common condition in this age of Quaalude-gobbling—and who find in Donaldson's beclouded prose an affirmation of their condition, an assurance that such feelings are the stigmata of a noble, suffering spirit. What I object to in *White Gold Wielder* is rather that neither in its moment-to-moment depiction of psychological experience nor in the broader operation of its plot at an allegorical level does it offer effective insights into the *miserablisme* it celebrates. Simply put, it wallows in self-pity, and the diffuse fogginess of the language provides a kind of smoke-screen that allows naive readers to wallow along without the discomfort of self-awareness.

And what is the harm in that? you may ask. If a book serves the purpose of a security blanket, is that such a terrible thing? Possibly not. There are times when all of us would rather flee our problems than confront them head-on with the heightened awareness that genuine art forces on us. For such times nothing will serve but escapism. Yet I can't help but think that a habit of tolerating such bad prose as Chalker and Donaldson offer, sentence by sentence, is more injurious to the mind's general fitness than an equivalent amount of time spent viewing *Magnum P.I.*, or *General Hospital*, or *Star Trek*, escapist entertainments that possess the minimal virtues of formal clarity and a professional execution.

Lest this year's sacrificial victims to the fires of St. Bradbury give the impression that genre fiction is generally sorry stuff, there is a newly published nonfiction book that provides a convincing case to the contrary. *Dream Makers, Volume II*, by Charles Platt, is, like the original, much-praised first volume of three years ago, a collection of interviews with (in this volume) some twenty-eight writers and editors in the field of sf and just across its boundaries (for instance, there are interviews with William Burroughs, Alvin "Future Shock" Toffler, D. M. Thomas, and Stephen King). The excellence of both volumes lies chiefly in Platt's Delilahlike knack of eliciting candid and lively responses from people of the most diverse temperaments and attitudes, and secondarily in his skill at compressing the resulting mass of dialogues and observations into a coherent, continuous narrative. The result is a book that provides livelier entertainment than most novels.

A few of the writers in *Volume II* kvetch an inordinate amount, and another few never leave off powdering their personas, though in cold print these evasive maneuvers turn out to be among the more self-revealing pieces in the book (e.g., the Robert Anton Wilson and Theodore Sturgeon interviews). Geographically, Florida would seem to produce sf writers of the highest in-person voltage: Andre Norton, prim amid the sea of her cats; Piers Anthony, speeding about his daily routines like the Road Runner of cartoon fame; Keith Laumer, who turns in a performance that Brando might envy for sheer stark-naked oomph; and Joe Haldeman, who's led the kind of life that TV docudramas are made of (the inspirational kind). By contrast, most of the Californians seem to have blanded out—except for Jerry Pournelle, who comes off as a one-man band doing a benefit for assertiveness training.

PART FOUR **ON SF** Selected Larger Trees

,

A Different Different World

Imagine another literary world, like the one we know in almost every way but different in one crucial respect. A world in which (for instance) Borges had written not the spare, idea-packed vignettes he's best known by but blockbuster novels on the scale of *Dr. Zhivago*. Or a world in which John Irving's first books were science fiction and fantasy novels, so that even when he wrote *Garp* he remained unknown beyond the confines of the genre ghetto. Or a world in which the Romantic novel in the grand manner of Hugo and Dumas was to be re-invented in our era of minimalist ambitions among "literary" writers and reduced expectations among their readers. Imagine such a world, and then read John Crowley's *Ægypt* and you will have begun to inhabit it.

The Ægypt of Crowley's title is also a world unlike the one we are familiar with: "It once worked in a different way than it does now; it had a different history and a different future. Its very flesh and bones, the physical laws that governed it, were other than the ones we know." There are literally thousands of fantasy novels that have such a premise, novels that recycle for the nth generation of readers the tropes of medieval romance: dragons, wizards, enchanted castles. There is almost as large a legion of contemporary occult novels that are modern-dress reenactments of traditional supernatural beliefs (*Rosemary's Baby*) or that exploit paranormal lore of more recent vintage (King's *Carrie* or *The Dead Zone*). Crowley's book is nothing like that. His world of Ægypt is different in an altogether different way; its strangeness is of that rare variety you feel on certain special days of your life when the sun seems to shine brighter on the ordinary sights of the world, making them extraordinary. There are no overtly supernatural events in his novel (or none that can't be accounted for by tricks of perspective), and yet the book is drenched in a sense of impending supernatural cataclysm. If the occult world had earthquakes, Ægypt would be found right on its San Andreas Fault.

The double plot-line is complex without ever becoming hard to follow. The contemporary half of the story concerns Pierce Moffett, a man coming of age in the sixties who has been born "with a talent for history, as

---

Review of *Ægypt*, by John Crowley.

you could be born with musical or mathematical talent." As a child, inspired partly by the work of the historical novelist Fellowes Kraft, Pierce invents his own fantasy realm of Ægypt, a world that he later comes to realize was not his unique invention but a myth with its roots in the Italian Renaissance, his area of specialty as a grown-up historian. Pierce, however, is also a child of the sixties and dissipates his talents, getting through grad school with a glib tongue, and ending up teaching at Barnabas College in New York, an academy that has so well adapted to the Age of Aquarius that it offers courses in judicial astrology. Its students come there "not to be disabused of their superstition, but to find new and different ones," and the central, seductive fascination of Pierce's story is to see how he comes to be enlisted, body and soul, in that most quixotic of all searches, the quest for some proof that the Ægypt of the imagination really did exist and still can be found hidden in the mists of history.

The other half of the plot, embedded in the first, takes place in the Italy of Giordano Bruno (burnt by the Inquisition for his refusal to recant the "heresy" of Copernicus) and in Shakespeare's England, and features these figures as characters in excerpts from the novels of Fellowes Kraft. As a historical novelist, Kraft is on a par with Renault or Yourcenar, and his account of the moment, at dawn in the Alps, when Bruno first comprehends the new Copernican universe is a set-piece that Berlioz would have wanted to set to music.

Crowley, writing of our own narrower-seeming times, not only is able to hold his own against the imaginary Kraft but even surpasses him, because Crowley—as in his earlier (and equally impressive) fantasy novel, Little, Big—is finally writing about something larger. Kraft is concerned with the conflict between faith and reason, between a mechanistic and a magical worldview. Crowley is concerned with these things, too, but only as they impinge on the eternal verities of love and lust, family life and solitude, death and re-birth, and in his depiction of these things Crowley writes with so much art and feeling that I won't embarrass myself by trying to make further and even more high-flown comparisons.

One caveat must be added: I am a friend of Crowley's (albeit a distant friend, since he lives like his protagonist in a rural fastness); a skeptic might, for that reason, ascribe some of my hyperbole to a personal partiality. However, my admiration for Crowley's books pre-dates our friendship, and I must say, in all candor, that it is on a different scale. I like Crowley, but I am in awe of his books. Nor am I alone in my enthusiasm. Crowley has yet to win his proper share of fame, but those who have read Little, Big (which is being re-issued in paperback in conjunction with

Ægypt) tend toward a similar missionary zeal. (Among those quoted on the book jacket are Ursula LeGuin and Russell Hoban.)

Another caveat: Ægypt is the first volume of a projected tetralogy, and it makes no pretense of bringing its plot to even a temporary resolution. Its cast of characters—both those in the present and those in the past—still have long lives ahead of them, hard choices, and (I'm sure) amazing destinies. Yet such is Crowley's artistry that the novel yields a satisfying sense of completeness if not of closure.

And what a pleasure to think that this story will continue! No first novel of a projected series has held such rich promise of good things to come since Justine, the first volume of Durrell's Alexandria Quartet. To defer reading until the tetralogy is complete would be as foolish as refusing to visit Venice on your vacation because you mean to live there when you retire.

Crowley's Poetry

Among the traditional postulates of sf the best loved, and most overused, may well be the regression of civilization into barbarism as a result of the Bomb. Indeed, the theme predates the splitting of the atom; in 1885 Richard Jefferies wrote *After London*, an account of Britain transformed into a gothic folly. In modern sf the avatars are John Wyndham's *Re-Birth* (in the U.K. *The Chrysalids*) and Walter Miller's *A Canticle for Leibowitz*. The seductions of the theme are manifold, not least the possibilities for set decoration as the woodbine pulls down the skyscrapers and every scrap-heap becomes a riddle book of misunderstood technologies. It allows the sf writer to revert to the idyllic imagery of Arcadia and put by the expository demands of the high-tech style. It provides a playground for day-dreams of Brute Power, one that is more plausible (and intellectually respectable) than alien planets concocted for such suspect pastimes. Finally, it can offer, as in *Canticle*, laboratory conditions for testing (or confirming) historical theories: Is civilization cyclical? Is the feudal three-tiered stratification of lord (power), priest (knowledge), and serf (forced labor) the inevitable solution to Hobbesian anarchy—or is it a false paradigm and therefore part of the problem? Will we, as predators doomed to aggress, finally drop our bombs? Good, solid, unanswerable questions guaranteed to lend dignity to even the most trivial fiction.

In 1976 St. Martin's published Steve Wilson's *The Lost Traveller*, which was recently reprinted by Ace with the irresistible blurb "A Science Fiction Western and Motorcycle Quest Epic" and an even more irresistible endorsement from Norman Spinrad, who promises that this is "unquestionably the best, most mature, most honest, fairest and most wise piece of fiction ever written about the Hell's Angels" and, what's more, "true science fiction in the highest sense—alien sensibilities rendered with conviction in their own terms, thereby expanding the reader's sense of the humanly possible." I mention this novel so much after the fact of its publication for two reasons: to second Norman's recommendation and by way of contrasting the much greater merits of another post-holocaust fantasy, John Crowley's *Engine Summer*, a novel that manages to use the

---

Review of *Engine Summer*, by John Crowley.

theme of post-atomic regression in so novel (and novelistic) a manner as to amount to a complete recension of that theme.

The Lost Traveller covers great tracts of familiar territory at high speed, moving from one familiar trope to the next with the quick editing, high color, and careful moral equivocation that allow one's own barbaric id a vicarious romp through an entire Disneyworld of macho high jinks, as the hero, a Hell's Angel with prophetic powers, kills rival motorcyclists with gun, crossbow, and knife (his own father among them, as they discover too late; an affecting moment); is initiated into an Indian tribe (a tip of the hat, here, to the ancient wisdom of Carlos Castaneda); rescues Professor Sangreal (White Science) from the evil clutches of East Coast totalitarians (Black Science); has exemplary sex with a barmaid who is a noble savage in disguise; and, with his buddy Milt, holds out against and defeats a small armada of villains. And even that isn't the topper. Revealing these elements of the story will not, I think, detract from any reader's pleasure in it, for Wilson's craft lies in deploying his archetypes in yes-of-course order, so that we know the moment a character enters exactly what role he must play. *The Lost Traveller* is predestined for Hollywood, and I hope Zelazny's slovenly and unpersuasive *Damnation Alley* hasn't spoiled its chance for the big screen. Meanwhile, all literate, would-be barbarians can enjoy this paperback.

To inventory the high points of *Engine Summer* similarly would be to perform an injustice to its future readers, for it's a novel full of genuine surprises, trapdoors that spring open under the feet of the mind at regular intervals all the way to the last chapter. Therefore, as much as possible I'll try to praise the book without betraying its secrets, though these, of course, are integral to its success sheerly as science fiction. Indeed, without a developed knack for the kind of decoding and riddle-guessing demanded by the more cerebral forms of sf, few readers are likely to get beyond the first two or three twists of the labyrinth. As Crowley explains, with customary indirection: "There is no way through Little Belaire to the outside except Path, and no one who wasn't born in Little Belaire, probably, could ever find his way to the center. Path looks no different from what is not Path: it's drawn on your feet."

Though full of surprises, *Engine Summer* eschews drama. There's not a single villain, not a fight, scarcely a line of dialogue that isn't redolent of goodwill. Is it then a kind of love story? No: though the narrator forms a rather forlorn attachment to a girl (who resembles Dickens's Estella a little too closely), is rebuffed, pursues her, and achieves a bittersweet and fleeting rapprochement, this, the largest dramatic action of the book, constitutes at most a subplot. Passion requires nutrients not to be found in the soil of *Engine Summer*. The best the hero can hope for, and what he finally achieves, is the stoic acceptance of an awareness almost congruent with despair.

What the book is poignantly, strenuously, and beautifully about is truth—how it is known and how spoken. The narrator is born into a society whose central value is introspection and plain-speaking, a kind of Quaker monastery populated by illiterate but exquisitely articulate aborigines, timid as rabbits, who support themselves by foraging for nuts and berries and dealing dope to other tribes who lack their horticultural resources. At an early age the narrator, Rush, forms the ambition of becoming a saint: that is, someone who in telling the story of his life evokes a universal truth, whose life, in its narrative form, is a paradigm for all human lives. *Engine Summer* is precisely the oral narrative by which we are to judge if Rush (and/or Crowley) has attained this so-novelistic ideal of sainthood. What the book is also about, by inference, is the art of the novel, the art of this novel. One can't read far without being reminded of Crowley's presence behind his narrator's persona: a modest, melancholy, quiet-spoken young man who occasionally reveals, as though inadvertently, an unshakable conviction in his own genius. The book's epigraph is from Kafka, but even without that hint it is of Kafka one is constantly made to think. Not the expressionist, shrill trance-medium of *Metamorphosis*, but the later, sedated Kafka who wrote such masterpieces of precision allegory as "Investigations of a Dog," the blandly lethal ironist, the master of dropped pins.

Most readers will have already leaped to the conclusion that I am urging them to read that anomalous and always suspect hybrid, a poetic novel. I confess it, but would add that Crowley's "poetry" is not what is ordinarily accounted poetic prose, a rhetorical commodity reserved for moments of maximum claptrap, as when Steve Wilson's hero has spent the *de rigeur* weekend fasting on a mountaintop so as to get in tune with the eternal rhythms:

> The sun's warmth was a smile on him, but an Indian smile, after nothing for itself, inscrutable—a mystery which was echoed in the mauve and violet shadows beneath the trees, the shifting blackness in the seas of evergreens, the cobalt of the sky above like a single abrupt syllable, a clapped hand.

That is fustian, cut from a long bolt of the same Nebula Award quality but sturdy enough to clothe a moment of naked ignorance. With the lighting right some readers may even mistake it for French gabardine; it's fustian, even so.

Crowley's "poetry" is of another ilk, descending from the scrubbed-bare, no-nonsense vein of modern mid-American poetry (represented by such poets as Williams, Creeley, Bly, and Simic), which has for its conservative aim the restoration of full emotional force to plain words grown slack with overuse. Such poetry, depending as it does on the running current for its luster, is not easily excerpted, but here, anyhow, is a passage from an early chapter in which Rush is explaining the totemic groupings of his people:

> Cords. Your cord is you more surely than your name or the face that looks out at you from mirrors, though both of those, face and name, belong to the cord you belong to. There are many cords in Little Belaire. Nobody knows exactly how many because there is a dispute among the gossips about cords which some say aren't cords but only parts of other cords. You grow into being in your cord; the more you become yourself, the more you become the cord you are. Until—if you aren't ordinary—you reach a time when your own cord expands and begins to swallow up others, and you grow out of being in a single cord at all. I said Painted Red had been Water cord, and her name was Wind; now she was larger than that and she had no cord that could be named, though in her way of speaking, in the motions of her hands, the matter of her life, in small things, she was still Water.
>
> Water and Buckle and Leaf; Palm and Bones and Ice; St. Gene's tiny Thread cord, and Brink's cord if it exists. And the rest. And Whisper. And was it because of her secrets that I loved Once a Day, or because of Once a Day that I came to love secrets?

The way the narrator struggles with his subject, his hedges and qualifications, and his final surrender to the wisdom of tautology have an almost anthropological ring of truth. There is the pleasure, as well, of being inducted into a private language (as in A Clockwork Orange), which becomes more complex and interconnected with each page; a pleasure that is heightened by the chemical purity of the vocabulary. There are glints of mystery (one never hears of the problematic Brink's cord again), as well as many minor, and ingenious, solutions to etymological riddles along the way. Nor are all the riddles minor: one of the story's most inspired ironies concerns the naming of the tribe known as Dr. Boot's List.

Engine Summer is exceptional in science fiction for being, first and foremost, a work of art. Its scale is small and the range of human possibility it encompasses is correspondingly narrow, but one doesn't fault Cézanne's *Card Players* for lacking *terribilità*. Within its carefully determined bounds *Engine Summer* succeeds at the first, and still the most difficult, task of art: it achieves formal beauty.

Wolfe's New Sun

Claw of the Conciliator is the second volume of a tetralogy-in-progress, *The Book of the New Sun*, which already seems assured of classic status within the subgenre of science fantasy. This alone would be faint praise, for science fantasy is a doubtful sort of hybrid in which the more decorative elements of science fiction proper—*Star Wars* hardware, dinosaurs, apemen, etc.—cohabit with the traditional chimeras of myth and legend. Characteristically, writers of science fantasy set wind-up heroes in quest of some grail across a bedragoned landscape quite as though Cervantes had not long since laughed picaresque romance off the literary map. Even when practiced by writers I ordinarily admire—Ursula LeGuin, Michael Moorcock, Brian Aldiss—science fantasy strikes me as inauthentic, coy, and trivial—circus costumery and paste diamonds, the lot of it.

Insofar as it is possible to judge any tetralogy by its first two volumes, *The Book of the New Sun* is a vast exception to that rule. Gene Wolfe has managed to do what no science fantasy author has done heretofore—he's produced a work of art that can satisfy adult appetites and in which even the most fantastical elements register as poetry rather than as pennywhistle whimsy. Furthermore, he's done this without in any way sacrificing the showmanship and splashy colors that augur a popular success. Quite a balancing act, as Wolfe notes himself in passing, when, toward the end of the first novel of the series, *The Shadow of a Torturer*, the narrator, Severian, an apprentice in the guild of torturers, relates a tale he was told in his school days

> of a certain Master Werenfrid of our guild who in olden times, being in grave need, accepted remuneration from the enemies of the condemned and from his friends as well; and who by stationing one party on the right of the block and the other on the left, by his great skill made it appear to each that the result was entirely satisfactory. In just this way the contending parties of tradition pull at the writers of histories. . . . One desires ease; the other, richness of experience in the execution . . . of the writing.

Review of *Claw of the Conciliator* and *Gene Wolfe's Book of Days*, by Gene Wolfe.

One could not ask for a tidier summing up of Wolfe's own achievement as an author—so long as one places the emphasis on "experience" rather than "richness" in the last phrase. Richness of imaginary detail is all too easily come by in a universe of unicorns and dragons: no sooner is one peril surmounted than Fancy, like the hydra, supplies a pair in its stead. But experience—in the sense of relevance to a real life intensely lived—is precisely what escapist fantasies are escaping *from*. In allegorical fantasies (and science fantasy is, in its nature, allegorical) it is only possible to achieve intensity and depth if each of the individual elements of the fantasy—the swords, ogres, magic jewels—bears a weight of meditated meaning that intensifies and deepens as the tale progresses (in the manner, say, of Wagner's *Ring* cycle). In most hands, these props are deployed with the artless caprice of children trimming a tree with their family's heritage of Christmas ornaments. Wolfe, however, is a Wagnerian, not a tree trimmer; his allegory actually has something to say, and it is said with art, acuity, wisdom, and wit.

At the risk of compressing it into extinction, I would submit that Wolfe's central theme is the nature of political authority and the use of terror as a necessary means to secure social stability in any society (but especially ours). "Here the master and I do our business still," says Severian, as he pantomimes his trade as torturer in a masque performed at the Autarch's court. "We do it still, and that's why the Commonwealth stands." This cannot be said to be his last word on the subject; rather, the first—the subject up for debate. Here at the center of the labyrinth it is impossible to second-guess the outcome of that debate, but that it will be satisfying can scarcely be doubted.

This is not to say that the web is flawless. I doubt that any tetralogy has ever been written in which the second volume didn't come off as second-best. There are chapters in *Claw of the Conciliator* that venture perilously close to pulp magazine hugger-mugger, and other chapters—one long interpolated masque, in particular—that are too archly Significant, after the manner of Thornton Wilder's *The Skin of Our Teeth*. (Wilder is a writer whom Wolfe resembles in other, and happier, respects.)

The acclaim and attention that *The Book of the New Sun* is winning among both critics and readers should further consolidate the reputation of Gene Wolfe as a writer of short fiction. Eighteen of his stories are assembled in *Gene Wolfe's Book of Days*, a collection that aspires to unity by the doubtful device of matching separate tales to national holidays: for Lincoln's Birthday a story about the reintroduction of slavery as a solution to the problem of overcrowded prisons; for Valentine's Day a whimsy about computer matchmaking; and so on through the calendar.

Actually, the stories suit their occasions fairly well, but sometimes I suspected that Wolfe was dipping toward the bottom of the barrel in order to accommodate his format. Even so, there are many first-rate stories, most notably the selection for Labor Day, "Forleson," a novella in which all the morose absurdities of a life devoted to middle-management job dissatisfactions are compressed into one day of high-speed, low-keyed nightmare.

A parting word concerning these books as items of commerce. Timescape Books has seen fit to wrap *Claw of the Conciliator* in a cover so lurid that only confirmed fans who have passed beyond shame will dare to be seen taking it from a bookshelf. The book itself is handsomely produced. By contrast, Doubleday (all too typically) disdains the decorums and amenities of book publishing so arrogantly that it might more honestly dispense the typesetting and binding altogether and simply market Xerox copies of its author's manuscript. Gene Wolfe deserves better, and so does anyone who pays ten dollars for a book.

The Champion of Cyberpunk: On Two Works by William Gibson

Cyberpunk is the label under which a portion of the younger science fiction writers of the eighties have been marketing their wares, and as neologisms go, it represents a fair description of their product. Cyberpunk sci-fi, in its ideal form, is compounded of (1) a re-envisioning of the consensual future in terms not of space travel and other feats of mega-engineering but of a plastic (i.e., wholly malleable) mental landscape that derives from the new possibilities of computer graphics, and (2) punk style, in clothes, hair, sexuality, and the abuse of controlled substances. Like punk rock, and like most traditional rocket-and-blaster sf, Cyberpunk caters to the wish-fulfillment requirements of male teenagers, but this is a job that can be done with varying degrees of panache, and in the whole field of sf there is presently no more accomplished caterer than William Gibson. He is the undisputed champion of Cyberpunk.

Mona Lisa Overdrive might be considered the concluding volume of a trilogy, except that the book's last chapter so patently advertises a sequel. These days nothing short of the author's death can keep a commercially successful work of sf from being cloned into sequels as long as the product moves from the shelves. A sense of closure, and so of narrative architecture, is not among the pleasures a reader should expect from *Mona Lisa Overdrive*. What Gibson offers in its place is "flash"—quick, high-intensity glimpses that linger on the retina of the imagination, like the sets (but not the narrative) of the movie *Blade Runner*, which Gibson has acknowledged as a formative influence. The new novel has plenty of flash, as in the following short travelogue from the inhabited ruins of a future Florida, seen from the point of view of the teenage hooker who is the novel's title character:

> About the only thing to like about Florida was drugs, which were easy to come by and cheap and mostly industrial strength. Sometimes she imagined the bleach smell [which pervades the beaches] was the smell of a million dope labs cooking some unthinkable cocktail, all those molecules thrashing their kinky little tails, hot for destiny and the street.
> She turned off the Avenue and walked down a line of unlicensed

Review of *Mona Lisa Overdrive* and *Virtual Light*, by William Gibson.

food stalls. Her stomach started growling at the smell, but she didn't trust street food, not if she didn t have to and there were licensed places in the mall that would take cash. . . . A soapbox evangelist spread his arms high, a pale fuzzy Jesus copying the gesture in the air above him. The projection rig was in the box he stood on. . . . The evangelist frowned up at Jesus, adjusted something on the belt at his waist. Jesus strobed, turned green, and vanished.

Decoded, the impacted inferences of this passage tell us that this is a world made nearly uninhabitable by industrial waste; a world under constant surveillance, in which almost all monetary transactions are controlled by computer; a world in which visual illusion is as cheap as canned sound today. Gibson excels at piling up such inferences to make a self-consistent, gritty-textured future junkheap of a world. In opposition to that world is the realm of cyberspace, into which humans who have been surgically adapted to interface with computers can go voyaging, as upon an ocean that is the confluence of all databases, a Pac-Man universe of infinite complexity.

Gibson's first novel, *Neuromancer*, offered more dazzling vistas of cyberspace than those that are to be found in *Mona Lisa Overdrive*, but at the expense of requiring more developed reading skills than many sf readers could bring to bear. *Mona Lisa Overdrive* seems to be written on purpose to admit a larger readership to the marvels of cyberspace. While Case, the hero of *Neuromancer*, was a professional computer "cowboy," a Ulysses of cyberspace, the four protagonists of *Mona Lisa Overdrive* are innocents and naifs, who move through the novel with all the autonomy of passengers on a ride at Disneyland. Indeed, one of the four, a Japanese teenage girl named Kumiko, is completely extraneous to the plot, her only involvement being to take a subway ride across London in order to make a long-distance phone call to warn the book's real heroine about a danger she has already dealt with.

Only in retrospect, however, is *Mona Lisa Overdrive* a disappointment. Zing by zing, its forty-five chapters provide a sufficiency of non-nutritive fun. As with *Neuromancer* the plot is strictly from 1946, but knowingly so, like a Brian de Palma film noir. Indeed, the book virtually begs to be filmed: there is a climactic duel between police helicopters and customized robots; a juicy double role for the leading lady; lots of martial-arts hugger-mugger performed by a leather-clad Wonder Woman; everything needful except the lyrics for the title song for Madonna or Cyndi Lauper to sing as the credits roll.

William Gibson may well be the last of the great science fiction writers. During the last decade, sci-fi has been wilting on its high-tech vine just like its over-hyped offspring, the "Star Wars" Strategic Defense Initiative. With SDI already smelling of mothballs, Outer Space looks like yesterday's future. So what future is left? The junky, postmodern urban sprawl of Cyberpunk, a territory across which William Gibson was one of the first to spray his name. He is still, on the evidence of *Virtual Light*, the fastest thinker. Other sf writers may write books that are just as good or even better, but none of them has generated a vision of the future that has spread through the whole culture like a computer virus. Gibson has made everyone else his imitator, and that is greatness in sci-fi.

This latest book shows Gibson in top form. Like his debut novel, *Neuromancer* (where he came up with the idea of cyberspace, the place where brains and software meet), *Virtual Light* is a mix of cyber and punk, where computer hackers are never nerds but get to wear the latest in low couture and designer tats. Corps of privatized cops patrol LA in tanks designed by Ralph Lauren, and clothes receive major attention. In Gibson you are what you wear:

The shirt was lemon-yellow and printed with life-size handguns, in full color, all different kinds. He wore a huge pair of navy blue shorts that came to way below his knees, Raiders socks, sneakers with little red lights embedded in the edges of soles, and a pair of round mirrored glasses with lenses the size of five-dollar coins.

As that fashion statement indicates, *Virtual Light* is not set in the far future, and it's all the scarier for that. Here is a day after tomorrow in which, after the earthquake California's been waiting for, the entire Golden Gate Bridge has to be closed to traffic and is then settled by hordes of squatters, who turn it into the honky-tonk at the end of time. Gibson makes it sound not only believable but worth trying. His special love is for what he calls "Thomassons," which is what Modern becomes after it's had a collision with Reality. More than any writer going today, he is the poet of assimilation, multiculturalism, and culture shock as good therapy.

What gives Gibson his special take on the global village is a disenchantment that is also on a global scale. He's scrapped the old utopian agenda of sci-fi that imagined a helicopter in every suburban garage, and he also has no truck with the eco-liberal fantasies of writers like Ursula LeGuin. In a world that just keeps getting more rotten, Gibson has decided he might as well try to learn to like how it smells. And no one, these days, has a finer nose for the decay of Western Civ.

Queen Victoria's Computers

This genre-transcending science fiction novel by the co-inventors of "Cyberpunk," William Gibson and Bruce Sterling, is set in an alternative version of Victorian London, circa 1855, with many of its familiar historical features intact: pea-souper fogs pierced with the dim glow of the first gaslight lamps, a war being fought in the Crimea, ladies in crinolines, gents in top hats, prodigies both of squalor and of nouveau riche excess. But then, and it is quite an enormous "but then," the authors have decreed that one crucial datum of history shall be other than it was: that sometime in the 1820s the mathematician Charles Babbage succeeded in constructing an operational Analytic Engine, a clockwork computer powered not by electricity, but by steam engines. The historical, cultural, and scientific repercussions are enormous, as they have been in our own time, and the resulting counter-Victorian era is elaborated with a Dickensian density of imaginative detail.

The crucial historical difference generated by this Difference Engine is an acceleration of the process of industrialization and its attendant political strife. In the 1830s, the Duke of Wellington confronts an Industrial Radical Party, headed by Lord Byron (although the real Lord Byron died in 1824). The Rads win, and Byron becomes the country's tyrannical prime minister, while Disraeli is only a Grub Street hack: "This fellow Disraeli, whose father founded *Disraeli's Quarterly*, you know. Bit of a madcap. Writes sensation-novels. Trash. But he's steady enough when he's sober." This is the verdict of T. H. Huxley, whose situation as a propagandist for Darwinism is not much altered, except that in this Victorian age, agnosticism is not a source of scandal but a mark of respectability.

This setting provides the background for a mystery-adventure plot with three distinctly separate, successive strands. The protagonist of the first is Sybil Gerard, the "ruined" daughter of an executed Luddite agitator, now a London dollymop (prostitute) who apprentices herself as an adventuress to the cunning press agent of Sam Houston, a political refugee from the independent state of Texas. Sybil's adventures continue just to the point where she comes into possession of the MacGuffin at the

---

Review of *The Difference Engine*, by William Gibson and Bruce Sterling.

heart of the plot—a box of celluloid punch cards containing a program not to be revealed, naturally, until the end of the book.

Meanwhile, like some immense, all-conquering parenthesis, we have the story of Edward Mallory, a foursquare Victorian hero of unimpeachable stolidity and rectitude. A paleontologist lately returned from an expedition to Wyoming, where he unearthed the bones of the first brontosaurus (and supplied guns to the Indians on behalf of the Foreign Office, which has succeeded in its policy of balkanizing the North American continent), Mallory comes into possession of the MacGuffin during a Derby Day encounter with Byron's daughter (and Babbage's protégée) Ada. Thereafter he is hounded by a whole rogue's gallery of villains bent on reclaiming the MacGuffin. He also picaresquely bumps into various representative eccentrics of the counter-era, among them a professional associate of Sybil Gerard's, with whom he enjoys a night of illicit love that is the most probable rendering of Victorian erotic seaminess this side of Anonymous's more comprehensive work, My Secret Life.

As Mallory's adventures mount ever higher, London succumbs to an ecological catastophe, the Stink, created by an inversion layer that traps the city's rampant and wholly unregulated pollutants. The rich flee, the lower orders run amok, and for fully one hundred pages there is a sustained set-piece of riot and anarchy that rivals the equivalent chapters of Dickens's Barnaby Rudge. Here, to hint at the flavor of that event, is the text of a broadside that is plastered on a wall near a scene of "rapturous looting":

AN APPEAL TO THE PEOPLE! Ye are all Lords of the Earth, and need only COURAGE to make triumphant WAR on the Whore of Babylondon and all her learned thieves. Blood! Blood! Vengeance! Vengeance, vengeance! Plagues, foul plagues, et cetera, to all those who harken not to universal justice! BROTHERS, SISTERS! Kneel no more before the vampyre capitalist and the idiot savantry! Let the slaves of crowned brigands grovel at the feet of Newton. WE shall destroy the Moloch Steam and shatter his rocking iron!

After Mallory's derring-do, the plot's shift to the viewpoint of the detective Laurence Oliphant can't help registering as a letdown, and this is compounded by the fact that the solution of the mystery represented by the MacGuffin is not a real mind-boggler. However, the authors have kept one major surprise in reserve, and it is an aesthetic one. The concluding chapter, "MODUS: The Images Tabled," is a montage of pseudo-historical texts and vignettes that unlooses a deluge of new data about the counterworld, opening up new vistas of extrapolation just as one expects the many loose ends of the plot to be tidied up. It's as if the authors had come right out and said their story was just a pretext for the real science-fictional excitement of building new worlds. The honesty is breathtaking.

The best science fiction has always worked by the power of suggestion, and seldom has that power source operated so effectively as in *The Difference Engine*. Working together, Mr. Gibson and Mr. Sterling have written a book that is even better than their earlier and considerable solo efforts. Grateful readers can only hope that this represents the beginning of a long and fruitful collaboration.

Dick's First Novel

There are, by now, many science fictions, but for myself (for any reader) there is only one science fiction—the kind I like. When I want to find out if someone else's idea of sf corresponds significantly with mine (and whether, therefore, we're liable to enjoy talking about the stuff), I have a simple rule-of-thumb: to wit—do they know—and admire—the work of Philip K. Dick?

An active dislike, as against mere ignorance, would suggest either of two possibilities to me. If it is expressed by an otherwise voracious consumer of the genre, one who doesn't balk at the prose of Zelazny, van Vogt, or Robert Moore Williams, I am inclined to think him essentially un-serious, a "fan" who is into sf entirely for escapist reasons. If, on the other hand, he is provably a person of enlightenment and good taste and he nevertheless doesn't like Dick, then I know that my kind of sf (the kind I like) will always remain inaccessible. For those readers who require sf always to aspire to the condition of art Philip Dick is just too nakedly a hack, capable of whole chapters of turgid prose and of bloopers so grandiose you may wonder, momentarily, whether they're not just his little way of winking at his fellow-laborers in the pulps. Even his most well-realized characters have their moments of wood, while in his bad novels (which are few), there are no characters, only names capable of dialogue. His plots may limp or they may soar, but they don't hang together. In short, he is not a bard in fealty to Apollo, not a "literary" writer.

What sets Philip Dick apart and lets him transcend the ordinary categories of criticism is simply—genius. A genius, what's more, that smells scarcely at all of perspiration despite a published output, over the last twenty years, of thirty-one novels and four collections of stories. Perhaps I'm being unfair to an art that conceals art, but the effect of his best books is of the purest eye-to-hand first-draft mastery. He tells it as he sees it, and it is the quality and clarity of his Vision that make him great. He takes in the world with the cleansed, uncanny sight of another Blake walking about London and being dumbfounded by the whole awful unalterable human mess in all its raddled glory. Not always an enviable knack.

Introduction to *Solar Lottery*, by Philip K. Dick.

Vision, if you're not well-trained in its use, is what bad trips are made of, and most of us, given the choice, will avoid the roads that tend in that direction. So, possibly, it is the very excellence of Dick's books that has kept readers away.

Not all readers, of course. There is a fair-sized and growing cult that faithfully buys each new book before it passes from the paperback racks into oblivion. But by comparison to the sf writers who have made a name for themselves in the Real World, who can be bought at the SuperValu and are taught in the trendier tenth-grade classrooms, by comparison to the likes of Asimov, Bradbury, Clarke, or Vonnegut, Dick might as well be an avant-garde poet or a composer of electronic music. The Public hasn't heard of him.

It isn't fair. If he were guilty of metaphors or some such elitist practice that makes books hard to read, you could understand people being leery of him, but Dick is as democratic as Whitman, as demotic as Spillane. When he's at his best he is—even by "literary" standards—terrific. His prose is as plain and as sturdy as Shaker furniture, his characters as plausible as your next-door neighbors, his dialogue as authentic as a Watergate transcript, and his plots go rattling along with more ideas per paragraph than the College Outline Series' *Introduction to Western Philosophy*. He makes you laugh, he makes you cry, he makes you think, and think again: who could ask for more?

So what went wrong? Why have so many sf writers who are clearly his inferiors (naming no names) been so much more successful in the marketplace—and even in attracting the attention of academics, who, after all, are supposed to be able to recognize Quality? The simplest theory is just—that's the breaks. A careless agent sold his first books to the worst of all paperback houses, and for years he was stuck on a treadmill of speedwriting to meet deadline after deadline, world without end. The wondrous thing is that instead of being broken by this system and declining into a stumblebum twilight of hackwork, drunk on the Gallo burgundy of fannish adulation (many the bright young writer who has vanished into that Saragasso!), Dick moved steadily from strength to strength with no other reward (excepting a single Hugo Award for *The Man in the High Castle* in 1963) than the consciousness of having racked up yet another Triple-Star Bonanza score on the great literary pinball machine in the sky.

That's one theory. The theory I prefer is that Dick's books have failed to win a mass audience precisely because of their central excellence—their truth to life. Not that Dick (or any other sf writer, for that matter) is in the Prediction Sweepstakes. Forecasting the future is best left to Jeane

Dixon and the Rand Corporation; sf has better things to do. The truths of sf (in its platonic form) and of Philip K. Dick are prophetic truths in the Old Testament sense, home truths about here, now, and forever.

Also, they're dark truths. Any reader with the least proclivity toward positive thinking, anyone whose lapel button shows a sappy grin, anyone, in short, who still believes in the essential decency, or even feasibility, of the System, is liable to experience one of Dick's novels as a direct assault on his sanity. Indeed, that, in a nutshell, is the plot of what many hold to be his most mindbending novel, The Three Stigmata of Palmer Eldritch.

For all that, Dick isn't really one of that infamous Brotherhood of Blackness that includes Swift, Beckett, Burroughs, and the suicide brigades of modern poetry. There is too much of the sunlight and wine of California in him to let Dick qualify for the deepest abysm of Literature.

Perhaps the problem is his evasiveness, the way his worlds refuse, iri-descently, to stay in any kind of unequivocal moral focus. (As against the clear blacks and whites of Heinlein's homilies, or even the subtly gradu-ated grays of Ursula LeGuin's.) Guys you thought were on Our Side end up acting like monsters—even, or especially, such guys as God. Dick is slippery, a game-player whose rules (what is possible, and what isn't, within the world of his invention) change from book to book, and some-times from chapter to chapter. His adversary in these games is—who else?—the reader, which means that as fun as his books are, as smooth as they are, they are also surprisingly strenuous.

There is a form of Monopoly called Rat in which the Banker, instead of just sitting there and watching, gets to be the Rat. The Rat can alter all the rules of the game at his discretion, like Idi Amin. The players elect the person they consider the slyest and nastiest among them to be the Rat. The trick in being a good Rat is in graduating the torment of the players, in moving away from the usual experience of Monopoly, by the minutest calibrations, into, finally, an utter delirium of lawlessness. If you think you might enjoy Rat a bit more than a standard game of Monopoly then you should probably try reading Philip Dick.

Where to begin?

Not, in fact, with the book in hand, Solar Lottery. While it is far from being one of his downright losers (by all accounts Our Friends from Frolix 8 takes the cake in that category), neither is it a book by which converts may be won. In this respect it is like the early work of many titans-to-be.

Few readers approaching Shakespeare by way of Titus Andronicus and Henry VI would feel awfully impelled to plunge on. Similarly, Henry James's first novel, Watch and Ward, does not represent the Master at his most enticing. First novels are interesting, usually, as grindstones for the sharpening of hindsight. They show us the size and shape of the still-unfaceted diamond, but to appreciate them properly one must first have some notion of the diamond in its polished state.

So, if there are readers of this introduction who are as yet unacquainted with Dick's masterpieces, I'd advise them to begin with two or three of those and then return to Solar Lottery. (An alternative course, and not necessarily a worse one, if you possess unbounded faith, is to begin with Solar Lottery and read all the rest in sequence.) Having read The Man in the High Castle, Martian Time-Slip, The Three Stigmata of Palmer Eldritch, and Do Androids Dream of Electric Sheep?, and the novella "Faith of Our Fathers," which are my nominations for Dick's quintessential and all-time classics, one may then return to Solar Lottery with an eye for all the excellences that exist here in, as it were, an embryonic state.

Solar Lottery is also illuminating with regard to all that Dick had in common with his predecessors and his peers in that long-ago year of 1955. Even the highest and loneliest artists are engaged in a communal endeavor. Art is a vineyard in which all contemporaries—Kyd and Shakespeare, James and the myriad manufacturers of penny-dreadfuls, Dick and . . . whoever—work side by side, in a perpetual condition of reciprocal influence and aid. Dick's influence on later writers is clear enough. It seems highly unlikely that Ursula LeGuin would have written The Lathe of Heaven without an example of such earlier adventures in solipsism as Dick's Eye in the Sky and The Three Stigmata of Palmer Eldritch. What his inspiration may have been is less evident, especially if one's acquaintance is limited to the works of his maturity, in which early influences have either been assimilated or eliminated. In Solar Lottery this is not the case, and it offers us an ideal middle ground from which to view both the heights of what is to come and the common grounds from which these were to spring.

Solar Lottery appeared in 1955 as half of a thirty-five-cent Ace Double Novel, and it is from the plates of that edition that the present book has been photographically reproduced. (A mutilated edition of the book appeared the next year in England from Rich & Cowan, under the title World of Chance. Its copy editor showed unerring literary tact in eliminating, wherever possible, all of the book's more inspired passages. Truly, a monument to what may be achieved by patient mediocrity!) Unlike the novel on the flipside, Leigh Brackett's The Big Jump, Solar Lottery was not published serially. A yellow blurb above the red-and-white title declares: "FIRST PRIZE WAS THE EARTH ITSELF!" (This, if inaccurate, does try to make sense of the title, a task that the novel itself never undertakes—probably because the title was not of the author's choosing.) The cover art shows a man in a spacesuit hurling a red boulder at a speck of a man (unsuited) below him on a cratered plain of celadon green. For a wonder, this scene does derive from the novel (the close of chapter 12), right down to the paradoxical detail of the person walking about on the moon without so much as a snorkel. There is this further Oddity, that the threatened figure is the villain, his threatener one of the minor heroes, and it is he who is actually in danger at this moment. Even this early, things aren't what they seem in a Dick novel.

What is being promised by such a cover, and what Dick in fact delivers (if somewhat grudgingly), is an action-adventure set in the Far Future (and Outer Space), a story with heroes and villians, a beginning, a middle, and an end. By comparison to almost any of his later books *Solar Lottery* seems conservative in dramatic conception and (except for the rare flare-up) restrained, even perfunctory, in execution. A journeyman space opera. It is, after all, the first published book of a young man who cannot know, at this point in his career, the degree to which he may be permitted to depart from the established ceremonies of an Ace Double.

The nature of that ceremony and the requirements it places on its celebrants are very much at issue here. As with other rigid dramatic forms, such as the Western or the Requiem Mass, the artist must find how to be sincere within the narrow bounds of the form given him. Most pulp sf never gets off the ground because most hack writers write cynically, parroting the early, genuine successes of the genre without tracing them back to their emotional, intellectual, and aesthetic sources. (Ditto for Westerns and Requiem Masses.) But it is always possible. Witness the Westerns of Bud Boetticher and Sergio Leone. Witness the requiems of Mozart (a Freemason) and Verdi (an atheist). Witness the science fiction of Philip Dick.

I've written at length elsewhere (in "The Embarrassments of Science Fiction") concerning the emotional dynamics of pulp sf, the ways in which the needs of the sf audience dictated the form and content of classic space opera. In that essay I maintain that through most of its history science fiction has been a lower-class literature that purveys compensatory power fantasies specially aimed at readers sensitive to their social and educational shortcomings. At its most intense and obsessive, in sf fandom, this purpose becomes so overriding that fans may well be likened to Jehovah's Witnesses, whose millennialist theology is likewise calculated to feed the insatiable hungers and nurse the unhealing wounds of those among the oppressed who would still resist their despair. If this is so, one may better understand why ordinary literary criteria are not only a matter of indifference to readers of sf but are actually a matter of alarm: the sheer urgency of their need is so great that so long as the need is satisfied nothing else signifies. The clarity that Art brings represents an unwanted degree of illumination. Some actions are best performed in the dark.

The sf writers who most perfectly fit the above description are L. Ron Hubbard and A. E. van Vogt. Hubbard left sf relatively early in his career to found his own religion (one which precisely occupies the interface of fandom and millennial religion). Van Vogt simply wrote. And wrote simply: his books make the productions of such other founding fathers of proletarian pulp as Hammett and Chandler look like mandarin poetry. His prose rises above the laws of rhetoric and approaches the condition of phatic noise, the direct communication of emotional states by means of grunts and groans.

Now, if there is a single writer who may be said to have exerted a forming influence on the author of *Solar Lottery*, it is A. E. van Vogt. It is possible, as well, to hear echoes of more sophisticated voices, specifically those of Bester and Kornbluth-and-Pohl. Like *The Demolished Man*, *Solar Lottery* is about a crime that must be carried out despite a corps of telepathic guards. Like *The Space Merchants*, it presents a world of systematic and ironic reversals, as in the contrast between the random choice of a world president and the convention called to elect that leader's assassin. (This Erewhonian procedure would reach its apotheosis in the geopolitical ingenuities of *The Man in the High Castle*.) Yet it would be several years before Dick could be said to have rivaled or beaten Bester and Kornbluth-and-Pohl at their own game. While in the case of van Vogt, Dick has certainly done just that. In a sense, *Solar Lottery* is van Vogt's best novel.

The opening of *Solar Lottery* is substantially identical to that of van Vogt's most characteristic work, *The World of Null-A*. In both books a down-and-out hero is on his way to what seems a cross between a final exam and a job interview. Though suffering momentary doubts as to his ability to Get Ahead, it is suggested that each hero's apparent lack of success so far has been due to bad luck and, possibly, lack of effort. But this time, the story promises, the hero will try, and he does, and as a result he ends up in the last chapter as President of the Universe. It is the plot skeleton of the Brave Little Tailor and a hundred fairy tales besides. But with this difference, that the readers of sf may be presumed to be older and to have a somewhat solider grasp on reality (where fantasies of infantile omnipotence don't stand much of a chance). Some reason, however spurious, must be offered for the hero's success. He is surrounded not only with rockets and blasters to tickle the reader's sense of wonder but also with such plausibilities as coffee cups and contemporary (to 1955) urban landscapes, like this one: "Across the street a looming hotel shielded a motley family of parasitic stores and dilapidated business establishments: loan shops, cigar stores, girl houses, bars." Further, pseudoscience is called on to explain the hero's specialness. In *The World of Null-A*, the hero, by his mysterious command of the non-Aristotelian logic of the title (an elusive discipline borrowed from a once faddish movement called General Semantics), is destined to triumph over those ignorant sods and highbrow Establishment Scientists still mired in the old-fashioned Aristotelian logic of either/or. In fact, not much is ever really made of Null-A logic, for the sufficient reason, I would think, that not much can be.

The *real* reason a van Vogt hero wins through is that his innate genetic superiority (and the author's predestining hand) has thrust greatness on him. *Slan* is the supreme example in his work of paranoid racism, while the Null-A books offer his most full-blown Superman. The political implications of these traditional sci-fi themes have been exhaustively and hilariously dealt with in Norman Spinrad's satire, *The Iron Dream*. Dick, in 1955, could not be so audacious as Spinrad in the seventies. He was committed to producing a novel of van Vogtian intrigue that would provide its readers with their traditional vicarious satisfactions. That he has found a way to do so that no longer need offend a liberal sensibility is no mean achievement.

Consider Dick's use of game theory. Though not so questionable a discipline as van Vogt's General Semantics, it was being used in the fifties as a kind of intellectual smokescreen for U.S. foreign policy decisions that would have appeared much more unseemly without such scholastic trappings. In an author's note in the frontmatter of the Ace edition, Dick writes: "I became interested in the Theory of Games, first in an intellectual manner (like chess) and then with a growing uneasy conviction that Minimax was playing an expanding role in our national life. . . . Both the U.S. and the Soviet Union employ Minimax strategy as I sit here. While I was writing *Solar Lottery*, Van Neumann, the co-inventor of the Games Theory, was named to the Atomic Energy Commission, bearing out my belief that Minimax is gaining on us all the time." This is certainly alarming, but then no more is made of Game Theory until well into the penultimate chapter of the book, when there is a flurry of Minimax terminology followed by some hugger-mugger between the leading ladies. There is a lottery by which the Quizmaster (President of the Universe) is selected, but it is the simplest kind of lottery, and in no way requires Game Theory to be understood. Game Theory, in short, has about as much to do with Dick's story as the logic of Aristotle, or its refutation, has to do with *The World of Null-A*. It is a bit of legerdemain calculated to give the guileless reader a sense that the book is about Something Important, a name to drop if not a whole idea. The difference is that in van Vogt such hocus-pocus is associated with the Good Guys; in Dick (as in real life) it is associated primarily with the Bad Guys.

Consider the social landscape of *Solar Lottery*. Like van Vogt, Dick is writing for the proverbial "little man," for readers who will feel an instant bond of kinship with the elderly Cartwright when he is challenged by the villain in these terms: "You can't operate this [the post of Quizmaster/President]. This isn't your line. What are you? I examined the records. . . . You had ten years of nominal school in the charity department of the Imperial Hill. You never excelled in anything. From high school on you dropped courses that dealt with symbolization and took manual shop courses. You took welding and electronic repair, that sort of thing." And here is Dick's epic catalogue of the unks (people who lack "classified" ratings, i.e., proletarians) who set off in a rickety ore freighter on a quixotic quest for the Flame Disc (the utopian planet promised to them by their prophet John Preston): "A bewildering variety of people crowded anxiously around [Cartwright]: Mexican laborers mute and frightened, clutching their belongings, a hard-faced urban couple, a jet stoker, Japanese optical workmen, a red-lipped bed girl, the middle-aged owner of a retail goods store that had gone quack, an agronomy student, a patent medicine salesman, a cook, a nurse, a carpenter. . . . These were people with skill in their hands—not their heads. Their abilities had come from years of practice and work, from direct contact with objects. They could grow plants, sink foundations, repair leaking pipes, maintain machinery, weave clothing, cook meals. According to the Classification system, they were failures." These are the Good Guys, clearly.

There are two Bad Guys, the super-rich multinational corporation director, Reese Verrick, whom Dick allows to glow with the glamour of power, a glamour entirely denied to the sub-villain, Herb Moore, who is obliged to represent so many of the things that Dick dislikes (the servility of the Organization Man, the desexed rationality of a behavioral scientist, etc.) that he never coheres as a character. Moore creates a kind of golem for Verrick, the purpose of which is to assassinate the usurping (but benevolent) Cartwright. Which is to say: Money rules the world and shores up its power, whenever threatened, by its control of Science (a Science that is, for that reason, dehumanizing). That is far from being the sole or even a primary "meaning" of *Solar Lottery*, but it is surely one of the book's underlying assumptions. The chief difference between then

(1955) and now (1976) is the degree to which, then, left-wing sympathies of any consistency had to be disguised and "translated" into politically neutral language. (Compare, in *The Space Merchants*, of 1953, one of the models for *Solar Lottery*, the authors' clever substitution of the imaginary "Consies" [Conservationists] for the dreaded "Commies." An uncannily correct extrapolation.) Again, Dick's use of the Pellig/superman figure may be contrasted to the work of van Vogt, in which the golem/superman is there precisely to afford his readers an unequivocal vicarious delight: If only it were me!

Solar Lottery, along with most of its successors, may be read as a self-consistent social allegory of a more-or-less Marxist bent. As such Dick's books are unique in the annals of American sf, whose brightest lights have either been outspokenly right-wing, like Heinlein, or blandly liberal in the manner of Asimov or Bradbury, or else they've back-pedaled after a fire-eating youth, like the post-Kornbluth Pohl. Doubtless this is what has enabled Dick to be excepted from the anathemas of Stanislaw Lem, the Polish sf writer and critic. But Dick's political imagination, though powerful, is not, I believe, his central strength.

Dick's big theme, the one that consistently calls forth his finest and most forceful work, is transcendence—whether it's possible, what it feels like, and whether that feeling ultimately represents wishful thinking or some larger reality. He is constantly torn between a rationalistic denial of the ultimate reality of transcendent experience and a (still ironic) celebration of the brute fact of it.

Viewed in the light of this concern, many of his themes take on shades of meaning that sort oddly with strict dialectical orthodoxy, or even any known variety of revisionism. Why, for instance, does he celebrate "people with skill in their hands—not their heads"? Not just because they're underdogs who perform vital work and are denied adequate recompense or recognition. Handicraft, for Dick, is a spiritual discipline, somewhat in the way it was for Shakers, whose motto, "Hands to work and hearts to God," might well be his own. The most fully developed of Dick's craftsmen/heroes is Frank in *The Man in the High Castle*, a maker of modern silver jewelry. Much of that novel's plot centers around the specifically spiritual quality of Frank's jewelry, a spirituality that in one instance allows another character than Frank to transcend the terrifying Nazi-dominated world of that novel (by, ironically, escaping into our own).

The Prestonites' voyage in quest of the Flame Disc and their discovery, en route, of the seemingly resurrected John Preston represent *Solar Lottery*'s initial sounding of this typical theme. It is not one of the stronger things in the book, in part simply because it is scanted in Dick's pell-mell rush to get the second half of his advance. But it may also be that the Flame Disc sequences fail because they haven't been sufficiently transformed from orthodox Christian eschatology. Dick is not about to make a declaration for Christ, though he always seems to be flirting with the possibility, symbolically. However, his confessional impulse is invariably contradicted by dramatic events of much greater emotional suasion. In *Solar Lottery* the exhumed body of John Preston proves not to be alive, as expected, but a simulacrum. Through all his novels Dick entertains the possibility that creatures of flesh and blood are all essentially robots, mechanical monads obeying laws of a mechanistic creation. *Do Androids Dream of Electric Sheep?* is his single most compelling vision of man's unredeemably material nature, but there is one moment in *Solar Lottery* when the later book's dark paradoxes are powerfully prefigured. It occurs on page 138: to say more would spoil *Solar Lottery*'s finest *coup de théâtre*.

This essay cannot begin to enumerate all Dick's characteristic motifs, much less to analyze their complex interactions. The best I can do is to suggest a context in which Dick's work may be viewed more fruitfully than that of other science fiction stories, and that is the context of Romantic poetry, especially the poetry of Blake and Shelley. Both were political radicals whose circumstances prevented them from translating their convictions into political action. Both demonstrated a profound and prophetic understanding of those realms that lay beyond the Age of Reason. Both were artists of process, prevented by the very urgency of their apprehensions from creating works of classic amplitude and concinnity of form.

This is not to say that readers will find no formal pleasures in Dick's novels, that it is all a matter of snuffling about for truffles of Meaning, as I've been doing here. But his commitment to an aesthetic of process means that, by and large, whatever he writes is what we read. There is no turning back to rethink, revise, or erase. He improvises rather than composes, thereby making his experience of the creative process the focus of his art. This is not a novelty, of course. It is the wager of Scheherazade, too, that she can be interesting and authentic absolutely all the time, and this tradition of the novel is as old and as honorable as the more Flaubertian idea of the novel-as-prose-poem that presently holds sway in academia. Within this tradition Dick is one of the inmortals by virtue of the sheer fecundity of his invention. Inevitably there are dull patches, days when his typewriter refuses to wake up, but on the whole these are few and the stretches of song, when they come, are all the more remarkable for being, so visibly, the overflow of a spirit . . . that from Heaven, or near it, pours its full heart in profuse strains of unpremeditated art.

In the Mold of 1964: An Afterword

In December of 1961 the U.S. Defense Department announced a fallout shelter program aimed at establishing 235,000,000 fallout shelter spaces. At that time the entire population of the country had yet to exceed 200,000,000.

In October of 1962, Kennedy had his moment of macho glory when he declared a quarantine around Cuba, where the Russians were building missile bases. For a few days everyone was waiting for the bombs to fall. The sensation of dread and helplessness was just the stuff nightmares are made of. For those who had read more than the government's bromidic brochures on the subject of nuclear destruction and who were living at that time in a major (i.e., targeted) city, there was little to be done but figure the odds for survival. Fifty-fifty seemed the general consensus among the New Yorkers I knew. The poet Robert Frost, legend has it, reckoned doomsday even likelier than that, and when he appeared at a symposium at Columbia University, he declared himself to be delighted that now he would not die alone (he was then eighty-eight) but would take all humanity along with him.

A year and a month later, in November of 1963, President Kennedy was assassinated—probably as a quid pro quo for his earlier efforts to play a similar dirty trick on Castro. However, at the time we were asked to believe that the deed was accomplished by a single bullet fired by Lee Harvey Oswald. Earl Warren, having been admonished by President Johnson that continued doubts of the scapegoat's sole guilt could lead to nuclear war, was directed to write a scenario to this effect. The Warren Commission issued its report in 1964, the same year in which The Penultimate Truth was published. Neither was nominated for a Hugo, for indeed both books were much too hastily written to deserve such an honor. But as a snapshot of the angst that characterized that period—and of the blackly humorous emotional antidote to that angst—The Penultimate Truth is an essential document.

According to the records of the Scott Meredith Literary Agency, the outline for The Penultimate Truth was received in March of 1964, and the

---

Afterword to The Penultimate Truth, by Philip K. Dick.

completed manuscript in May. Conceptually it represented the splicing together of two short stories Philip K. Dick had written in the earliest years of his apprenticeship. The first of these, "The Defenders," appeared in the January 1953 issue of *Galaxy*. It duplicates, in miniature, the Nicholas St. James portion of the plot, in which all humanity has been tricked into believing it must continue living underground to escape the radiation and other dangers of a nuclear war. In this story it is the leadies (robots) that have perpetrated the deception in order to keep mankind from self-extinction, and the story's last wistfully liberal tableau represents two groups of escaped U.S. and Russian troglodytes blasting off into the sunset, reconciled by the rational leadies:

> "It has taken thousands of generations to achieve," the A-class leady concluded. "Hundreds of centuries of bloodshed and destruction. But each war was a step toward uniting mankind. And now the end is in sight: a world without war. But even that is only the beginning of a new stage of history."
>
> "The conquest of space," breathed Colonel Borodsky.
>
> "The meaning of life," Moss added.
>
> "Eliminating hunger and poverty," said Taylor.
>
> The leady opened the door of the ship. "All that and more. How much more? We cannot foresee it any more than the first men who formed a tribe could foresee this day. But it will be unimaginably great."
>
> The door closed and the ship took off toward their new home.

The second source story for the novel was published in *If* (August 1955), and its title, "The Mold of Yancy," was intended, in a slightly emended form, "In the Mold of Yancy," as the original title of the book. It concerns the conspiracy of the yance-men of Callisto, a satellite of Jupiter, to brainwash the guileless Callistotes into a condition of abject conformity by means of the televised speeches of a (nonexistent) homespun philosopher who is a cross between Arthur Godfrey and George Orwell's Big Brother. The problem is resolved not by revealing the deception to the gullible population but by using the Yancy mannikin to inculcate a preference for Greek tragedy and Bach fugues among those who formerly were satisfied by Westerns and the songs of Stephen Collins Foster.

It is clear, even in that early story, that Dick's interest in the premise is more with the secret power exercised by hidden persuaders, such as advertising copywriters, speechwriters, and filmmakers, than with the moral question of the legitimacy of such persuasion. It's less clear whether, as he wrote "The Mold of Yancy," Dick recognized his personal fascination and identification with the yance-men of Callisto, but surely by the time he had decided to rework that old material into a novel, he knew himself to be a yance-man—albeit one employed in the lower echelons of the power structure—as a hack writer producing sci-fi paperbacks. By way of signaling that fact and of sharing it with the unhappy few who could be counted on to read his hack novels as a phantasmal form of autobiography, Dick gave the Agency that is responsible for this global deception the then-current address of his own literary agent, Scott Meredith, at 580 Fifth Avenue.

What it meant, for Dick—as for his novel's protagonist, Joseph Adams—to be a yance-man was that he knew, as most of his fellow citizens did not, that the real sociopolitical function of the cold war and the arms race was to guarantee comfortable "demesnes for corporate executives and other officials of the military-industrial establishments." Only as long as there was the menace of an external enemy would a majority of people agree to their own systematic impoverishment. But if one's "enemy" was in the same situation with respect to its captive populations, then a deal could be struck to keep their reciprocal menace everthreatening—not at all a difficult task with the unthinkable power of the nuclear arsenals both sides possessed.

In another novel, The Zap Gun, conceived and written in the same few months of spring 1964 that produced The Penultimate Truth, Dick hypothesized a very similar conspiracy between the superpowers. The hero of that novel, Lars Powderdry, is a weapons fashions designer whose imposing but impotent creations are derived, telepathically, from an Italian horror comic, The Blue Cephalopod Man from Titan. The moral of both novels is clear: government is a conspiracy against the people, and it is maintained by the illusion of a permanent crisis that exists, for the most part, as a media event.

Such a view of world affairs was much less common in the early sixties than it has become since Watergate, but it was surely not original to Philip Dick. Its most forceful expression is probably found in George Orwell's 1984, in which a perpetual state of war and shifting alliances among the three superpowers provide the basis for totalitarian rule, and in which the head of state is, like Talbot Yancy, a chimera. Many critics have pointed out that 1984 is intended, not as a prediction or a warning against some dire possible future, but rather as a nightmarishly hyperbolic picture of the actual state of affairs at the time it was being written, a meaning concealed in the title: 1984 = 1948.

The great difference between Orwell's world-nightmare and Dick's is that the possibility of nuclear holocaust has not yet informed Orwell's vision, while it dominates Dick's—and often obscures it. Never mind that the future Dick has imagined could not come into being, that the radiation released by a nuclear war would have had far more awful and widespread consequences than the singeing represented in The Penultimate Truth. The emotional basis of the inability to comprehend nuclear reality has been compellingly discussed by Jonathan Schell in The Fate of the Earth, where, after demonstrating the virtual certainty of human extinction as a result of a large-scale nuclear war, he argues:

> It thus seems to be in the nature of extinction to repel emotion and starve thought, and if the mind, brought face to face with extinction, descends into a kind of exhaustion and dejection it is surely in large part because we know that mankind cannot be a "spectator" at its own funeral, any more than any individual person can.

Might not the congruent sense of "exhaustion and dejection" pervading the first chapters of The Penultimate Truth be symptomatic of Dick's natural inability to think the unthinkable—that is, to imagine the aftermath of nuclear war in plausibly dire terms?

Of course, Dick never intended to write a plausible, realistic post-holocaust novel. Readers who want a verismo version of their own future deaths might read On the Beach (novel, 1959; movie, 1959). Dick has another zeitgeist to summon, a new wisdom that is at once happier and blacker, the Spirit of '64. He simply denies that the cold war is happening.

It is a denial we all learned to make, having passed through the twin crises of 1962 and 1963: the Missile Crisis and the Assassination. Robert Frost died alone, after all, and the rest of us, by and large, survived. If we'd never bothered listening to the news, there'd have been no reason to be fussed. Life went on. The Beach Boys produced new and better songs. Ditto Detroit and cars. That segment of the entertainment industry devoted to politics had an election, Johnson versus Goldwater, and the plot was that Goldwater would lead us into war. So we voted, by and large, for Johnson.

But that's getting ahead of the story, since this cannot chronicle the entire unreality of the nuclear era, but only the particular slice represented by The Penultimate Truth—spring of 1964.

Consider our presidents. Up to the age of fifteen, Dick would have known but one, FDR, and he would undoubtedly have shared in the idolatry accorded Roosevelt in the war years, Dick being eleven years old in 1941. It can be maintained (and often has been) that two of the next three presidents—Truman, Eisenhower, and Kennedy—achieved their success because of the image they projected rather than through some special competence. Indeed, Eisenhower's nomination in 1952 was denounced by Taft's supporters as a triumph of showbiz over politics, while, with the benefit of hindsight, Kennedy's entire career seems a pageant choreographed by the yance-men about him—Schlesinger, Bradlee, even Mailer. Christopher Lasch writes, in the October 1983 issue of *Harper's* magazine: "Never was a political myth so consciously and deliberately created or so assiduously promoted, in this case by the very people who had deplored Madison Avenue's participation in President Eisenhower's campaigns." As Norman Mailer wrote in his account of the 1960 Democratic convention, which helped to fix Kennedy's image as an "existential hero," the "life of politics and the life of myth had diverged too far" during the dull years of Eisenhower and Truman. It was Kennedy's destiny, Mailer thought (along with many others), to restore a heroic dimension to American politics, to speak and represent the "real subterranean life of America," to "engage" once again the "myth of the nation," and thus to bring a new "impetus . . . to the lives and the imaginations of the American."

If this is how one of the man's vassals speaks of him, in public, in his lifetime, Lasch's case—and Dick's—seems fairly unassailable. Of course, those intellectuals who promoted Kennedy for his mythic potential felt with a certain complacent knowingness that they were privileged to see the reality beyond the myth (for that is a yance-man's greatest reward). Mailer begins his teasingly self-revealing, self-concealing *An American Dream* (which first began to appear, serially, in *Esquire* in January 1964) with a paragraph calculated to make all true yance-men swoon with envy:

> I met Jack Kennedy in November, 1946. We were both war heroes, and both of us had just been elected to Congress. We went out one night on a double date and it turned out to be a fair evening for me. I seduced a girl who would have been bored by a diamond as big as the Ritz.

In every respect but one *An American Dream* is a more accomplished novel than *The Penultimate Truth*, but that one respect is crucial to its (failed) ambition. *An American Dream* does not succeed as an evocation of the zeitgeist of the dawn of the assassination era—for the sufficient novelistic reason that Mailer has murders to discuss much closer to his own heart. However, both novels share the same courtier's fascination with the intrigues presumed to be the reality behind the myth of Camelot/Talbot Yancy, and both find something glamorous in the ruthless exercise of power by well-placed criminals.

It must be admitted, however, that the hugger-mugger surrounding the Machiavellian schemes of the smarmily villainous Brose and the Byronic David Lantano is the central weakness of *The Penultimate Truth*. Brose's plot for entrapping Runcible is so unnecessarily preposterous, and involves such needless multiplication of hypotheses, and is at last so irrelevant to the outcome of the story, that one might wonder at Dick's willingness to permit such an obvious blemish to remain, except that one knows, from his own admissions and from other internal evidences, that Dick's method of work was to plunge on ahead and never look behind. If he'd been Orpheus, Eurydice would have had nothing to worry about backwards-looking-wise (as Dick would say).

I'd like to intrude a long parenthesis here concerning the faults of the book, which are, pretty obviously, the result of Dick's chosen manner of writing, a manner comparable to downhill racing. The results can be spectacular, though often the spectacle provided is one of disaster. But rather than appearing to guess at Dick's technique of composition on the basis of internal evidence, let me quote his account of the matter, written to an editor at Harcourt, Brace early in 1960:

> I wonder why you say I write so much; that is, produce so much. My anxiety is that I produce too little—that if I bore down I could produce a lot more. Most of the work, for me, lies in the pre-typing stage, in the note-taking. I generally spend five to six months doing no typing, but simply outlining. At best I can now bring forth no more than two novels a year. . . . Under certain conditions, however, I can write very fast, even without notes. The Lippincott book was written in two weeks, proofread and then retyped in two more. . . . My work tends to force a pace on me; I'll do forty to sixty pages a day for days on end, until I'm exhausted, and then not uncover the machine for several months.
>
> I wait until I am sure of what I want to put down, and then away I go.

After winning a Hugo for *The Man in the High Castle* in 1963, Dick was actually able to increase his rate of production to a little better than three novels a year, a rate he maintained almost to the end of the sixties.

The downhill-racing style of novel-writing is not uncommon in science fiction or other genres, and when it is brought off well, there is a fizziness and exhilaration to such books that is not to be found in more carefully wrought novels, however favorably they might otherwise be compared. Often, however, speed-written novels run out of steam sporadically. Forty to sixty pages a day means a week's continuous work for a novel the length of The Penultimate Truth, and it is difficult to scintillate virtually nonstop for an entire week. Often it is all that bleary eyes and weary fingers can do to type coherent sentences. Take as a for-instance chapter 14, four labored pages of dialogue in which two minor characters rehash a situation the reader is already well aware of, arrive at no conclusions, and can't refrain from dropping hints right and left as to how low Phil Dick is feeling at that late hour, after his seventeenth cup of coffee: "A Yance-man, female, named Arlene Davidson, who has a demesne in New Jersey; the Agency's top draftsman. Died of a massive coronary during the past weekend. Late Saturday night. . . . She may have been given a deadline, for something major; overworked. But that's conjecture." And then, a page later: "Still shuffling his documents, trying to come up with something of use, trying and unhappily failing, the abstract-carrier Footeman said, 'I wish you good luck. Maybe next time.' And he wondered if, for Runcible, there would be a further report. This inadequate—admittedly so—one today might well be the last. . . ."

The wonder is how often Dick was able to produce work of real interest and wit in these marathons of typewriting. For readers who read at a pace proportioned to his speed of writing (as most sf fans learn to do, or else cease being fans), the dull patches disappear into a haze of white powder as they careen down the slopes of the narrative. It is the ideas they are after, and Dick always provides more than a sufficiency of these.

Indeed, for slower readers like myself, who are so old-fashioned in their tastes as to demand some kind of consistency and continuity in the plot of a book, this profusion of ideas often is a bigger stumbling block to the enjoyment of Dick's lesser novels than the chapters written on automatic pilot. Take the way Dick picks up, and throws away, and again picks up, the idea of time travel in The Penultimate Truth. First he posits a "time scoop" that can propel objects back into the past, a device Brose intends to use to plant false archaeological "proofs" of an extraterrestrial invasion of fifteenth-century North America. Brose's plot comes to nothing, though several chapters are devoted to its preparation. Then, fudging the explanation like mad, Dick asks us to believe (1) that one of the yance-men, David Lantano, is actually a Cherokee Indian who has managed to ride the (now two-way) scoop back into the twenty-first century; (2) that in a manner never fully explained this Lantano's physical age oscillates between young manhood and old age, when he becomes the real Talbot Yancy; and (3) that he has taken a few starring roles in the intervening five centuries.

None of which has much to do with what the book set off to be about, nor does it impinge very much on the resolution of the plot. Yet, it is clear from scattered footprints, broken twigs, and other spoor of the downhill-racing novelist what Dick would have liked this stew of impossibilities to accomplish. Lantano first appears as the yance-man most likely to succeed—and to succeed the hero, Joseph Adams, as the Agency's most accomplished speechwriter. Adams envies the way Lantano, in one of the speeches he has written for the Yancy simulacrum, is able to "openly discuss the fact that those tankers down there are systematically deprived of what they're entitled to." Here is how Dick, using the mask of Lantano (who is using the mask of Yancy), describes the characteristic deprivation of the tankers' (i.e., working-class) lives:

> Your lives are incomplete, in the sense that Rousseau had meant when he talked of man having been born in one condition, brought into the light free, and everywhere was now in chains. Only here, in this day and age . . . they had been born onto the surface of a world and now that surface with its air and sunlight and hills, its oceans, its streams, its colors and textures, its very smells, had been swiped from them and they were left with tin-can submarine—figuratively—dwelling boxes in which they were squeezed, under a false light, to breathe repurified stale air, to listen to wired obligatory music and sit daylong at work-benches making leadies for a purpose which—but even Lantano could not go on here.

But Lantano's place in the scheme of the novel isn't limited to his rhetorical abilities. He is meant to be the redeemer of a humanity not simply downtrodden but buried, a Christ figure whom Nicholas St. James, his evangelist, at once recognizes as such, murmuring when they first meet, "He was oppressed and despised," a misquotation that Lantano himself corrects to "despised and rejected of men." However, about the only way that the Cherokee Lantano resembles Christ is in having been appointed the task of harrowing hell—that is, of being the agent by which the subterranean tankers will win release and inherit the earth. Yet, the means Lantano adopts resemble those of Danton much more than those of Christ, for Lantano proves to be the sneakiest and most ruthless of the book's sundry schemers, and in this he represents Dick's own ambivalent—and unformulated—feelings on the question of how human liberation is to be achieved.

The same ambivalence is mirrored—but more coherently—in the opposition between the two chief protagonists of the novel. Nicholas St.

James is an ideal proletarian, the "president" of his ant tank, resourceful, courageous, and a dupe. Joseph Adams has only one thing going for him, apart from a certain ineffectual "liberal" goodwill—the fact that he is not a dupe. Dick admires Nicholas St. James, but he identifies with Joseph Adams (who is, accordingly, the only character in the book with an intermittently plausible inner life).

With regard to plot construction, therefore, Lantano is an unnecessary complication, a *deus ex machina* whose powers prove almost as illusory as those of the figurehead of Yancy with which he is identified. At the end of the novel, as a result of Lantano's coup, humanity is to be released from its bondage, but this has been accomplished without any recourse to Lantano's special characteristics as a time-traveling, Christ-like Cherokee warrior.

What, then, was the purpose of such "ideas"? Were they no more than a kind of conceptual padding, a way to pump up the premise of the original stories to novel length? After the fact, perhaps yes, but in the pell-mell of writing I think Dick's throwaway ideas represent a kind of self-pitched curve ball that he honestly hopes to knock over the stadium wall. There are similarly transcendental elements in the plot of another novel from 1964 (and one of his best), *The Three Stigmata of Palmer Eldritch*.

If Dick had stopped to think (but that's something a downhill racer can't do), he might have realized that there was an essential dramatic disparity between the two stories he was trying to weld together. The Yancy part of the plot generated a story about dirty tricks in high places, a genre for which Dick possesses little flair (compare Le Carré and his better imitators), while that element of the story that all readers remember, after the lapse of however many years, is the notion of the human race imprisoned in underground factories because they've been tricked into believing that a nuclear war has destroyed the world. It's an extraordinarily resonant idea. One thinks of the dwellers in Plato's cave who know nothing of the reality but the shadows cast on the wall; of the similar destiny of Wells's Morlocks; of the prisoners in Beethoven's *Fidelio*; and of ourselves, living in the shadows of a nuclear threat that is only bearable when we pretend that it does not exist. To have recognized that our situation is a kind of madness ("What, me worry?" sang the *Titanic*'s passengers) has not helped us toward a solution, for our situation with respect to the bomb is not much different in 1983 than it was in 1964. And for that reason *The Penultimate Truth*, for all its flaws, remains a book that can speak to the terror that is the bedrock of our social order.

PART FIVE ON SF Crazy Neighbors

The Village Alien

If Whitley Strieber isn't fibbing in his new book, Communion (and the book's cover boldly affirms that it is "A True Story"), then it must be accounted the most important book of the year, of the decade, of the century, indeed, of all time. For what Strieber recounts in Communion is nothing less than the first contact of the human race, in the person of Whitley Strieber, with an ancient alien civilization that abducted him from his cabin in the Catskills on the nights of October 4 and December 26, 1985 (and on various other occasions over the years), and took him aboard a flying saucer, where he communicated with a variety of alien beings and was subjected to surgical and sexual indignities. To cover their tracks the alien abductors then implanted false "screen memories" in Strieber's mind (as they have been doing, he has come to suspect, throughout his life). Only later, in March 1986, did hypnosis reveal the true character of what had happened to him.

There have been other, similar reports of UFO sightings and contact with aliens, but Strieber's is unique in two important respects. First, as he notes himself, "If mine is a real experience of visitors, it is among the deepest and most extensive as yet recorded." Second, this is the first time a best-selling author has written his own extensive, firsthand account of a UFO experience. Strieber's early novels were horror stories, taking traditional figures like werewolves (The Wolfen, 1979) and vampires (The Hunger, 1981), and placing them in contemporary urban settings.

Both books became successful movies. Two later science fiction novels were written as collaborations with James Kunetka: Warday (1984) is a fictional "documentary" of nuclear holocaust, and Nature's End (1986) treats global ecological catastrophe on a similar panoramic scale. Communion seems the end of a logical progression, leading Strieber from the fiction side of the bestseller list to the nonfiction side. That assumes that Communion will make it onto the list, but with a one-million-dollar investment in the book, William Morrow would seem to have confidence in its success.

Skeptical readers (and I freely confess that I began as one) may feel

---

Review of Communion, by Whitley Strieber.

that the million-dollar advance paid for the book is in itself reason to doubt the good faith of the author. For there certainly could be writers who might be tempted for such a price to invent such a tale out of whole cloth and swear to its truth. Strieber does not address this question directly in his book, but he makes it clear that he deplores charlatanry and pseudoscience, and those who profit from the public's credulity:

> One of the greatest challenges to science in our age is from modern superstitions such as UFO cults and people who are beginning to take instruction from space brothers. Charlatans ranging from magicians to "psychic healers" have tried to gather money and power for themselves at the expense of science. And this is tragic. When one looks at the vast dollars that go each year to the astrology industry and thinks what that money would have done for us in the hands of astronomers and astrophysicists, it is possible to feel very frustrated. Had the astronomers been awash in these funds, perhaps they would have already solved the problem that I am grappling with now. I respect astrology in its context as an ancient human tradition. Still, I wish the astronomers could share royalties from the astrology books.

Strieber is aware that there will be those who may doubt what he is saying, and even admits: "I did not believe in UFOs at all before this happened. And I would have laughed in the face of anybody who claimed contact." He maintains, furthermore, that until impelled by his own experience to examine other UFO literature, he had taken no interest in such matters. If he had read widely in the literature, the striking correspondences between his own UFO experience and that recorded by others could be ascribed to imitation. A case in point: *Science and the UFOs*, by Jenny Randles and Peter Warrington, a book that by happy coincidence he'd received from his brother at Christmas of 1985, just hours before the visitation of December 26. He did not read it at once, for "I was surprised to find that *Science and the UFOs* frightened me. I put it aside with no more than the first five or six pages read." Later, however:

> I finally finished *Science and the UFOs*. Toward the end of the book I was astonished to read a description of an experience similar to my own. When I read the author's version of the "archetypal abduction experience," I was shocked. I was lying in bed at the time, and I just stared and stared at the words. I, also, had been seated in a little depression in the woods. And I had later remembered an animal [a screen memory].
>
> My first reaction was to slam the book closed as if it contained a coiled snake.

Throughout the book, the correspondence between Strieber's and other contactees' experiences constitute one of the main criteria offered for our believing that Something Must Be Happening, something bigger than Whitley Strieber:

What may have been orchestrated [by the aliens] with great care has not been so much the reality of the experience as public perception of it. First the craft were seen from a distance in the forties and fifties. Then they began to be observed at closer and closer range. By the early sixties there were many reports of entities, and a few abduction cases. Now, in the mid-eighties, I and others—for the most part independent of one another—have begun to discover this presence in our lives.

Even though there has been no physical proof of the existence of the visitors, the overall structure of their emergence into our consciousness has had to my mind the distinct appearance of design.

There does, indeed, appear to be a design, but could it not be accounted for by the tacit collusion of the witnesses? Of course, we have Strieber's assurance that he was innocent of earlier testimony until his own experiences prompted him to do research. But by his own account Strieber's memory is an erratic instrument, due (it may be) to the aliens' implanting, virtually on an annual basis, of false "screen memories," the weeding out of which constitutes a very large part of *Communion*:

Many of my screen memories concern animals, but not all. I remember being terrified as a little boy by an appearance of Mr. Peanut, and yet I know that I never saw Mr. Peanut except on a Planter's can. I said that I was menaced by him at a Battle of Flowers Parade in San Antonio, but I now understand perfectly well that it never happened. For years I have told of being present at the University of Texas when Charles Whitman went on his shooting spree from the tower in 1966. But I wasn't there.

Then where was I? And what is behind all the other screen memories?

Perhaps on some level I do know. Maybe that's why I spent so much time peeking into closets and under beds. If I really face the truth about this behavior, I must admit that it has been going on for a long time, although in 1985 it became much more intense. Now that I have uncovered these memories, though, it has ended completely.

As a matter of fact, I cannot remember a time in my life when I have felt as well and as happy as I do now.

That is not to say that Strieber's life has been untroubled since the surfacing of the aliens. *Communion* records so much distress, suffering, agony, anguish, and pain that in undertaking to write of the book I dreaded to think that I might be adding to it by taking a tone that would suggest that I am scoffing at the author. Strieber has had the same dread and in his introduction cautions against making light of "people who have been taken by the visitors": "Scoffing at them is as ugly as laughing at rape victims. We do not know what is happening to these people, but whatever it is, it causes them to react as if they have suffered a great personal trauma. And society turns away, led by vociferous professional debunkers whose secret fears apparently close their minds." Here is a sampling of the sufferings, both physical and mental, that Strieber has had to endure:

> [Aboard the saucer] the next thing I knew I was being shown an enormous and extremely ugly object, gray and scaly, with a sort of network of wires on the end. It was at least a foot long, narrow, and triangular in structure. They inserted this thing into my rectum. It seemed to swarm into me as if it had a life of its own. Apparently its purpose was to take samples, possibly of fecal matter, but at the time I had the impression that I was being raped, and for the first time I felt anger.
>
> My wife reports that my personality deteriorated dramatically over the following weeks. I became hypersensitive, easily confused, and, worst of all, short with my son. . . . I had a feeling of being separated from myself, as if either I was unreal or the world around me was unreal. By December 28 I was so depressed and in such a state of inner conflict that I sat down and wrote a short story in an effort to explore my emotions. . . . I called it "Pain."

This story appears in an anthology of horror stories edited by Dennis Etchison, *Cutting Edge*, and a most revealing exploration it is. See below.

> [After hypnosis by Dr. Donald Klein] I recalled seeing a landscape with a great hooked object floating in the air, which on closer inspection proved to be a triangle. Then there followed a glut of symbolic material, so intense that even as I write I can feel how it hurt my whole brain and body to take it all in. I don't remember what this was—triangles, rushing pyramids, animals leaping through the air.
>
> Are such experiences the source of the performance anxiety that has been detected in psychological tests I have taken, or does that have to do with the many recollections I have always had of sitting in the middle of a little round room and being asked by a surrounding audience of furious interlocutors questions so hard they shatter my soul?

Finally, this *cri de coeur*, wrested from the author during hypnosis as he relives his examination by the aliens aboard the saucer. Dr. Klein has asked, "Are they paying attention to you?" and Strieber replies:

> "Yes. There's one of them now sitting down in front of me staring right at me, and she's completely different from the others. The others are all very small people. This one is tall and thin. And she's sitting down. She's all gangly. I don't know what to make of that. I don't know what to make of this. Where the hell—how the hell—you know, it's like I can't see. I just don't know what the hell to make of this. It's just impossible. It's totally impossible. It can't be like this."

What the aliens are actually up to zipping around in their UFOs and inserting probes into the orifices of selected citizens never becomes very clear. Although he often has had the opportunity, Strieber rarely has the presence of mind to ask his aliens where they come from or what their intentions are. Once they volunteer the information: "You are our chosen one." A more ambitious chosen one than Strieber might want to know what such an announcement portends. Does it mean he is the single person chosen from the whole human race to be the aliens' go-between? If so, what an awesome destiny! But Strieber declines to speculate, though the bulk of the book is given over to his speculations: whether the visitors come from outer space or from some other dimension; whether they are archetypes or ancient gods conjured up from the communal unconscious; whether their natures are insectlike; and questions even more improbable:

> What might be hidden in the dark part of my mind? I thought then that I was dancing on the thinnest edge of my soul. Below me were vast spaces, totally unknown. Not psychiatry, not religion, not biology could penetrate that depth. None of them had any real idea of what lives within. They only knew what little it had chosen to reveal of itself.
>
> Were human beings what we seemed to be? Or did we have another purpose in another world? Perhaps our life here on earth was a mere drift of shadow, incidental to our real truth. Maybe this was quite literally a stage, and we were blind actors.

Perhaps. Who can say? Perhaps I only *dreamt* I read Strieber's book. Perhaps James Landis at Morrow only *dreamt* he paid a million dollars for it. Or perhaps (it occurred to my ever-skeptical mind) human beings *are* what they seem to be, and Whitley Strieber is embroidering the truth.

Certainly in the last passage quoted he looks remarkably like a hack writer padding out a thin story with a lot of guff. Some novelists do that. Even Whitley Strieber. Perhaps (we ought to at least consider the possibility) he is making up the whole story just as if he were writing fiction! Novelists, especially horror novelists, know all kinds of ways to make the implausible seem plausible. It's what they're paid for.

Another thing novelists have been known to do is to enlarge, develop, or inflate a short story they have written to novel length. Sometimes they do this because they feel the story's theme has not been fully realized; sometimes simply because they have no better hook to hang the next novel from. If *Communion* were a novel and not A True Story, anyone who had also read the short story "Pain" would feel certain that there was such an acorn-to-oak relation between the two works, and for that reason it is worth examining in detail. It begins with a professional narrative hook: "When I encountered Janet O'Reilly I was doing research into the community of prostitutes." The narrator is circumstanced much like Strieber himself: he is a professional novelist living in Greenwich Village with his wife and three children. (Strieber himself has one child, a son, age eight, who is reported in *Communion* to have shared, with Strieber and his wife, in some of the close encounters the book describes.)

> For my new book [the narrator relates], to be called *Pain*, I wanted to know not only about prostitution but also about the various perversions that attach themselves to it. There are sexual desires so exploitative that people will not gratify them without being paid even in our exploitative society. These have to do for the most part with pain and death. For death is connected to sexuality—witness the spider. Who hasn't wondered what the male spider feels, submitting at the same time to the ecstasy of coitus and the agony of death?

There follows a male spider's précis of Western culture, from the ritual sacrifice of kings and Roman emperors to Hitler's death camps and the Kennedy assassination. Then comes a fairly extensive consideration of "ufology," which is surprising in view of Strieber's claim in *Communion* that he had not been concerned with such matters at the time "Pain" was written—and had, indeed, been a skeptic. The narrator of "Pain," by contrast, sounds quite convinced that Something Is Happening:

> There is evidence all around us of the presence of the hidden world. We reject it, though, as silliness and foolery.
> Because it knows that this hidden civilization feeds on us, the gov-

ernment does everything possible to hide reality. It does not want us to know that our lives, our culture, our very history has been designed for the purpose of causing us suffering, and that there is nothing whatsoever that any of us can do to relieve ourselves of this burden.

I was astonished to see in 1983 that NSA had been approached by CAUS (Citizens Against UFO Secrecy) under the Freedom of Information Act to divulge what it knows about UFOs. Officially, the government has made a massive effort to debunk the whole notion of "flying saucers," claiming that they are all either hoaxes or misperceptions.

After these discursive preliminaries the story begins again at its first beginning:

I met Janet O'Reilly at the Terminal Diner at the corner of Twelfth and West streets in Greenwich Village. I was there because of my research. The Hellfire Club is nearby, a haunt of New York's sadomasochistic community. I particularly wanted to connect with some of the people who went there to make money. I wasn't interested in the compulsive participants, but rather in the men and women who preyed on them.

Well, one thing leads to another, and before he knows it the narrator has been lured to Janet's apartment, "a miserable filthy cellar on Thirteenth Street," where the library contains books by Proust and Céline. She invites him to crouch at her feet, and when he demurs she kicks him in the chest. She is verbally abusive: "Unlike you, I don't lie about myself. Now you're here and you're still having difficulty submitting." Eventually, however, he comes around, only to learn this sorry wisdom:

When I go to her and submit myself, a part of my suffering will be the certain knowledge that all of their lives [i.e., those of his wife and children] will be damaged by my act. My pain will be infinitely greater for understanding that It will lead to theirs. To know that you will cause grief to those you love is a very hard thing.

As True Stories go, "Pain" has more of a ring of truth than Communion, but possibly that is because Strieber has had more experience as a writer of fiction than of nonfiction. It is at times hard to remember that Janet O'Reilly is an alien and not just a fly-by-night dominatrix. The narrator's visit to her flying saucer is over almost before it begins. One minute he's having a beer behind a cabin (how life does imitate art), and then: "The next thing I knew I was in a tiny, droning airplane with Janet. At first I didn't recognize her. Then I saw that she was flying the plane, watching me out of the corner of one eye. She spoke in a language I could not quite understand."

The textual parallels between "Pain" and *Communion* are even more extensive and systematic than this synopsis can indicate, but it would be hard to deny the virtual identity between the fictive Janet O'Reilly and the nameless alien who abducts Strieber and, in one rather breathless paragraph of hypnotic transcript, has something like sex with him.

There are two ways I can think of to account for this. The first is that Strieber, having made the imaginative equation between the "archetypal abduction experience" and the ritual protocols of bondage and domination, realized he'd hit a vein of ore not previously tapped by ufologists, who have been generally a pretty naive lot. To have drawn such an explicit parallel in *Communion*, however, would have risked alienating the audience at which such a book is targeted, and so among Strieber's many speculations there are none that examine or allude to the metaphorical premise of the story and its relevance to the "abduction experience," a relevance that is only to be found, once again, beneath the longer narrative's surface, like a prize bone dug up and then reburied.

A second possible explanation is that the story represents the first surfacing of materials repressed by the aliens, who had, only days before the story's writing, taken Strieber aboard their saucer and given him such a hazing. This is undoubtedly the explanation Strieber would adopt if the question should ever come up, though in *Communion* he is content to let that sleeping dog lie.

That Strieber appreciates that "Pain" poses an awkward question was confirmed early this morning (Monday, February 23) by a telephone call from Strieber in Chicago, the latest stop on his extensive promotional tour. He had earlier agreed to be interviewed in New York on Saturday, but then called to cancel that meeting. I decided to begin this essay without the benefit of speaking with Strieber, but I still wanted to know more about the chronology of the composition of story and book. Yesterday, to that end, I telephoned Dennis Etchison, in whose anthology "Pain" appeared, and asked when Strieber had been solicited for a story and when Etchison had received the completed manuscript. There was nothing in the dates to contradict Strieber's account, and Etchison was full of praise for his friend and contributor (who had been "a national debating champion and studied for fifteen years with the Gurdjieff Foundation"), and for "Pain," confiding that Strieber had told him that he regarded it as "a major turning point in my life and my career."

Etchison inquired for what magazine I was writing my piece: *Omni?* I had to admit it was the *Nation*, and this produced a resonant silence and an expressed wish that his remarks were all off the record. I would certainly have complied with his wish if he had not himself at once sent out an SOS to Strieber, who then left the following message on my answering machine:

Tom, it's Whitley at 8:30 on Monday morning. I'm calling you from Chicago. I still have got time problems. I also understand from other people who you've talked to that you're planning what is apparently a really vicious hatchet job on *Communion*, and I'm not sure I even want to talk to you about it. It's an awful, ugly, terrible thing to do. The book is so obviously from the heart! To think that it was written for money—it shows an absolute lack of sensitivity, and also a lack of understanding of the book market. You know, the book was turned down by its original publisher [Warner], and I had to write it knowing it had no publisher. The fact that I got . . . a good price for it . . . I shouldn't be punished for that, Tom, nor should the people that this strange experience— [Here the machine stopped recording.]

About an hour later, he called again, and this time I was doing my own answering. Without any prompting or argument, Strieber repeated his reproaches, deploring all those flaws in my character that he'd first observed when I'd taken over the PEN table from him at the 1985 Small Press Fair at Madison Square Garden. Even from our brief time-filling conversation he'd sensed a lack of human decency and feeling that had made him feel . . . sorry for me, nothing but that. He suggested that it was not too late to show some elemental respect for human feelings, that I didn't have to subject him to the agony my essay would surely cause. When he'd lost his first head of steam, I pointed out that, not having read what I'd not finished writing, he was arguing with straw men. No, he said, he could tell where I was heading just from my condescending tone of voice, and from the questions I'd been asking about "Pain." It became clear that "Pain" was a sensitive area, and without my having to state my sense of its relevance, Whitley volunteered his own, which corresponded to the "second possible explanation" given above, that the story had just bubbled up from his subconscious as a result of his encounters with the aliens. It wasn't the acorn, so to speak, but the first little oak.

What Whitley could not have imagined at that moment (and what I certainly was not going to tell him after so many minutes of vituperation) was that I was no longer a skeptic about UFOs, that, in fact, in the course of writing this essay I have been in contact with alien beings, and though my aliens—the Winipi (pronounced Weenie Pie; singular, Winipus)—are not of the same race as those in touch with Strieber (who are known, and feared, throughout the galaxy as the Xlom), they, the Winipi, are well informed of the purposes of the Xlom and the grave danger they represent.

However, before I relate what I've learned about the Xlom and their human minions, I should give an account of how I encountered the Winipi and was taken aboard their flying saucer. It was on the same Saturday I was to have seen Strieber. I had gone downtown to get coffee at my favorite coffee store on Bleecker Street, and, realizing that I was only a few blocks from the address Strieber had given me to call at, I thought I would see where he lived. It was a brick building larger than a brownstone but smaller than the massive piles of Washington Square Village, which it faces. Its facade was paneled at ground level with squares of black slate, and the lower doors and windows were secured with heavy ornamental iron gratings. On an impulse I went down the short flight of steps and entered the foyer. I pushed the buzzer marked "Strieber," thinking that he might find time to see me after all. No response. I pressed the buzzer a second time, and as I released it I felt a strange shuddering vibration pass over me, which I ascribed at that time to static electricity.

Leaving the foyer, another unconsidered impulse made me turn right (instead of left, toward home), and within minutes I found myself beside a fenced-in quarter-acre of wasteland, which a signboard declared to be a "Time Landscape." The sign went on to explain that this was "an environmental sculpture of a primeval forest, showing how this area looked in the fifteenth century." If the Time Landscape was any clue, Manhattan was in pretty sorry shape in the fifteenth century. Stunted oaks, scrawny maples, a few empty beer cans, and a broken umbrella contested with one another for the parched bare dirt.

In the middle of this primeval squalor I observed a strange phenomenon, which at first I assumed to be no more than a metallic-hued Frisbee gliding slowly in a long curve through the sickly branches of the dying shrubs. But why did it not reach the end of its trajectory? Why did it seem to hover inches above my head, emitting a pallid cinnamon-scented effulgence? (Strieber notes that the scent of cinnamon is often associated with alien contact.) Why did I seem to hear an eerie contralto voice whispering in my ear, "Sleep! gigantic Terran, sleep!"?

And then, nothing, blackness, snores. I awoke *inside* the wire enclosure of the Time Landscape with my green spiral notebook lying beside me in the dirt. And Strieber's words were echoing in my ears: "I don't know what to make of that. I don't know what to make of this." I walked home in a daze. I dined in a trance. I went to bed in my pajamas—and when I awoke, that same eerie contralto I'd heard earlier ordered me, in implacable accents: "Go to your desk."

The next morning, after breakfast, I discovered that I had filled an entire floppy disk with what must be thought of as a kind of automatic word-processing. Are the words on the disk my own writing? I cannot say. They are on the disk. A brief prefatory note declares that they were written on "Washington's Birthday, February 22, 1987, 3:34 A.M.: I cannot tell a lie!" They seem to be the transcript of the dialogue I had carried on with my abductors the previous afternoon. They are, like Strieber's transcriptions of his testimony under hypnosis, unedited:

Me: Where am I? Who are you? What's happening?

Winipus I: [Giggles; then] Hello, Terran. You are in the Time Landscape on La Guardia Place between Bleecker and Houston, aboard our spacecraft, *Winipi Frisbee IV.* Welcome! And what is happening, Terran, is your own archetypal abduction experience. [More giggles; scurrying sounds; a burp]

Winipus II: [Speaking in a deeper, masculine voice, with a strong scent of peanuts on his breath] Welcome to the club. Just as Whitley warned you, right there in the endpapers of his book, "Don't be too skeptical: somewhere in your own past there may be some lost hour or strange recollection that means that you also have had this experience."

Me: I can't believe this! I'm in your flying saucer. But it was no bigger than a Frisbee.

Winipus I: That is because we Winipi are no bigger than peanuts. The tallest of us is not quite one centimeter. We had to use our shrink-blasters to get you inside the ship.

Me: [Confused] Shrink-blasters? But Strieber doesn't say anything about shrink-blasters. This is some kind of practical joke, isn't it? You're not aliens. You're—oh my God, no! I see you now! I smell you! You're . . . Mr. Peanut! It *wasn't* a screen memory that Strieber had. You *were* at the Battle of Flowers Parade in San Antonio!

Winipus II: We were there, yes, but we weren't threatening him. We were trying to save him from the Xlom. You see, Terran—do you mind if we call you Tom? You see, Tom, there are two alien races, us and the Xlom. The Xlom are, as Whitley intuited, humanoid insects with a hive mind. They have only one goal in their group mind, one all-consuming purpose, one hunger that drives them from star system to star system—Arcturus, Antares, Vega, Venus, and now Earth. They want money.

Me: Money? But if they're aliens . . .

Winipus I: [Twirling his cane] It's ridiculous, isn't it? Why would a Xlom need dollars? We've never understood that side of their characters. We only know they're insatiable, and utterly without a sense of humor.

Winipus II: That's why we have been following them everywhere through the universe. Because what we Winipi love more than anything else is comedy. The Xlom are just so funny. And in combination with you earthlings! I mean, what you never said in all those pages about Whitley's wonderful book is how funny it is. It's a classic, right up there with McGonagall's poetry or the Ninja thrillers of Eric Van Lustbader. Caviar, absolute caviar!

Me: But if what he says is true, then it isn't that funny. Clumsily written perhaps, but there's a point to all his nebulous fears. He may be in grave danger, if—

Winipus I: [Chuckles] Oh, it's much too late to save Whitley from the Xlom! He's one of them now himself. Surely you've seen *Invasion of the Body Snatchers.* Well, that's what the Xlom have done with Whitley. All those sessions of forced feeding that he reports? That's how it was done. Whitley's consciousness now is 95 percent Xlom. Even back at the parade in San Antonio it was too late to help him.

Me: Wait a minute. Why would the Xlom be letting Whitley reveal all their secrets? That's the major logical objection to his book in the first place: if the aliens are so wise and powerful, why is a [characterization deleted] like Strieber their "chosen one"?

Winipus II: First, there was money to be made, and as we've explained, the Xlom will do anything for money. They nearly became extinct a millennium ago when they began selling their children to the Arcturans for spare parts. But that's a separate story. There's not just the money for the book. There are already movie offers. Whitley's certain to write a sequel. And there's an outside chance he can get a whole cult going for himself on the order of that woman in Washington, the one who's been reincarnated so many times. Didn't you notice that *Communion's* last page is an invitation to write to Whitley at 496 LaGuardia Place? What better way for the Xlom to make mass conversions of humans into Xlom minions? As to his book letting the

Xlom's cat out of the bag, do you think most sensible people will believe it? Of course not. Oh, talk-show hosts treat him politely enough. In the broadcast time allotted to Silly Season celebrities like Strieber, they're content to let him tell his tall tale, take his bow, and head back to the airport. A wink and a smile will convey their sense of what kind of goods are being sold. But to call him to account would be like trying to swim in a swamp. It's more than they're paid for. As for what we've revealed to *you*, your readers will just dismiss the whole thing as satire, a story you've invented as a demonstration of how easy it is to make up any nonsense and call it A True Story as long as its only probative basis is the good faith of someone who'll swear he's not lying.

Here the transcript of my conversation with the Winipi breaks off. I can dimly recall other things that took place aboard the *Winipi Frisbee IV*, including a grueling tap-dancing lesson with a large group of Winipi, for which I was forced to wear a Mr. Peanut costume. (My feet hurt terribly the next day, so strange as this memory seems, I know it must be true, and not a screen memory.) I also learned the names of many other humans who have, like Whitley Strieber, been transformed into Xlom. Some of the most notable or notorious figures in modern society are Xlom, from Wall Street arbitragers to movie stars and high-ranking White House officials! The Xlom are everywhere, and there is no way they can be detected except with the Xlom-detecting technology developed by the Winipi—which I alone, of all humanity, have been entrusted with! After the Winipi had tuned the Xlom-detector (which is in itself undetectable) to my neural patterns, and as I was about to leave their saucer and be de-shrunk, one of them said to me, "You are *our* chosen one."

And then they laughed!

UFOs and the Origins of Christianity

That all Cretans are liars is a proposition that isn't generally disputed except by Cretans themselves, who can take refuge in the paradox that if they simply admit to being Cretans, the first term of the syllogism has to be called into question. Yet we, who are not Cretans, recognize that there are whole classes of people who are egregious and inveterate liars and who make their living by it. Preeminently our president, but also, in the same spirit, the spokesman for Isuzu, flying saucer abductees, Egyptic Pharoahs reincarnated as actresses and professional astrologers, Oral Roberts and others whom the living God speaks to familiarly, Kurt Waldheim, Oliver North, and suchlike candidates for indictment. We understand that their position requires the lies they tell, and to the degree that their lies appear harmless or sanctified by the established decorums of National (and self) Interest or Religious Liberty, the media report their prevarications with no more than a knowing wink. It is understood that they are Cretans, but what the hell, we live in Crete.

In such a situation, jesting Pilate's poser "What is truth?" becomes, increasingly, an impropriety. When a club is called a spade, the man who wields it isn't a goon but an honest farmer, like James Jordan Denby, down there on the border of Nicaragua, whose putative connection to, and funding by, the CIA is deniable, by definition. In England these matters may not even be mentioned, thanks to that nation's superior command of Good Form and the police. And then there's France.

And so the paradigm of manly virtue, here in Crete, becomes not merely the raffish con man pulling one's leg, but the macho mobster breaking one's kneecap, who in his most paradigmatic moment, at the end of *The Godfather*, swears to his spouse that he is innocent of what she, and we, and every Cretan, knows is so. But she's married to the bastard, so what can she say except, "Darling, I believe you." And then revenge herself with an appropriate adultery. And who's the wiser? That's life, among the Cretans.

Though it's not in the OED, nor even in the big Random House dictionary dated 1967 (well after Eisenhower's U-2 embarrassment), "deniability" can be found in the 1962 *Roget's Thesaurus*, as the penultimate synonym in section 513.2, which begins with "doubtfulness" and concludes, logically, with "disbelief." Logically, because deniability almost always implies that what can be denied did nevertheless happen. Nixon was never such a fool as to suppose anyone thought he was innocent; deniability was all he asked. Capone was proud of his criminal empire and indignant when the Feds betrayed his trust in the social order by nailing him for the wimpy crime of tax evasion, and lately history has been repeating itself, comically, in the figure of John Gotti, who manifests an evangelic sense of personal righteousness and good tailoring that must be the envy of even such a washed-in-the-blood Tartuffe as Pat Robertson. Donald Manes died in a pool of tears shed in the solemn conviction that he was doing only what everyone did, what had to be done if the world was to keep turning on the axis he'd spent his whole life helping to grease. Doubtless, his widow, in the dark mansion financed by his malfeasances, still adds her tears to that pool.

Perhaps the most delectable (because silliest) instance of deniability in the annals of contemporary business-as-usual is Michael Deaver's insistence that he is innocent of perjury because, thanks to his quart-a-day alcoholism, he can't remember the crimes he committed. Waldheim must wish he'd thought of that one.

The assumption behind the concept of deniability is that the entire public realm is a criminal conspiracy, in which it is common knowledge that cops deal dope and the CIA sells ammo to those who will use it to scramble our own expendable eggs, without whose sacrifice history's omelette could not be made, nor yet the profits that accrue to such transactions. Money rules: who's so naive as not to know that?

But let us, a moment, restrict our view to the domestic plane. Here too deniability exerts a noticeable force. Rape is such a loaded question because it hinges, both ways, on the issue of deniability. Did Jennifer Levin consent to, or somehow provoke, the nice young man who, as it were, spasmodically, took her life? He says so, and she's dead: deniability. Was Jessica Hahn the helpless victim of Jim Bakker's lust, or was she, like Mary Magdalene before her, an experienced prostitute and, hence, fair game? Jim is strongly motivated to hope the latter is the case, for therein lies his hope of Adamic deniability: the woman tempted him. For similar reasons child molesters must take comfort in the incoherencies of those they have molested, and felons of all kinds, making the same calculation, prudently endeavor to murder the victims who might become their witnesses.

Lasting success in business, government, or organized crime depends, as every good team player will tell you, on cooperation. The police force's blue wall of silence is only as strong as its crumbliest brick.

If every Watergate conspirator had had the team spirit of G. Gordon Liddy, children today might still have some respect for constituted authority. A semblance of ethical behavior can only be maintained in a society where there are material advantages for those who blow whistles and tell tales out of school. Sensibly, such behavior is ordinarily reprobated and punished by exile to the vast, invisible metropolis of Coventry. Those who want to belong learn early in life that they can do so only by keeping mum.

The moral imperative of keeping mum extends beyond the narrow confines of the Teamsters local and the quality-control task force of Morton Thiokol and encroaches on our smallest social interactions. Meeting Mormons socially, it is not *comme il faut* to inquire too closely into their honest opinion of the revelations Joseph Smith received from the Angel Moroni, nor is it considered polite to snicker at the pretensions of those who think there may be something in astrology. The realm of protected idiocies is as large as all Lilliput—and its boundaries are being continually extended.

I know this from recent personal experience. Earlier in 1987 I reviewed the first in a recent spate of books about UFO "abductions," Whitley Strieber's *Communion*, and suggested, on the basis of internal evidence in that book and an earlier work of fiction by Strieber, that his purported "nonfiction" book was a transparent hoax. Subsequently, it spent many weeks on the nonfiction side of the *Times* bestseller list, and received the kind of polite, not overtly skeptical attention that is accorded any piece of charlatanry that has earned money in the seven-digit range. The review written for the *Sunday Times Book Review* had its most deflating judgments deleted by editorial *force majeure*, and both *Publishers Weekly* and *Omni* have published articles that bent over backwards to accommodate the author's second line of defense, which is that if he wasn't literally abducted, he was having a Significant Spiritual Experience. That he might simply have been telling a whopper is a supposition that durst not be expressed, given the author's gifts for litigious saber-rattling.

My own fascination with Strieber's case and that of other copycat abduction claimants is due not just to the sheer scale of the chicanery but to my conviction that ufology constitutes an invaluable scale model of the origins of the Christian faith. The four gospels are based, like Strieber's *Communion*, on the obdurate insistence of a small circle of witnesses that *they saw* what they saw. Since no one else was in the vicinity of the witnessed event who might contradict them, these witnesses are guaranteed deniability. This is not only a necessary precondition of any miraculous witness but, implicitly, a template for the stage management of future miracles.

Contemporary fundamentalists claim to find the accounts of the resurrection persuasive as to the literal truth of the event witnessed, while those of more elastic faith tend to interpret the resurrection stories as shared visionary experiences. Similarly, Strieber offers two ways in which his UFO stories may be understood, as events that really did happen, and as mystical experiences somewhat on a par with receiving the stigmata. Neither Christians nor ufologists care to examine the likeliest possibility, that the mere collusion of many liars accounts for the congruence of one witness's testimony with another's. (Assuming such congruence exists; actually, there are versions of the UFO gospel that out-Strieber Strieber in their covert salaciousness.)

Indeed, a new religion's first concern, after its gospel has been proclaimed, is to secure the faithful against the scorn of skeptics. "Smite a scorner," advises the author of *Proverbs*, "and the simple will beware." And "Judgments are prepared for scorners, and stripes for the back of fools." Strieber is not yet so confident of his young faith as openly to brandish the knout, but he does sound this note of warning in the "Prelude" to *Communion*:

> There has been a lot of scoffing directed at people who have been taken by the visitors. . . . Scoffing at them is as ugly as laughing at rape victims. We do not know what is happening to these people, but whatever it is, it causes them to react as if they have suffered a great personal trauma. And society turns away, led by vociferous professional debunkers whose secret fears apparently close their minds. . . . I suffered from this experience. Others suffered, and are still suffering. It is essential that effective support be developed to aid those who have it. The scoffing has to stop.

In practice it is not that difficult to engineer a social environment in which true believers can enjoy the illusion of their triumph over scoffers. Churches are built for precisely that purpose, and till there's enough money for a proper nave, one can rent a lecture hall. In the summer of '87, a panel of ufologists convened at American University in Washington, D.C., where Strieber had an opportunity to intimidate ufology's most persistent debunker, Philip Klass. "There is a gentleman here tonight," he is reported as saying (*Omni*, December 1987), "who has seen fit to call me a liar in public on a number of occasions: Mr. Philip Klass, right here, in case anyone doesn't recognize him." After the audience booed and hissed Klass, Strieber read aloud from one of the sacred texts of his creed, a polygraph text in which he swore he was telling the truth, that he wasn't fibbing for dollars, and that the aliens really and truly had touched him. Strieber's enactment of these scenes of testimony and rebuke to unbelievers serve, like the perorations of a Jimmy Swaggart, both as entertainment and as a model of how the faithful are to confront a world of unbelievers.

For a certain kind of person such confrontations must be fun, especially if they lead to such a satisfying conclusion as that reported in *Omni*, where Klass denied having called Strieber a liar and offered to make a public apology if Strieber could produce a tape of the TV show in which the charge was made. I imagine that McCarthy, in his era, felt the thrill of the circus aerialist as he ascended to the heights of national fame on the tightwire of lies he walked each day before the media. And how much more amusing for Gary Stollman (another UFO evangelist) to have secured his moment before the TV cameras by intimidating the TV crew with a *toy* revolver.

Strieber's rewards, both financial and psychological, are clear enough, but what do lesser, Johnny-come-lately abductees stand to gain from accepting Strieber's standing invitation to add their UFO testimonials to his? They won't have bestsellers and movie sales; they won't be interviewed by prime talk-show hosts. They will, however, know the primal satisfaction of telling the same Big Lie without the strain of having to invent and promulgate it themselves. It is now, so to speak, in the public domain. Within the smaller public sphere of his or her own personal acquaintance, each self-proclaimed abductee can be a mini-celebrity, a person important enough to have been taken up by the living gods into the high-tech heaven of a genuine flying saucer.

A scam, even so? skeptics may urge. Assuredly, but why (these claimants may assuage the doubter within) should not they enjoy their moment in the spotlight of inauthenticity, along with the nation's official dramatis personae: Poindexter and North, Nixon and Reagan, Oral Roberts, Jim Bakker, and Pat Robertson, all proven and approved liars and all still officially respectable and accorded kid-glove treatment by the media. So might an early Christian have assuaged his or her doubts anent the resurrection of Christ and all latter-day saints, themselves especially included. Had not the emperors of Rome regularly proclaimed their own divinity? Had not Caligula testified to having had (much like Strieber) sexual congress with the moon-goddess? (Even at the Roman court, however, there were skeptics, though they recognized the need for diplomacy. Vitellius, when asked to corroborate Nero's claims, answered, "No, only you gods can see one another.") An ordinary citizen confronted with such imperial effrontery had few options more personally satisfying than to declare an equivalent demi-divinity: if not Godhead, at least co-immortality with the crucified and resurrected God. So much for the divine pretensions of Caligula, Jimmy Swaggart, Nero, Nixon, Heliogabalus, and their anointed successors.

Science Fiction as a Church

I exhort you to meditate with me on the subject of science fiction considered as a religious experience and as a church. This is Easter Sunday; we are gathered here to celebrate our peculiar rites; and so I'm going to begin the service now.

The first time I tried to deliver this talk was in Minneapolis, in the spring of 1973, when I went to a very small science fiction convention (it must have been around Easter time). Two or three people were delivering their message, their testimony, before I spoke. As they were talking, it dawned on me that this was a religious meeting, something I'd never understood about conventions till then. It didn't closely resemble the Catholicism I was brought up in (I'd grown up in the period of the Latin Mass), but there were great similarities between the convention in Minneapolis and certain Pentecostal services that I had seen in Guatemala.

Now that I have the hook in, I'll digress to tell you about my experiences in Guatemala. I was traveling through with Tony Clark, a professional con man who sold solid gold watches from his van, and the van got stuck in the mud. The only way to get where I was going was to take a plane that for political reasons stopped at the border of British Honduras and would go no further. There was no public transportation from the border to the only city, Belize. So I started hitchhiking, and there's not much traffic far inland in British Honduras. When finally a Land Rover came along and picked me up the driver was very friendly, and I was very friendly too. It turned out that he was there as a Pentecostal gospel missionary to the people of British Honduras, and he realized that Divine Providence had placed me there on the highway for him to pick up. I could not very well gainsay that. He took me to his home, and to his services. They were very nice services. They sang and they danced and they were exhorted to consider their own specialness: the fact that, of the few people of the human race who were going to be saved in times to come, this enclave right here in central British Honduras were among the privileged who wouldn't go to hell and would instead go to heaven.

That is the parallel that I observed in Minneapolis. Blessed was the text they preached; blessed are those who read sf for they shall inherit the future. There were also hints of secret powers that some few people possess, and hints that these secret mental powers of various sorts are observably related to one's reading of science fiction. Such powers are not uncommonly associated with religious experience. There is also the promise made to Noah. Like Noah, many sf writers and their fans feel they have the inside track on the approaching catastrophe, whatever it may be, and they're counting on being among the happy few who survive it. Need I cite chapter and verse?

Then there is the matter of healing—and here I will indulge in another digression. The very first science fiction "do" on a large scale that I went to was the Milford Writers' Conference in 1964. I hadn't known anybody in Milford beforehand and no one there, literally, had ever heard of me, because I was invited there as Dobbin Thorpe. Dobbin had published one story in *Amazing*. Damon Knight had liked the story, and so Dobbin was invited and wrote back saying he'd be happy to come. I was billeted with Walt and Leigh Richmond, who owned the Red Fox Inn about ten miles outside of Milford, in the country. After the first day at the Anchorage, where the Knights were, I arrived at the Red Fox and met Walt and Leigh Richmond. I entered on a scene that was to me unfamiliar. Walt Richmond was examining a young sf writer who had also been invited there. He had a malady that was focused in his knee, but it related to a childhood trauma that Walt was investigating. It turned out that this fellow had had all sorts of unresolved problems with his father, and they were all concentrated in engrams in his knee. I didn't know the theory behind all of this very well, but I was impressed with the fact that they both understood what they were doing and that they expected me to do it too. I was shy and I didn't let Walt get at my engrams.

But I have to tell the story because the Richmonds were among the people who possess psychic powers of a strange sort. They were collaborators on several books, and Leigh explained the method of their collaboration at one of the writing sessions. Often when you collaborate other people want to know how you actually do it. Walt and Leigh had found a very unusual and effective technique. He would think of what they were going to write and he would project it to her psychically. She would sit down at the typewriter and write the story that he had projected to her. They never had to exchange a word!

This was as near as I got to the inner arcana of the temple of True Believing in science fiction. The Richmonds understood all sorts of things about Atlantis. They'd written books about it, books that were visions of things that had actually happened. They were a little miffed when people regarded the books as fiction, because they knew they weren't. But on the other hand they had to make a living, and so they published them as fiction.

Now that doesn't at all exhaust the parallels between science fiction and religion. That's about as far as I got in Minneapolis, and it wasn't well received. But since, over the years, I have thought about all the ways in which the religious nature of sf fandom and its many conventions is a good thing—especially if one doesn't have other religions going for one. If you think about some of the purposes that religions serve for people, and try to think of how science fiction may serve those purposes for us, there is rather a large number.

The obvious side of it is the social life. Surely when Methodists get together and decide that they're going to bake cakes and sell them to each other and then sit down and eat them, they're not *really* thinking about salvation at that moment. They're enjoying coffee and cake with their friends. And it is good to have occasions to get together and have coffee and cake, even if you're Presbyterian, or Unitarian—or science fiction fans.

Then there's the question of pilgrimages. On the way up here to Leeds I realized that it was April and (you'll forgive my Middle English, I hope) "then longen folk to go on pilgrimages." I realized that I was this moment on a pilgrimage. We were in that queue (I expect there were others of you there with us, it got in the newspapers), ten miles of endless traffic jam on the M1 that just went on and on. Pilgrims, all of us. And as in Chaucer one of the purposes of making a pilgrimage isn't to get there, it's to trade stories along the way.

Then there's the aspect of what theologians call Agape, or communion—or, as it was practised by the Romans, drunken orgies. This is an important aspect of religion. People who have read about the history of religion will find that there's scarcely one recorded that does not make allowance for this at periodic intervals during the year when the pressure mounts up and people need a little break. And so we have holidays.

There's also the nationalistic aspect of religion. Nowadays it's considered quite unhip to even remember that we belong to nations, but like it or not, nationality is one of the chief ways people have of sorting themselves into groups. In the course of the different times I've been to conventions in England—the first one was at Bristol, and then it was at Buxton—I have seen an awful lot of England that I would not otherwise have seen. I kept thinking, "Well, that's me being a tourist." But if you're English you can't really think of yourself as a tourist in that way. Religions and the pilgrimage system provide one of the ways in which you get to know your nation, as it were, through direct experience. You visit other cities and you see what they're like and you live there a while. With people converging from all over the same nation, you mix together and you hear other people's funny accents and you ask them to repeat themselves till you can understand what they're saying. After a while you actually have a sense of the larger social group. As a social unifying force, one of the functions of religion has always been to make you aware of the larger groups you belong to.

Those are what I think of as the really good things about "the convention system" in science fiction, in its religious aspect—things nobody can take exception to. If you don't have another religion accomplishing those purposes, then this is terrific. But it leaves out one thing, obviously. The central idea of religion is supposed to be about the human experience of our relationship to something else: God, the infinite, or however your own religion will put it. The question is, can the parallel continue to be extended? If there are all these other resemblances to religion, then won't science fiction reflect this central aspect of religion as well?

(There are very many science fiction stories *about* religion, and I will just recommend to you that worthy book *The Science Fiction Encyclopedia*, where Brian Stableford has written an absolutely definitive article on the subject. It's a long subject; there is a lot of it. But that's not quite what I am getting at here.)

What I have in mind is this. Every sf fan will tell you that the basic element that has to be there in sf is Sense of Wonder—or "sensawonda," as I've seen it printed recently. Sense of Wonder can easily be related to religion if I can give it a different name, Sublimity. There is a book I started lately called *Turner and the Sublime*. Sublimity is instantly recognizable in Turner's paintings, or John Martin's (if you've seen that magnificent painting of the Apocalypse in the Tate Gallery, with the lightning bolt striking the cliff side and the giant rock falling). Martin did deluges and catastrophes on a large scale, and there are a lot of Turner landscapes and seascapes, with storms at sea and vast swirling distances. Boundlessness is part of it, but also just *size*, the sense of looking into huge distances and losing yourself in awe. It's like stargazing in a way, but stargazing that involves a bit of thought. If you have no imagination, a black sky with little dots in it that blink could be construed as a kind of light show, a dome with lights shining through the punctured tin. When you begin to speculate about what the sky really is, how far away the stars are and how big each of them is, when you start getting lost in those ideas, that's when Sense of Wonder starts happening.

I guess the archetypal science fiction books are the ones that appeal directly to that feeling, and help you form a vision of the vastness of space. There is Stapledon, and another that immediately comes to mind (that compares directly to a John Martin picture) is Clarke's *Rendezvous with Rama*, where you have an artifact that is mysterious, explored at great length, totally awesome in its dimensions, and which disappears without having been explained—it is just contemplated. *Ringworld* is another obvious example of the satisfaction that contemplating a very large-scale phenomenon can give. On a smaller scale, I did a story about an elevator that just goes down forever, nonstop.

You can take it back all the way to the beginning of the gothic novel— not science fiction but one of our kissing-cousins. *The Castle of Otranto* is an absolutely silly book that I don't think anybody nowadays could read without giggling, but at *one* point it just knocks everybody out. The only thing that happens in it that's interesting or yields Sense of Wonder is that a giant helmet appears out of nowhere and lands in the middle of the city square, killing the intended bridegroom of the heroine. This happens on page 2. Nobody can explain it; it's a very large helmet. Later on other pieces of an entire suit of armor appear, similarly gigantic. There has to be something in the notion of *bigness* that is innately inspiring, that stirs the sense of awe and makes us all kneel down and pray.

All of this ties in with what Freud wrote about as "oceanic experience"—which is just religion without a theory, the feeling that you get on a starry night. But that's not all there is to the Sublime, because there is no system to that yet: one is just relating to the universe. Religions always look out at the universe and they discover gods. And gods invariably have a very human shape. It is in forming the idea of the human shape that gods should have that we get into the business of writing stories.

The scale of time is another aspect of Sublimity—the fact that you can look back in history the way you can look out in space; or you can look forward in history across vast dimensions, like Stapledon's huge projections through eras and eras of futurity. Wells was the first writer to begin a universal human history going back to the period of cavemen or even to the geological formation of the earth. It's the new sense of history we have, of the dimensions of time, that needs to be celebrated somehow, to be understood and grasped and thought about. So that's another aspect of Sublimity, historical Sublimity.

But there's still one more, and it's where the word really got into its stride. Before landscapes were considered Sublime (according to Reynolds) Michelangelo was credited with being the *great* Sublime painter. That also relates to what he was supposed to have that Raphael and other people didn't have: *terribilità*, which is a wonderful Italian word. "Terribility" does not work in English the same way that "terribilità" works in Italian. It means that you look at a Michelangelo and you relate to the image that you're seeing as you might relate to the Sense of Wonder you get out of the sky: a human image so powerful and so profoundly meaningful that you look at it and you sense something *beyond* the human in that human image, something God-like. And of course that's what Michelangelo was busy painting: pictures of gods. Now, to paint a picture of a god well isn't actually to tell fibs. You don't even have to be a Christian to understand that the human image can be boundlessly significant for human beings, that it can condense everything that is meaningful and wonderful and soul-shattering in an image—or a tale.

The human Sublime can be found in literature as well as in painting. The artists Reynolds compared Michelangelo with weren't other painters: they were Homer and Milton. Nowadays, novelists rarely write about gods as such; they seldom even write about heroes in the decorative sense of people wearing something appropriate for a fancy-dress ball. Aside from military heroes and cowboys, who each have their own uniform, heroes in modern novels tend to be ordinary folk.

There are also aspects of ritual observation connected with the evocation of extraordinary heroes in fancy-dress plots. Wagner's *Parsifal* has more than a little in common with a High Mass in Latin. Or there's the Society for Creative Anachronism, which organizes real jousts for those who crave rituals at a higher energy level. I have my own suggestion for a ritual observation that could be returned to and renovated for modern-day use: building pyramids. I feel that they've been neglected for a long time. I was once in a cathedral in Italy, and it looked so easy to do. It was a really early cathedral and not very well built. There wasn't much that distinguished it as a work of architecture, and I couldn't help thinking, "Hey, I could do *that!*" Then I thought maybe I couldn't but I could surely do *something*. It must have been nice to live then and have one of those things going up in the town—and to help out. However, if you don't have a religion you probably wouldn't want to build a cathedral, because then you'd be locked into a whole system that you didn't agree with. But if you built *pyramids*, you would have the satisfaction of building something without having to be a true believer. So I wrote an article proposing that they build pyramids in Minnesota, and it was published and very well received. I called for volunteers and got a whole lot of mail from people who wanted to build pyramids in Minnesota and were volunteering to be a sort of slave corps for the purpose. Unfortunately none of the people who wrote in were offering to fund it, and that's where it bogged down. I funked out really, because I should have got busy organizing a fund-raising drive. Then there would be pyramids in Minnesota today, and I wouldn't just be presenting a daydream.

I don't mean to suggest that the parallel I'm observing between science fiction and religion is always a good thing. There are aspects of religion that many people have had trouble with historically. For instance, there was the Inquisition, a time when if you had notions that could be considered heretical, it could be most unfortunate. Religion is often organized to make trouble for people who have the wrong ideas. This is true in science fiction as well. There are orthodox influences in the field that I have felt in my own experience, and others have felt as well. Like most heretics, I tend to think of Orthodoxy as being opposed to the free exercise of the imagination. The Orthodox themselves, of course, are defending The Truth.

I do think that when we're talking about art as against religion (if we're not considering religion a branch of art) the artistic imperative to make things new, to create an image that isn't just an echo of yesterday's success, is necessarily opposed to the *other* dictate, namely to do it again the same way. As a writer, what one often feels from editors, and sometimes from readers, is that one should do it again: it feels so good, do it like you did it the last time. This often is done; people do write what seems to me substantially the same book all over again. The process is called Orthodoxy, and the result can be a paperback novel or an icon.

Most orthodox paperback novels are based on a book called *The Hero with a Thousand Faces*, by Joseph Campbell. Campbell shows how all myths can be boiled down into one all-purpose myth for all seasons. Moses is the same story as Theseus, and that's the same as every other famous story. So, since there really is only one story to tell, writers need only tell that one story. And what is that story? It's the questing adventure! Scratch any one of them, such as *Lord Silverberg's Castle*, and under its coat of new paint is a chassis straight out of *The Hero of a Thousand Pages*. Silverberg, of course, doesn't have the only copy of Campbell's book. My own "The Brave Little Toaster" is a questing tale with the same ur-plot. There's nothing necessarily wrong with questing tales—indeed everybody probably will write one some time or other, maybe without knowing it, because it's a pretty basic pattern—but it is not the *only* pattern for telling a story. Try and tell that to a painter of orthodox icons, though, and you'll only get a blank look.

There's another aspect of always telling one story, and that's not a question of the plot but of the moral of the story. It has sometimes been suggested that I am a nihilist, and I feel that's tantamount to saying a heretic. Nihilists believe in nothing, and that means that there is therefore something to believe in, i.e., an orthodox position. What my nihilism seemed to boil down to among those who pointed it out was that I had written a book called *The Genocides* in which the earth is destroyed by alien invaders. I didn't mean to suggest in the book that the earth *should* be destroyed by alien invaders, or that it *will* in all likelihood be destroyed, or even that we *deserve* such a fate. I meant to write what you might call an epic tragedy, and while that may be a rather highfalutin' ambition for a slim book, the notion that one could write a tragedy was the error of my way, as I have been made to understand since. Not that I am recanting, mind you, but when the Grand Inquisitor had me down in the cellar he pointed out that problems don't exist in science fiction unless they're going to be solved, and that men can look toward a future of immortality and that it's quite possible that we will none of us ever die.

Though I remained unpersuaded, I don't object to the Grand Inquisitor, or others of his faith, publishing books expressing the orthodox, cheery view of mankind's destined immortality and the consequent irrelevance of tragic experience, but I think we heretics should be allowed to hand out our pamphlets and publish our novels too.

What all this boils down to is a plea for pluralism—and that seems to be a very English plea. Historically, England was the first country in which several religions learned to live side by side successfully. Indeed, they would even meet sometimes at ecumenical congresses, or, if not there, they would all live in the same village and sneer at each other's churches in a neighborly, peaceful, pluralistic spirit, the spirit of a good con.

So that seems to be my happy ending. Except—it occurred to me to wonder if I might on the basis of these ideas qualify as a religious thinker myself. And if so, whether I could solicit you to become members of my own congregation. The tax benefits to me would be simply amazing.

The Evidence of Things Not Seen

"Faith," declared Paul in his epistle to the Hebrews, "is the substance of things hoped for, the evidence of things not seen." "Faith," declares Alexander Cruden, at the head of a lengthy list of biblical citations under that heading in his concordance to the Old and New Testaments, "is a dependence on the veracity of another." It could be that faith is simply an agreement to be deceived, a proposition that neither Paul's definition, nor Cruden's, necessarily contradicts.

Since one man's faith may be another's folly, it is generally considered impolite to question openly even the dottiest supernatural beliefs of one's fellow citizens. Those who entertain peculiar or millennial beliefs can usually be counted on to assemble in some congenial fastness, where they will not be embarrassed by public scrutiny unless they misbehave, as in cases like Jim Jones's cult in Guyana or the Aum Shinrikyo sect in Japan. For the most part, no one pays fringe faiths much attention, and so the generations of gurus, ascended masters, Mahdis, and other self-proclaimed Messiahs sail into the ether of religious history, shrinking to the size of footnotes and then vanishing from sight altogether.

Thanks, however, to the industry and intelligence of Peter Washington, the editor of Everyman's Library, the snow jobs of yesteryear have been compacted into a single multi-biography, *Madame Blavatsky's Baboon*, with an irreproachable scholarly apparatus (forty-seven pages of notes and bibliography) and, more importantly, with an irresistible narrative brio. Has anyone before Washington undertaken the Augean labor of writing a coherent history of the intellectual antecedents of the New Age? Professional doubters, such as those who write for the *Skeptical Inquirer*, have their hands full controverting the absurdities of the passing moment—UFO claimants, Satanic child abusers, and spoonbending psychics. And those who are busy tilling New Age fields will not wish to call attention to their shabby ancestors, who were, with few exceptions, a disreputable lot in the conduct of their lives, while their immense tomes, full of bygone flummeries, do not decant well.

Review of *Madame Blavatsky's Baboon*, by Peter Washington.

That is what makes *Madame Blavatsky's Baboon* such a delight for readers who look to history for a higher form of gossip. The Merchant/Ivory film team could refine half a dozen good screenplays from the ore Washington provides—beginning with the raffish career of the title character, the author of *Isis Unveiled* (1875), co-founder of the Theosophical Society, and an archetypal con artist of the sort who can't resist glorying in her trickster capabilities.

Blavatsky regularly arranged for the Hidden Masters with whom she was in communication—Koot Hoomi, Serapis Bey, et al.—to "precipitate" sealed letters from the immaterial realm into the pockets of her acolytes. One such missive to a wavering recruit, Colonel Henry Olcott, instructed him that Blavatsky "had a special mission in the world, and must be cared for at all costs, even if caring for her meant sacrificing the colonel's other interests, such as his wife and children." Olcott dumped his wife and sons and became Blavatsky's lifelong patsy and her shill. After many wanderings they pitched their tents at Adyar, in India, and established the Theosophical Society. Blavatsky thrived as a spiritualist in Anglo-Indian circles, performing conventional psychic tricks, "making a brooch appear in a flowerbed, finding a teacup and summoning music out of thin air." Often detected in her impostures, Blavatsky loftily maintained that her seeming scamming was actually an integral part of the Hidden Masters' higher plan—which only she could apprehend. Even today she has her remnant of true believers: a review of Washington's book in the *New York Times Book Review* occasioned a reproachful letter from one such diehard. As Washington observes, "There are those who argue still that if Blavatsky is a figure of scandal, it is only because the slanders on her reputation are signs of grace: the stigmata that all great martyrs must bear." There is even a kind of heroism in such loyalty, as who might say, "Well, yes, he was crucified, but I had dinner with him yesterday."

For Blavatsky the highest wisdom, as set forth in her books, transcended both Christianity and its then blackest *bête noire*, Darwinism. (The baboon of the title was a cherished bibelot, a stuffed "bespectacled baboon, standing upright, dressed in wing-collar, morning-coat and tie, and carrying under its arm the manuscript of a lecture on *The Origin of Species*.") "It was necessary," Washington argues, "for someone to show the way forward by denouncing both the Darwinians, who stood for false ideals of progress, and the Christians, who believe in false myths of salvation. Blavatsky's supporters argue that attacking both parties with their huge vested interests was bound to provoke a bitter response: hence the personal attacks on their idol."

Washington spends more of his time on the page recounting scandals than interpreting them, but in that passage he begins to suggest not only Blavatsky's appeal but that of the whole New Age mindset. New Agers want the best of both worlds, Here and Hereafter. They want a pleasant afterlife, which requires some recourse to the miraculous, but they don't want it to be conditional upon their own good behavior. They applaud the libertinism of the Enlightenment but deplore its irreligion. The scandal of God, as Madame Blavatsky sensed (along with her countryman Dostoevsky), is that he can be capricious, dispensing grace to reprobates and withholding it from the righteous.

This was, then as now, a gender-specific issue. Blavatsky, simply by asserting herself as a prophet and high priestess of a new religion, was making a feminist statement, one with which those who followed in her footsteps concurred: Annie Besant, initially an early advocate of contraception; Katherine Tingley, an American actress in the mold of Shirley MacLaine, who formed her own apostate, California branch of Theosophy; and innumerable others, down to the legions of lady psychics, seers, tarot readers, and astrologers in our own time. Women, as any woman knows, have as good a claim on Godhead and/or priesthood as men, and if this age won't acknowledge the justice of their claim, then let's have another. Believe in the Goddess and viva Blavatsky!

But the women have not been entirely alone in their mystic fane. There was, in those days (the *fin de siécle*), a love that dared not speak its name, but was, even so, hot to trot. Enter the pedophile and psychopathic liar Charles Webster Leadbeater, whose biopic might more suitably be filmed by Ken Russell. Leadbeater's account of his own early life is, like Blavatsky's and Gurdjieff's official CVs, a parcel of succulent lies, but the life the lies were designed to camouflage was just as juicy. Pedophilia was to be, more than once, the spur to travel, both before and after Leadbeater's ascension to the rank of bishop in the Liberal Catholic Church, an apostate institution in which bishoprics were to be had for the asking. Liberal Catholics chiefly believed in candles, incense, and glitzy vestments, along with Atlantis, Mu, and all that is divinely decadent. It was an enduring tradition. In the early sixties I came upon a remnant of the creed, one Bishop Itkin, who was often noted, in the newspapers of the day, for his prominent episcopal presence at rallies of the peace movement. Like Leadbeater, Itkin found that if you called yourself a bishop and wore a pectoral cross you would be treated with the same deference as the genuine article, both by the media and by altar boys.

Leadbeater is the Mr. Micawber of *Madame Blavatsky's Baboon*, a deliciously predictable reprobate and opportunist. In the course of his career he scored at least as well as Father Bruce Ritter in our own era. He was disgraced repeatedly, but he would just expatriate himself and keep on scoring. Theosophy, by shrugging off a moral code, possessed a special attraction for homosexuals who wanted to love both God and man. Now that the more liberal Protestant churches have welcomed homosexuals into the ranks of the clergy, gays of a religious bent need not venture as far afield as Theosophy to enjoy the rites and consolations of the Christian faith. Only time will tell if Theosophy is strong enough to survive that loss.

Leadbeater's penchant for ephebes leads to the next, and most amazing biopic opportunity of this history—Krishnamurti. "One evening in the spring of 1909," Washington recounts, "Leadbeater noticed an extraordinary aura surrounding one of the Indian boys paddling in the shallows. The boy was dirty and unkempt . . . . The boy took his fancy, and within days Leadbeater had told his followers that this child was destined to be a great teacher. . . ."

The charm of Krishnamurti's story is much like that of the movie *Forrest Gump*, a fairy tale in which a simpleton, after only a little adversity, is blessed with all possible blessings because his heart is pure. Leadbeater intuited that young Krishna, known in the spirit realm as Alcyone, had lived thirty lives already, ranging in time from 22662 B.C. to A.D. 624, which Leadbeater began to chronicle in the pages of *The Theosophist*: "It turned out that in each of these thirty lives everyone else known to Leadbeater also figured, but with different identities and sometimes different sexes. Some had been famous historical characters. Others had lived on the moon and Venus." Alcyone's long saga became the means by which Leadbeater revenged himself on old enemies and theosophical rivals. Thus, in an earlier life, Mrs. Besant (in this life, too, a serial monogamist) "acquired twelve husbands for whom she roasted rats." Another Leadbeater scoop: Julius Caesar's marriage to Jesus Christ. The bishop could out-tabloid even the *Weekly World News*, and in this he prefigured the can-you-top-this spirituality of our own era, in which sheer imagination is confused with causality. Such fads as creative visualization, UFO abductions, and incest survivalism all conflate dreams and matters-of-fact, and they are licensed to do so by the intellectual deference long accorded to crackpot religions.

Leadbeater's tales of his divine Alcyone soon put the teenage Krishnamurti on the theosophical map. Mrs. Besant adopted "Krishna" and his sibling, Nitya, transported them to London, and put them on a new dietary regimen of porridge, eggs, and milk. Leadbeater, a fanatic about good hygiene, personally attended their daily ablutions. The boys' father sued for repossession of his offspring, charging Leadbeater with "deification and sodomy." That is only the beginning of Krishnamurti's golden legend. By the sound of it, he was a rather nice fellow, his God-head notwithstanding—a bit like Bertie Wooster in his happy blindness to his own astonishing privilege.

Three further gurus round out Washington's dramatis personae: George Ivanovich Gurdjieff (1873?–1949), Peter Ouspensky (1878–1947), and Rudolf Steiner (1861–1925). Gurdjieff was the most audacious of the lot, the self-appointed Svengali to several generations of mystical Trilbys. He bootstrapped himself from an impoverished childhood in Armenia to become, by 1912, the spiritual drillmaster of his own small sect in Moscow. He kept his followers busy with a regimen of chanting and breathing exercises, modern dance, and character-building drudgery, a program of summer-camp monasticism much emulated by later gurus: submission = inner peace.

At the height of his notoriety, in 1922, Gurdjieff had established his own school-cum-commune at the Chateau du Prieuré, forty miles outside Paris. Many noted intellectuals of the era made pilgrimages to the Prieuré—A. R. Orage, a prominent magazine editor who was chiefly responsible for Gurdjieff's celebrity; D. H. Lawrence, who wasn't about to be someone else's Trilby and didn't stay long; and most famously, Katherine Mansfield, who died there after a brief sojourn, her faith in Gurdjieff not being sufficient to cure her tuberculosis. Because of its unities of time, space, and action, Mansfield's few weeks of discipleship would be the best bet for a *Masterpiece Theatre* offering. Mansfield's *Liebestod* would supply the plot, and here is the *mise en scène:*

> Society ladies who had never done a day's work would be set to peel[ing] potatoes or weed[ing] a flower border with teaspoons while learning a few Tibetan words or memorizing Morse code. Others were given complicated exercises in mental arithmetic while performing certain movements. A Harley Street doctor was deputed to light the boiler, writers cooked and chopped, and eminent psychiatrists shoveled manure or scrubbed the kitchen floor. The place had the atmosphere of a savage boarding school run by a demented if genial head-master and most of the pupils loved it—for a while.

Peter Ouspensky was as drab a personage as Gurdjieff was colorful. Ouspensky's lifelong search for the miraculous began in the mists of pseudoscience, where he inferred from the mathematical postulate of time as "the fourth dimension" (the title of his first publication) the necessity of a Nietzschean eternal recurrence. This brainstorm shaded by degrees into an acceptance of reincarnation, occultism, and all the rest of the theosophical agenda. A visit to the Theosophical Society's headquarters at Adyar only left him longing for a social environment large enough to swallow him whole. His wish—perhaps the essential impulse of a religious vocation—echoes Donne: ". . . bend / Your force to break, blow, burn, and make me new. . . . Take me to You, imprison me, for I / Except you enthrall me, never shall be free / Nor ever chaste, except You ravish me."

Ouspensky's prayers were answered when, just before World War I, he was taken before Gurdjieff and their long game of Captain-may-I began. Imprisoned, enthralled, and ravished, Ouspensky became Gurdjieff's John the Baptist and general dogsbody. His daily witnessing of his master's scams and caprices only snugged the bonds of love tighter, as in The Blue Angel. Just as their platonically sadomasochistic romance reached a rolling boil, the Russian Revolution kicked in, and Gurdjieff's little band of disciples, along with a small tribe of gypsy relatives, became refugees, seeking escape into Turkey. They caromed about the steppes of central Asia between the contending Red and White armies, giving modern dance recitals, living on mushrooms and berries, and gathering about the campfire at night to drink in the master's wisdom. It would require the budget of another Dr. Zhivago, but the dance sequences on the battlefield could be stunning. Le Sacre du printemps? George C. Scott is Gurdjieff. Gene Hackman would pass muster as Ouspensky, though, really, it's a role anyone could handle. That was Ouspensky's problem.

Rudolf Steiner—a guru only insofar as that was one of the duties he imposed on himself as a universal genius and world redeemer—was the son of Austrian peasants and had a childhood that would have been the envy even of Wordsworth. Nature spoke to him incessantly. As he matured, Steiner tried to translate these intimations into a theory that would controvert positivistic science, and so, with some scraps of Goethe's errant optical and biological theories and with deep draughts of Kant, he began to construct his Summa. Then Madame Blavatsky's Secret Doctrine blew his Summa out of the water. He converted to Theosophy in 1902 and became the Society's leader in German-speaking lands.

Of all Washington's leading actors, Steiner was the dullest, the most conventionally respectable, and the most successful. He lived to see two cathedralish Goetheanums built according to his own Art Nouveau–like specifications (the first one, of wood, burned down), and the system of Steiner schools is still around to offer progressive education with a theosophical flavor. Should the government ever establish a National Endowment for Occult Science, it would have to find someone like Rudolf Steiner to be its chairman.

As the chronicle approaches our own time, the roster of theosophical dabblers and day-trippers multiplies. There are index entries for Aldous Huxley, Christopher Isherwood, Bob Dylan, and recent leaders of the Liberal Party in England. The last of Washington's gurus, Idries Shah, seems to have been sent down from on high specifically to prove the theory of eternal recurrence. Like Blavatsky, Shah was in touch with "an invisible hierarchy which had chosen him to transmit their wisdom to suitable individuals. He was now looking for European pupils and helpers, and for introductions to the rich and powerful whose help he needed to transform the world. To this end he had founded SUFI: the Society for Understanding Fundamental Ideas."

Shah managed to connect with one of Gurdjieff and Ouspensky's most devoted disciples, Captain J. G. Bennett. Now an old man and a spiritual orphan, Bennett was persuaded in the 1960s to turn over a valuable English estate at Coombe Springs, which had served for many years as a Gurdjieff-style Prieuré. When the other trustees of the estate balked, Shah was adamant: there must be an outright gift or nothing at all. Bennett tried to negotiate, but the more conciliatory his behavior, the more outrageous Shah's demands became. The new teacher wanted to know how Bennett could have the nerve to negotiate with the Absolute. Once the Absolute had got his way, "Shah's first act was to eject Bennett and the old pupils from their own house, banning them from the place except by his specific permission. His second act was to sell the property to developers for £100,000 in the following year, buying a manor house at Langton Green near Tunbridge Wells in Kent with the proceeds."

Why do they do it? Why do fools fall in love—and believers believe, even as they're being fleeced? I think it is Pascal's wager applied to the realm of personal finance. Just as gamblers gamble from a secret desire to know the thrill of utter ruin, so believers need to immolate themselves upon the altars of the Absolute in order to prove themselves worthy of the sacrificial fires. The experience may not last long, but the thrill must be exquisite. For those who prefer to experience that thrill vicariously, *Madame Blavatsky's Baboon* gets you close enough to smell the singed hair.

The Road to Heaven: Science Fiction and the Militarization of Space

Readers of the Sunday *New York Times* on March 30, 1986, may have come upon a full-page "Letter to the American People" in the "News in Review" section of the paper, in which it is urged that the most fitting memorial for the seven astronauts killed in the explosion of the *Challenger* would be:

> The restoration and enhancement of the shuttle fleet and resumption of a full launch schedule.
>
> For the seven.
>
> In keeping with their spirit of dedication to space exploration and with the deepest respect for their memory, we, the undersigned, are asking you to join us in urging the president and the Congress to build a new shuttle orbiter to carry on the work of these seven courageous men and women.

> AS LONG AS THEIR DREAM LIVES ON,
>
> THE SEVEN LIVE ON IN THE DREAM

Following this appeal are four columns in fourteen-point type of the names of the ad's eighty-eight "underwriters," plus a ten-point type rabble of nearly two hundred "other contributors." Most readers will recognize the first name on the list of underwriters, that of Isaac Asimov, and there is a sprinkling of other "name" science fiction and fantasy writers, but the extent to which the list of underwriters is comprised of science fiction professionals—writers, editors, agents, and fans—would only be evident to someone familiar with the field. By my own census, fifty-four of the eighty-eight underwriters have some connection with sf, as do a much smaller proportion of those in small print. Undoubtedly many of the names I don't recognize are present through the same connection.

For many science fiction writers and fans the perpetuation of a manned space program stands as the central tenet of their faith in mankind's destiny as explorer and colonizer of outer space—the solar system today, tomorrow the stars. This faith was promulgated long before NASA. Its adherents vary in their sophistication, from Trekkies dressed in the pajamas of their gods to engineers and physicists in the employ of NASA and related agencies, but it is for all concerned a literal and often fervent faith, and NASA has become the church at which its worship is conducted.

Sf writers have a legitimate claim to be considered not only the prophets of that faith but the builders of the church. If poets are the world's unacknowledged legislators, sf writers have been its unacknowledged civil and mechanical engineers, doodling their designs for rocket-ships and spacesuits on that most plastic medium, the adolescent mind. The influence of such sf writers of the thirties and forties as Robert Heinlein, Asimov, and Jack Williamson (all three still alive, productive, and signers of the *Times* letter) on the teenage readers who would grow up to staff the space agencies has been widely attested to. The symposiasts at the recent PEN Congress who took as their theme "The Imagination of the State," only to lament that Imagination was what the State specifically lacked, evidently had read little science fiction or failed to consider its relation to the space program. Such an oversight is not to be wondered at, for most literary intellectuals regard sf as Dr. Pritikin would a Twinkie, while a majority of political liberals have similarly disregarded the space program, considering it a relatively harmless boondoggle, useful, if at all, as a sop to the Cerberus of the defense industry. Better a man on the moon than another missile silo in Kansas.

The enthusiasm expressed by President Reagan for the Strategic Defense Initiative, or "Star Wars" program, and his ability to translate that enthusiasm into budgetary reality has made both dismissions—of sf and of the space program—intellectually indefensible. Whatever its merits or demerits as literature, sf's role as a debating society, moral-support system, and cheerleading section for the present and future personnel of space-related industries and military services makes it worth examining simply for what it can show us about the high-tech experts whose expertise will shape the foreseeable future.

The most remarkable of sf's ancestral voices in this regard, and one that is still with us, is that of Robert Heinlein. Heinlein's stories of the near-future conquest of space, which first began to appear in the late thirties, were written in a manner more naturalistic and verisimilar than the naive space operas common at that time. For Heinlein, outer space was not a realm of faery but simply the next frontier, and he was its recruiting sergeant. In 1952 he wrote, "What one man can imagine, another man can do. Youths who build hot-rods are not dismayed by spaceships; in their adult years they will build such ships. In the meantime they will read stories of interplanetary travel."

Heinlein was not alone in this ambition, nor was he even the chief prophet laureate of the conquest of space. Those laurels must go to Arthur Clarke. However, claims of priority, preeminence, or uniqueness obscure one of the genre's salient strengths, that much sf inhabits a consensual future that is open (since ideas can't be copyrighted) to all comers. Michel Butor in an essay on sf written in 1960 deplored the heterogeneous nature of the genre's too individualistic writers. He called for the genre to become "a collective work, like the science which is its indispensable basis":

> Now, let us imagine that a certain number of authors were to take as the setting of their stories a single city, named and situated with some precision in space and in future time; that each author were to take into account the description given by the others in order to introduce his own new ideas. This city would become a common possession to the same degree as an ancient city that has vanished; gradually, all readers would give its name to the city of their dreams and would model that city in its image.
>
> Sf, if it could limit and unify itself, would be capable of acquiring over the individual imaginations a constraining power comparable to that of any classical mythology. Soon all authors would be obliged to take this predicted city into account, readers would organize their actions in relation to its imminent existence, ultimately they would find themselves obliged to build it.

Dismaying as Butor's agenda may sound in its zeal for imaginative conformity, the consensual future that evolved in the natural process of sf writers reading over, and standing on, each other's shoulders very nearly fills Butor's prescription—and has had much the effect that he predicted for it: the city is being built.

Since Hiroshima there has been another element of sf's consensual future that cannot be contemplated with the same hypothetical good cheer and bravado with which mankind's future in space is envisioned. The possibility of nuclear war and its potential for annihilation on a planetary scale have become the defining nightmare of the twentieth century, a consensual future no one admits to consenting to but which no one can resist imagining, and recoiling from. On the whole, sf writers have been as reluctant to think about the unthinkable as anyone else, and their reasons may be rooted in the nature of fiction, which must concern the lives and actions of people, and in the nature of atomic holocaust, which brings all lives and actions to an end. Only a few novelists, and those not within the genre, have described the worst-case (but not so unlikely) scenario of universal annihilation. The common practice has been to depict a post-holocaust world as a kind of damaged Eden, where a few survivors scavenge a subsistence living from the wreck of civilization. Literally hundreds of novels have been written on this theme, a virtual massed choir of whistling in the dark.

One of the most remarkable of these post-holocaust fantasies is by Heinlein, *Farnham's Freehold* (1964), a book that was to become Holy Writ to the survivalist movement. It was Heinlein's peculiar inspiration to find a silver lining in the prospect of nuclear holocaust. Here his hero (who, with his family, mistress, and Negro servant, has survived a Russian sneak attack by virtue of his prudence in having provided a suburban home with a fall-out shelter) states the case for nuclear Armageddon:

> ". . . Barbara, I'm not as sad over what has happened as you are. It might be good for us. I don't mean us six; I mean our country."
>
> She looked startled. "How?"
>
> "Well—it's hard to take the long view when you are crouching in a shelter and wondering how long you can hold out. But—Barbara, I've worried for years about our country. It seems to me that we have been breeding slaves—and I believe in freedom. This war may have turned the tide. This may be the first war in history which kills the stupid rather than the bright and able—where it makes any distinction.
>
> "Wars have always been hardest on the best young men. This time the boys in the service are as safe or safer than civilians. And of civilians those who used their heads and made preparations stand a far better chance . . . that will improve the breed. When it's over, things will be tough, and that will improve the breed still more. For years the surest way of surviving has been to be utterly worthless and breed a lot of worthless kids. All that will change."
>
> She nodded thoughtfully. "That's standard genetics, but it seems cruel."
>
> "It is cruel. But no government has yet been able to repeal natural laws, though they keep trying."
>
> She shivered in spite of the heat. "I suppose you re right. No, I know you're right."

The events that follow in *Farnham's Freehold* don't bear out this blithe new application of Social Darwinism (Black Africa, it turns out, has inherited the earth, and enslaved the surviving whites, whose children supply the choicest delicacies at their cannibal feasts—no kidding), but Farnham's words are not intended ironically. When Heinlein's heroes speak out (the superiority of the warrior caste and the social and biological benefits to be derived from war are among their other recurrent themes), they speak out unequivocally on behalf of their creator.

In recent years, though Heinlein has continued to write in spate, his novels have taken sex as their theme, and while he continues to be able to amaze and appall the liberal imagination like almost no other sf writer, one must turn to the work of those who have inherited his mantle as a concerned and active right-wing ideologue to see the specific and very direct relationship between contemporary sf and the Strategic Defense Initiative. Specifically, the work of Jerry Pournelle.

Pournelle came to science fiction from the space program, having worked for both government agencies and the space division of Rockwell International. Early in the seventies, he began to publish stories in *Analog*, an sf magazine whose editor, John W. Campbell, had discovered and nurtured Heinlein some thirty years before. Pournelle is not a writer notable for inventiveness, thematic range, or dramatic skill. His artlessness may derive in part from a principled aversion to literature, a word with bad associations among those sf writers who identify themselves as "hard-core" (i.e., technophilic and, usually, ultra-right). "Truthfully," he declared, in a 1979 interview, "I don't pay much attention to style. In fact, some people might say they can believe that after reading one of my books, I'm not particularly interested in creating 'literature,' per se. . . . I enjoy writing science fiction. It's easy to write and I'm familiar with the material. It also lets you get across your view of the world, which is something I like doing. In addition, there is the phenomenon of fandom, which is extremely gratifying."

Pournelle's view of the world has been succinctly expressed by the title of a series of anthologies he edits for Tor Books (the fifth volume will appear in September): There Will Be War. This series offers its readers nonfiction polemics on that perennial theme of the military-industrial establishment, the need for arms, more arms. Only a strong defensive posture (i.e., SDI) can prevent nuclear Armageddon; a further benefit of SDI is that it will make possible the kind of limited wars that furnish the scenery for the fiction, hairy-chested sf adventures of space-age Rambos. Virtually all of Pournelle's own (non-collaborative) fiction falls into this category, and his enthusiasm for the right defense posture has even led him to creative efforts in the field of military fashion. I remember attending an sf convention in Seattle at which Pournelle, a man of Falstaffian proportions, was boasting that the paramilitary uniform he was wearing (he and his particular fans, of which there were some two dozen in attendance, all armed to the teeth with an arsenal of toy weapons) had been tailored to his own exacting specifications. None of your off-the-rack camo for the author of *The Mercenary*!

The plot of that book, his first success in the sf field, and those of his later novels are as calculated to offend and outrage liberal sensibilities as a biker's tattoos. In *The Mercenary* (1977) the denouement features the wholesale slaughter of a planet's criminal or unemployed elements (easily decoded as the "permanent underclass" of today's inner cities), who have been assembled by the wily heroine to a vast sports arena for this purpose. When he is not gunning for welfare mothers, Pournelle's favorite villains include traditional Reds and Pinkos (even on the planet Tran in the far future, in the novel *Janissaries* [1979], the threat to liberty comes from "Cuban advisors and Nationalist Front native Marxists"). But his *bêtes noires* are Greens, or "ecosymps," as he prefers to style those who oppose the advance of Science, Technology, Nuclear Power, NASA, and the corporate interests of Rockwell International.

In *Oath of Fealty* (1981), his most readable novel (because it was written in collaboration with Larry Niven, a better storyteller and a cannier ideologue), ecosymps provide the plot with that paranoid requisite, an external enemy whose unremitting and unreasoning malice is the mortar binding together an otherwise doubtfully viable utopian city of the near future. *Oath* represents the fictional apotheosis of Festung Los Angeles, and its story revolves around the moral right of the affluent to create a polity that excludes the poor; this time round, however, the denouement does not decree death to all the losers but has them instead tattooed with the book's recurring slogan: "THINK OF IT AS EVOLUTION IN ACTION."

Most liberal readers would feel as little incentive to read Pournelle's work as to study the writings of Lyndon LaRouche. So long as their tribes do not increase at an alarming rate, why worry? Boys with toy guns at sf conventions pose no substantial threat to democracy or global survival. Not, that is, until they grow up to become the scientific advisors of the president and the defense industry. And that is what has been happening.

In 1984 Pournelle published (with a new collaborator, Dean Ing) a nonfiction book, *Mutual Assured Survival*, that marshalls the arguments that can be made in support of the Star Wars program and presents them in language that can be grasped by the scientific layman. These arguments are not original to Pournelle, but the fervor and pugnacity that he brings to bear have won for the book commendation from no less a blurb-writer than President Reagan, whose letter to Pournelle is presented in full on the back jacket of the book. Reagan writes:

You and your associates of the Citizens Advisory Panel on National Space Policy [a group of experts that includes among its members Pournelle's collaborators, Ing and Niven, his mentor Heinlein, his son Alexander, Alexander's girlfriend Jennifer, and James Baen, Pournelle's editor at Simon & Schuster, the publisher of the book], deserve high praise for addressing with verve and vision the challenges to peace and to our national security. Efforts like this can assist us in achieving a safer and more stable future for this country, for our allies, and, indeed, for all mankind. Thank you, and God bless you.

With this presidential blessing and his chairmanship of the policy-making Citizens Advisory Council, Pournelle must be considered as more than another polemicist or popularizer writing about SDI. He has become a semi-official spokesman for that initiative. No one would challenge his right to the fictional promulgation of his views, but having entered the arena of a national debate, a debate that will ultimately be resolved by the "experts" on each side, the worldview he evidences in his other writings is not beside the point. Reagan is choosing his team; it would be well to know where that team is coming from.

This is not to suggest that sf as a whole, or even most of the under-writers of the Times letter, has become a lobby for NASA and the defense industry. Many sf writers, notably Frederik Pohl, have been outspoken opponents of SDI.

But the Times letter does reflect the strong emotions of that part of the educated public that sees in the space program a compelling national purpose. The desire to get Man into Space may become so overriding an imperative for those who share the "dream of the seven" that they may be willing to advocate SDI solely on the basis of that desire, calculating—probably correctly—that only by ceding the space program to the military will it receive the funding required for such a mammoth effort. Such a calculation would be, perhaps fatally, a mistake.

As to the immediate issue of the rescheduling of the shuttle program, that decision surely must be based on a rational estimation of the program's safety, the soundness of its management, and a cool assessment of the value of the shuttle program as against less costly, unmanned alternatives. None of these questions are addressed in the Times letter, which implicitly endorses NASA's position that things are basically still A-OK.

"The production facility still exists," the letter states. "The assembly process can be reactivated. The experiments designed for the orbiter bay are waiting. We can recover a program which is one of our nation's greatest resources and mankind's proudest achievements." The *Challenger* disaster was undoubtedly a national tragedy, but the "Challenger Campaign" is an ill-judged response that reflects little credit on the science fiction community.

Speaker Moonbeam: Newt's Futurist Brain Trust

At some point in his presidency Richard Nixon posed for a photograph in which he can be seen holding a copy of the Modern Library edition of *The Sound and the Fury*. The moment I saw it, I thought: "Nixon? Faulkner? Not very likely."

But Newt Gingrich might just get away with striking such a pose. Here is a politician who actually does read books; who has said "ideas matter"; who even draws up lists of required reading for his fellow legislators. OK, *The Federalist Papers* is on the list, which is a bit like including the Holy Bible. More significant is the presence on Gingrich's list of two popular futurologists, Alvin Toffler and John Naisbitt, writers who had not till now been identified with a particular political agenda.

More significant still—though not included on the reading list or much noted—has been Gingrich's connection with another, less celebrated school of futurology, the writers of sci-fi and high-tech, gung-ho military romance, who have been and continue to be his collaborators on both nonfiction and fiction projects. Of them, anon.

Gingrich's most noticed and commendable co-optation has been his enlistment of Toffler, the author of *Future Shock* and now a spokesman for the Progress and Freedom Foundation, a Gingrich franchise. *Future Shock* was published in 1970 and established Toffler's bona fides as a "futurist." In that book and its successors, *The Third Wave* (1980) and *Power Shift* (1990), Toffler managed to look beyond the polarizing us-or-them antinomies of the cold war imagination to descry, with remarkable foresight, the postmodern future we postmoderns now inhabit. He observed the ways that advances in cybernetics and media technology had already transformed daily life and power politics and extrapolated from there. His books are informed, judicious, and thought-provoking.

Toffler's major competitor in the futurology business has been John Naisbitt, author of *Megatrends* (1982). His work differs from Toffler's more in style than content. Toffler is discursive and sequential; the print in his books is smaller, the footnotes more abundant, and he assumes a goodly attention span. Naisbitt writes in info-bites for a later, more impatient breed of reader. His pages have the disjunctive inputs of *USA*

Today, with paragraphs regularly interspersed with explanatory headlines and bulleted lines, as though to say, "Skim me, I'm an easy read."

Both Toffler and Naisbitt have worthwhile points to make. The world is changing in ever-exfoliating ways, thanks to computers and satellite technology and the simple yens, of people and of corporations, to do whatever they want. These changes cannot be withstood or gainsaid, if only because they are, so often, *faits accompli*. In their way, Toffler and Naisbitt represent the chilly common sense of cyberspace: the future will be the exclusive domain of computer-literate managers of multinational corporations; the rest of us will be consigned to the Rust Belt.

As so often with common sense, appetite dictates what is perceived. Toffler, and Naisbitt even more, accentuate the welling-up of nutrients in the churning waters of history, heedless of (or indifferent to) whole flotillas liable to sink. Thus in *Global Paradox* (1994) Naisbitt, who believes that "travel is and will continue to be the world's largest industry," only once makes significant reference to AIDS, noting how it has reduced tourism in Kenya and Gambia. Warfare rates almost as little attention: "Escalation of armed conflict in certain regions around the globe can have a negative impact on worldwide tourism. The Gulf War demonstrated just how much of an impact armed conflict can have." Naisbitt is a resident of the ski resort and mountain fastness of Telluride, Colorado, and boasts that he can interface with current events without ever stirring from his monitor. Those who access information electronically have a privileged perspective but not necessarily a clearer one. Gingrich's attitude of "Let them eat laptops" and Marie Antoinette's "Let them eat cake" are both memorable for their delicate positioning between naivete and irony. From the perspective of the trailer park and the inner city, a free ticket to cyberspace has all the allure of a half-off coupon for a Berlitz course in Japanese conversation.

Toffler's take on the problem of evil isn't so blithely New Age as Naisbitt's. His role model is Machiavelli and not Marie Antoinette, but even so he has a penchant for finding ponies at the bottom of every dungheap. Thus the "personal political views" of a media baron like Rupert Murdoch are inconsequential because such giants are necessarily committed to an "ideology of globalism . . . or at least supranationalism which must operate across national boundaries, and it is in the self-interest of the new media moguls to spread this ideology." Such a McLuhanite focus on the medium as against the message accommodates the needs of power.

It is not surprising, then, that Toffler and Naisbitt should now be advanced by Gingrich to the rank of official government-accredited gurus. Their works had already been garlanded with blurbs from the international press and U.S. senators and CEOs. Recruiting them was a respectable sort of recent acquisition, on the order of a Monet or a Cézanne. What is much more revealing is Gingrich's alliance with another kind of futurist in the persons of Jerry Pournelle, Janet Morris, David Drake, and William Forstchen. In the work of these four once-and-future Gingrich collaborators one confronts the unnerving and sinister shadows implicit in Toffler and Naisbitt's sunshiny scenarios.

Do their names ring bells? Probably not, unless you are a science fiction fan. All four follow in the bootprints of Robert A. Heinlein, both as partisans of sending Man (and Woman) into Space as the priority for a viable future (Heinlein's first book, in 1950, was *The Man Who Sold the Moon*) and as scenarists of high-tech warfare. In *Starship Troopers* (1959), his seminal work, Heinlein uses the gosh-wow conventions of pulp-era space opera to advance a political agenda that celebrates America's future as the Rome of the space age. With the skill of Leni Riefenstahl, the author glamorizes the trappings of military power—the uniforms and macho rituals—while lecturing the reader, as if he were a raw recruit, on the need to obey one's officers and to exterminate the enemy (the Bugs, in this novel) utterly. After Heinlein, Buck Rogers and other guys with blasters would never look the same. Space opera = NASA = a blank check for high-tech research.

Pournelle, Heinlein's heir apparent, was an early advocate of Star Wars technology. His inspirational tract of 1984, *Mutual Assured Survival: A Space-Age Solution to Nuclear Annihilation*, earned him a pat on the back, and a blurb, from no less than Ronald Reagan. That book did not elevate him to the dignity of being an official policy guru, but it was published in the same year, by the same entrepreneur, Jim Baen—long the principal patron of these and other Heinleinite sf writers—as a much less noticed book, *Window of Opportunity: A Blueprint for the Future*, which identifies its authors as "the Honorable Newt Gingrich, with David Drake and Marianne Gingrich." The preface is written by Pournelle, who salutes Gingrich's (and Drake and Gingrich's) work as "a remarkable book, almost unique in that, without the slightest compromise with the principles that made this nation great, Gingrich presents a detailed blueprint, a practical program that not only proves that we can all get rich, but shows how."

Gingrich, on his acknowledgments page, thanks Pournelle for introducing him to his publisher. Baen, in turn, is complimented for "matching" the Gingriches with "our co-author, David Drake, and Janet Morris. Money alone could not buy the creativity, skill, and effort that Janet contributed to the final draft. David's contribution, of course, cannot be overstated."

Needless to say, politician-authors usually do little more than talk into a tape recorder and let their ghosts take it from there. But they are expected to stand by what they've signed their names to. And what Newt Gingrich signed his name to back in 1984 is a document worth pondering. For it shows much more vividly than transcripts of his recent speeches, which are necessarily more circumspect, more "politic," his sense of his constituency—who they are and what they can be sold.

Right-wing politicians traditionally offer a mix of two flavors: ressentiment and hope. And while the Republican resurgence of 1994 employed vitriolic attacks on the entire liberal spectrum, hope is Gingrich's special note, as it was Ronald ("Morning in America") Reagan's. The difference is that Reagan's optimism looked back to the idyllic past of the mythical frontier in which he'd acted as a Hollywood cowboy, while Gingrich places his hope in a sci-fi future. Gingrich sounds that motif at full diapason in the introduction to *Window of Opportunity*: "Breakthroughs in computers, biology, and space make possible new jobs, new opportunities, and new hope on a scale unimagined since Christopher Columbus discovered a new world. . . . There is hope for a continuing revolution in biology which will allow us to feed the entire planet; hope for jobs, opportunities, and adventures in space."

Adventures in space turn out to be a major component of what we are to hope for. One can't help but sense the influence of Gingrich's sci-fi collaborators, especially at such moments as this: "Congressman Bob Walker of Pennsylvania [now Chairman of the House Committee on Science, Space, and Technology] has been exploring the possible benefits of weightlessness to people currently restricted to wheelchairs. In speeches to handicapped Americans, he makes the point that in a zero-gravity environment, a paraplegic can float as easily as anyone else. Walker reports that wheelchair-bound adults begin asking questions in an enthusiastic tone when exposed to the possibility of floating free, released from their wheelchairs. Several have volunteered to be the first pioneers."

This "Arise and float!" is evangelism with a canny subtext, not unfamiliar to sci-fi professionals. Space is envisioned as that New Frontier where the indignities of ordinary life—onerous no-future jobs and low status—are to be remedied, as they were by an earlier expansion into the American West. Space is Texas, only larger. In the twenty-first century, Gingrich (or his ghosts) declares, a third-generation space shuttle "will be the DC-3 of space. From that point on, people will flow out to the Hiltons and Marriotts of the solar system, and mankind will have permanently broken free of the planet." In short, vote for me and someday your children will inhabit the *Star Trek* of their video dreams.

As hopes go, that might seem to be on a par with the Rapture awaited by fundamentalist Christians, and indeed, the demographics are not mutually exclusive. The same audience/electorate that polls tell us expects the Third Coming sometime soon might well settle for a visit to the Venus Hilton as a good second-best. It's only a fantasy, after all.

But people buy fantasy, as Gingrich's ghosts well know. And the fantasies they can be sold are by no means limited to space as the last frontier. All four of the Gingrich ghosts have specialized in military fantasies that skillfully meld high-tech weaponry with the kind of gung-ho glamour one associates with recruiting posters. Indeed, the cover of *Star Voyager Academy*, by William Forstchen (the contracted collaborator on Gingrich's much-tsked-over forthcoming novel, set in 1945 and featuring a "pouting sex kitten"), takes the literal form of a recruiting poster, including the pointed finger and "We Want YOU!" As its title suggests, Forstchen's novel is a lineal descendant of Heinlein's *Starship Troopers*, a young-adult-level paean to the joys of military life. The enemy now is not hive-dwelling "aliens" (Heinlein's shorthand for the Communist menace) but the United Nations of Earth (shorthand for government bureaucracies other than NASA). In this, Forstchen reflects the dilemma faced by the right wing as it searches the landscape for an internal enemy to replace the Communist menace.

David Drake, a co-author of *Window of Opportunity*, had his first notable success with the Hammer's Slammers series, begun in 1979, which is a hybrid of TV's *Star Trek* and *Soldier of Fortune* magazine.

Janet Morris, likewise, has specialized in future war scenarios from the perspective of a female guerrilla. If women are not suited to foxholes, as Gingrich recently suggested, they may still wreak havoc from behind a computer monitor. With her husband, Chris, sometime co-author and once-upon-a-time partner in a jazz-fusion band, Morris also works as a consultant in weapons development, specializing in "weapons of mass protection"—like the sticky foam that can be sprayed on demonstrators in lieu of bullets.

The bibliographies of Forstchen, Drake, and Morris are as impressive as that of Balzac, but Pournelle, their senior by a generation, has outdone them all in his ability to cater to their target audience. He is, quite simply, the best writer of the lot, and if not the most prolific (only a computer could crunch those numbers), surely the most successful.

Characteristically, Pournelle's best books are collaborations. Drake,

Forstchen, and Morris have collaborated not only with Gingrich but with one another, and others still, in a manner as complex as a cable-knit sweater. They have not as yet had the good fortune to collaborate with Pournelle's regular partner, Larry Niven, with whom Pournelle has produced some classic sci-fi titles, including *Inferno* (1976), a modern recension of Dante's book of the same name; the best-selling *Lucifer's Hammer* (1977), a futuristic disaster novel; and *Oath of Fealty* (1981), the tale of a right-wing utopia that seer Gingrich himself would be proud to set his name to.

Oath of Fealty is unique in the annals of utopian literature in offering a plausible depiction of the Orwellian nightmare from the point of view of Big Brother. In its blueprint of a privileged Fortress America—called Todos Santos, a self-sufficient "arcology" plunked down in the middle of a feral Los Angeles, where the wealthy can live protected from the promiscuous mob of undesirable anarchists, terrorists, and other paupers—*Oath of Fealty* echoes Jack London's *The Iron Heel* of 1907 and foreshadows the "custodial state" commended in *The Bell Curve*.

The plot pits the arcology's security chief against ecoterrorists who will go to any lengths to monkey-wrench Todos Santos. As one terrorist explains in her confession to the TS police, "Todos Santos is beautiful, Tony, but it uses too many resources to support too few people. The more successful Todos Santos is, the worse it will be for everyone else. . . . Don't you understand that technology is not the answer, that using technology to fix problems created by technology only puts you in an endless chain?" Tony, the security chief, has a clearer view of what is at stake: "If Todos Santos goes broke then it can't run any longer, expenses, expenses, expenses, it's property rights against human rights, money against lives and I'm defending the money. I'm defending my city!"

Pournelle regularly uses the medium of his fiction to take revenge on his ideological enemies. That is, after all, a novelist's prerogative. In *Inferno*, he and Niven have a field day in devising suitable Dantean torments for such enemies of the corporate state as the woman responsible for banning cyclamates (an early alternative to saccharine); another woman who, for reasons like those of the "ecoterrorist" quoted above, prevented the building of power plants and oil wells; and a man whose sins were vegetarianism and jogging. Pournelle's enemies list, like Rush Limbaugh's, includes anyone who would keep the rich from getting richer as fast as they can. But he understands that more is required than a loser's vindictiveness. One must offer hope, and what can that be in a future in which, as even he is willing to admit in his darker fictions, Third

World immiseration must be imported to America by the rigors of corporate logic?

It must be Outer Space, the final utopia, where the Rapture is to be achieved by the wonders of modern technology. Whether the promise is a conscious or unconscious scam on Pournelle's part, or on Gingrich's, can be known only to their confessors. It is probably intended as a benign deception, as when a faith healer promises to cure afflictions of all kinds. He knows that for a certain percentage the placebo effect will kick in. As for the rest, well, it's their own fault if they still need crutches. They didn't believe hard enough.

Whatever happens to the cripple, the faith healer's coffers will be filled. In that regard it is interesting to learn that there is a new collaborative novel on Pournelle's hard disk, and this time his collaborator is none other than Newt Gingrich. This new collaboration is to be a Tom Clancy Yellow Peril adventure, an account of a future war between a perfidious Japan and a guileless USA.

When the book does appear, it is guaranteed a large-scale commercial success. *Window of Opportunity* flopped eleven years ago because Gingrich wasn't yet a media star and because it's basically no more than a very long-winded speech. But a sensational premise and the professional polish that Pournelle can supply could make the novel a bestseller such as even popes might envy. The recent film *Bob Roberts* hypothesized a *fin de siécle* demagogue who uses folk-rock music as his entrée to high office. But for an electorate with sufficient reading skills and attention spans, the novel is probably still, as it was for Disraeli, the art form best adapted for political propaganda, if only because it has built-in deniability. A politician will get in trouble by calling Barney Frank a fag; a novelist always has the excuse that it is his characters who say all those terrible things. A collaborative novel offers a further margin of deniability.

After the Yellow Peril has been dealt with and we've all seen the movie version, what then? In an era of franchised fiction there is really no limit except what the market will bear. There must be dozens of other authors as eager as Pournelle to join their craft with Gingrich's marketability.

But why stop there? Andy Warhol was a master franchiser. He solicited ideas for pictures from people with a knack for ideas and had them silk-screened by people with a knack for that. Gingrich could do the same. He could merchandise, under his own trademark, sandwich spreads, skateboards, mousepads, bullets, aftershave.

Marketers, this is your Window of Opportunity. Offer him millions and promise the Moon.

A Closer Look at CLOSE ENCOUNTERS

Admirers of science fiction have a paradoxical disposition to be literal-minded in their discussion of sf, to resist the possibility of interpretation, and so very often to miss the point even of those works they admire. Perhaps the paradox is built into the genre, for what does the sci of sci-fi promise us but that there is a logical, "scientific" legitimacy to fantasies that we might otherwise blush to entertain? So, in all the talk about Star Wars, I never once heard mention of what seemed the salient feature of the story-line—that it retold, on a larger scale but quite transparently, the sperm-as-spaceman skit from Woody Allen's Everything You Ever Wanted to Know about Sex But Were Afraid to Ask. The film is a virtual sex manual for nervous teenage boys who need to be reassured that if they will only relax a little, all will be well and the force will be with them. Perfectly sound advice, and glad tidings, evidently, to millions of viewers. But how did the critics view Star Wars? As a jolly old-fashioned conflict between Good and Evil of which nothing more need be noted. Enough to praise the special effects and to vie with each other in tracking down the sources they supposed Lucas to be plagiarizing, an exercise on a par with tracing the iconographic influences on modern automobile showrooms: decor, after all, cannot be copyrighted.

In not wishing to interpret Star Wars, its critics showed themselves to be staunch clerics and preservers of their culture's most hallowed (and therefore unspoken) traditions, which are to be understood as self-evident and above interpretation. Now the same thing has happened with Close Encounters, with this difference—that as its subtext is subversive of many of our most cherished values, deceits, and social arrangements, it has been dismissed (with some faint praise for its special effects) with the same cavalier inattention to what it means as Star Wars was welcomed with. Which is to say that it doesn't mean anything.

Or rather, that it only means what its ads have proclaimed—that we are not alone and that the UFOs are up there, biding their time until They're ready to bliss us out. The critics have been abetted in their self-blinkered nescience by the film's director, Steven Spielberg, who maintains in his interviews that maybe UFOs really are real. Mr. Spielberg is a young man with a manner as guileless as four-year-old Cary Guffey's in his film, and his protestations have been accepted at face value. After all, it isn't in the interest of his interviewers or anyone else in the publicity machine to probe too deeply into Spielberg's good or bad faith in this matter. It may be wondered whether his movie would have made quite so many millions of dollars if Spielberg hadn't thrown these sops to his literal-minded audience, who in this way are able to enjoy.

I, for one, don't believe in the extraterrestrial origin of UFOs, any more than I believe in ESP, reincarnation, or the divinity (or satanic maleficence) of whatever guru has most recently won space in the Sunday supplements—though all of these are viable and potentially significant premises for fantasy. However, as Richard Dreyfuss keeps insisting as he models his mashed potatoes into truncated pyramids, it must mean something. I would submit that what Spielberg *means* in *Close Encounters* is much the same as what R. D. Laing means in *The Divided Self*. Less familiar though even closer to Spielberg's general drift is *Mount Analogue*, an allegorical novel by the French surrealist René Daumal, in which the quest for transcendental experience is likened to a mountain-climbing expedition—an analogy so precise it may amount in at least one direction (mountain climbers *are* pursuing transcendence) to an identity.

Interpreted in this light, *Close Encounters* may be seen as a story about the pursuit of God by an Everyman called Roy Neary (as in "Neary My God to Thee"). It is not an easy pursuit, for it requires acts of faith that look to his employers, family, and neighbors like madness. Indeed, Neary *is* mad, for God is not approachable in the clothing of rationality. (When the police cars try to follow the first set of flying saucers they plunge over a precipice.) Neary's first experience of Something Else is a gratuitous visitation, an act of grace, but because Neary insists on following the saucers whither they lead, he loses his job: you cannot serve God and Mammon. When the saucers have departed, Neary has no very good idea of how to continue the pursuit. He has an obscure impulse to model shaving foam, mashed potatoes, and finally the entire fabric of his house and grounds into an Object of mysterious, numenous significance. In short, he becomes an artist, a decision that entails for Neary (as for that other representative all-sacrificing artist Gauguin) the abandonment of his family. Christ demanded no less. The TLS's reviewer, S. Schoenbaus, writes that "Neary's willingness to give up wife and children for a fabulous voyage may be comprehensible, but his ability to do so without an internal conflict betrays the psychological poverty of the script." On the contrary, it is precisely the heedless, headlong, joyful way that Neary smashes up his own suburban household in the pursuit of his vision that evidences the psychological acumen of the script. Converts, and madmen, are people who have passed beyond internal conflicts.

At length, Neary is rewarded for his persistence by a Sign that the form he has been modeling and remodeling has an objective existence outside his imagination (a sign it is every artist's hope some day to be vouchsafed). It is shown on television, Devil's Tower, a mountain in Wyoming. Naturally, he sets off at once for the spot. However, the forces-that-be would prevent him from going there. (Mammon, after all, has his own interests to look after.) They say the area has been contaminated with nerve gas and that he will be poisoned unless he wears a gas mask. In other words, it is unsafe to pursue wisdom along the paths of excess, and madness is not only bad but fatal. The dramatic high point of the film occurs when Neary decides to take off his gas mask. This leap of faith immediately liberates him and his two companions to make their attempt on the Devil's Tower (a name, like the story about the nerve gas, that is meant to act as a deterrent; religious authority is always suspicious of do-it-yourselfers), and his reward at the mountain top is a vision of . . . something ineffable.

If the movie can be faulted, it is for its vision of Neary's reward. Spielberg demonstrates technical mastery in establishing the scale and physical reality of Devil's Tower, so that when the mothership eventually makes its entrance, dwarfing the mountain, the effect is truly awesome. But the concert that ensues is not, to my ear, the music of the spheres. I'd have preferred a score by Beethoven—or, lacking that, by Terry Riley. But after all, art always fails at conveying the Divine Presence in the fullness of its glory. Art offers an image, not the real thing, and that image, finally, takes a human form, as it does in the Sistine Chapel, or in Blake's drawings, or in the "aliens" who come out of their ship to wave hello to the audience. If the effect is risible, the laughter is inherent in all anthropomorphic representations of the divine.

Why, if this is indeed the subtext of the film, has the film been so popular? Surely, it does not portend a mass exodus from suburbia into the desert. It has been popular, I think, for the same reason Christianity has been—not because the audience is persuaded to take its precepts to heart, but because it offers an impressive *picture* of God, a graven image, a Golden Calf. We are all hungry to see His face, and at the same time reluctant to become a madman for His sake, which so many authorities have claimed to be one of the requirements. What we can't do, however, we can enjoy watching in simulation, especially if the endeavor has been masked in the sanitized imagery of conventional sci-fi and we aren't required to think about it, since, by definition, sci-fi can never mean anything important.

Primal Hooting

Whitley is back! Those who treasure the more exotic forms of untruth will need no further prompting.

Communion, Whitley Strieber's 1987 account of his abduction by aliens, was a primal hoot. Its sequel, *Transformation*, recycles the same whoppers with only minor variations, but it offers generous portions of the same shameless charlatanry and page after page of Whitley's patented prose with its peanut-butter-and-jelly mix of penny-dreadful horror and saccharine sanctimony. Here's a taste of the peanut butter:

> Andrew [his seven-year-old son and coabductee] started screaming. The shock that went through me this time was absolutely explosive. . . . His screaming filled my ears, my soul. Listening to it, I wanted to die. . . . I thought I was going to suffocate. My throat was closed, my eyes were swimming with tears. The sense of being *injured* was powerful and awful. It was as if the whole house were full of filthy, stinking insects the size of tigers.

And here's the jelly:

> The visitors are sweeping up from where we buried them under layers of denial and false assurance to deliver what is truly a message from the beyond. . . . They have caused me to slough off my old view of the world like the dismal skin that it was and seek a completely new vision of this magnificent, mysterious, and fiercely alive universe.

UFO stories are generally not accorded serious media attention, but Strieber was a special case. He had already published best-selling horror novels that had gone on to become movies. Here was a bankable Name Writer willing to go on record as a UFO abductee. "It's rather doubtful that a non-writer could spark the kind of enthusiasm that you find in this book," his editor at Morrow, James Landis, confided in the August 14, 1987, *Publisher's Weekly*. Whitley got a million-dollar advance for *Communion*. Morrow and Avon aren't ballyhooing what they're paying for the

---

Review of *Transformation*, by Whitley Strieber.

sequel, for such publicity might confirm doubts among those inclined to believe that Whitley's motivation is mercenary rather than his declared desire to seek a completely new vision of our mysterious universe. Surely it is hard to account for Whitley's and his publisher's conduct on any other basis. Read as a factual account of alien contact, Communion and Transformation have the verisimilitude of a Paul Bunyan legend. Taken as a strategy for commercial and psychological self-aggrandizement, however, they make perfect sense.

Consider only the internal chronology and publishing history of the two books. Communion tells of Whitley's encounters with the aliens on October 4 and December 26, 1985, events the aliens had made him forget until the memories were retrieved via hypnosis in March of 1986. Between March and the fall of that year, Whitley must have made and sold the book proposal and written the book, which appeared in bookstores promptly in January 1987. Meanwhile, on April 2, 1986, Whitley now reports in Transformation, his seven-year-old son, Andrew, underwent his own UFO abduction, which was the source of the paternal anguish quoted above. Readers of Transformation won't learn much about little Andrew's sufferings at the hands of the aliens, since Whitley is extremely respectful of his son's privacy in this matter. For the inside story on that one, we'll probably have to wait another couple of years until Andrew is old enough to appear on talk shows to sell his own searing account. Does it not seem strange that Whitley would not have mentioned these latest tricks his aliens were up to in the book he was then writing? This is a question not addressed in Transformation, but I can hypothesize two answers: (1) Andrew's abduction was held in reserve for Transformation because of its can-you-top-this, sequel-making value; or (2) Whitley did not want to expose his boy to the merciless scrutiny of the press at that time, but then, coming to realize the awesome significance of his revelations, decided that he would sacrifice these paternal scruples in the interest of the Truth.

Transformation differs from Communion in several significant ways. Whitley no longer accesses his abduction memories via hypnosis. Indeed, he is now critical of the practice and of his fellow UFO expert Budd Hopkins, whose competing and more lurid account of abduction—and rape—by aliens, Intruders (Random House, no less), appeared in bookstores shortly after Communion. "I feel," Whitley warns, "that the present fad of hypnotizing 'abductees,' which is being engaged in by untrained investigators, will inevitably lead to suffering, breakdown, and possibly even suicide." Hopkins's book reported that women were being impregnated by aliens, returned to earth, and then reabducted for the harvesting of the fetuses, and while Whitley wisely refrains from questioning the literal truth of such claims, he does take Hopkins to task for his view of the aliens as a destructive force:

> I cannot agree with this. Certainly it is clear that our response to an encounter is often one of fear and terror. Our perceptions are distorted by panic at the high level of strangeness we observe.
>
> But it is premature to assume that our experiences are actually negative in content.

Whitley is now promoting an upbeat UFO abduction experience. Fear is to be a key that opens up a cosmic funhouse:

> We must learn to walk the razor's edge between fear and ecstasy. [The visitors] made me face death, face them, face my weaknesses and my buried terrors. At the same time, they kept demonstrating to me that I was more than a body, and even that my body could enter extraordinary states such as physical levitation.

In *Communion* Whitley solicited readers to come to the front of the church and testify about their UFO experiences, an invitation that yielded a brief fad of abductee support groups. In *Transformation* Whitley extends a more enticing possibility, a form of transcendence that doesn't depend on the whims of aliens, who are notoriously undependable, never appearing when they're invited. How about out-of-body travel? It's safe, it's cheap, and it's semi-reliable, if, like Whitley, one uses the methods developed at the Monroe Institute in West Virginia, where Whitley went to learn methods for entering a "mind awake/body asleep" state that allows the wakeful sleeper to shuffle off this mortal coil and visit friends in a discorporate but not imperceptible condition. Two people Whitley tried to contact in this way didn't receive his vibrations, but then, in February of 1981, Eureka!

> A friend in Denver called me to report an odd experience. She had awakened and seen the outline of my face across the room from her. Later she wrote me, "What I saw exactly was the impression of your face wearing the glasses you wear amid the leaves of a plant hanging near the door of my bedroom for about three seconds in the dark. I turned on the light and nothing was there."
>
> I probably would not have mentioned the incident had it not kept happening. Chicago radio personality Roy Leonard awakened on the

night of June 7, 1987, to find my presence in his bedroom. He reported that he could "almost" see me.

That night I had an extremely strange dream of moving like a ghost through an endless, dark woods and entering a little room that was so dark I couldn't see a thing. How Roy Leonard ended up on the receiving end of that dream I do not presently understand.

What Whitley's out-of-body capabilities have to do with his UFO experiences is never precisely spelled out, but it makes good sense intuitively. To paraphrase Judy Garland, "If UFOs fly beyond the rainbow, why, oh why can't I?" In any case, there is no need to speculate about Whitley's intentions and supernal powers, for I have been able to discuss all these matters in confidence with Whitley's disembodied spirit! Only last night—October 13, 1988—Whitley's ecoplasmic, night-wandering self visited me in my bedroom, and this time it was no mere three-second, now-you-see-him-now-you-don't fugitive vision. His pale, tormented visage hung around for several minutes, and though I lacked the presence of mind to tape-record our dialogue, you can take my word for it that what follows is substantially what Whitley confided to me. Whitley himself may not recall our conversation, just as he seems to have forgotten his visit to Roy Leonard; he may even deny that it took place, but I am entirely persuaded it was Whitley I spoke to and no one else, though a skeptical friend has suggested to me that what I perceived as Whitley was only a product of my own overheated imagination. Or then again, it may be, as Hamlet surmised:

The spirit that I have seen
May be a devil: and the devil hath power
To assume a pleasing shape; yea, and perhaps
Out of my weakness and my melancholy
As he is very potent with such spirits
Abuses me to damn me.

I had just laid aside the volume of Browne's *Pseudodoxia Epidemica* with which I had been beguiling the sleepless hours when I began to feel a curious sensation, not unlike one recounted by Whitley: "It felt as if I had come unstuck from myself. The experience was strange in the extreme—almost beyond description." At the same time I heard an unearthly mewling sound that seemed to come from outside the window screen. It was inconceivable that a cat could have made its way to my window ledge, eleven stories above ground level, for there is no fire escape, and yet I could distinctly see a dark shape on the ledge—a shape that, even as I watched, dumb with horror, proceeded to drift through the screen and to hover above a spider plant in the far corner of the room. Slowly the dark cloud coalesced into the mirthless face I had seen on so many television talk shows.

"Whitley!" I gasped. "Is it possible?"

His face trembled as though molded of colorless Jell-O and solidified into a sneer. "Of course not. You must be one of those fantasy-prone personalities I've read about. You must be having a hypnopompic hallucination."

Whitley was undoubtedly referring to Robert A. Baker's discussion of *Communion*, which had appeared in the winter 1987–88 issue of the *Skeptical Inquirer*, a journal put out by CSI-COP, the Committee for the Scientific Investigation of Claims of the Paranormal, an organization devoted to the thankless task of debunking all the varieties of supernatural and pseudoscientific fraud. According to Baker, Whitley's UFO stories are textbook cases of hypnopompic hallucination:

> complete with the awakening from a sound sleep, the strong sense of reality and of being awake, the paralysis (due to the fact that the body's neural circuits keep our muscles relaxed and help preserve our sleep), and the encounter with strange beings. Following the encounter, instead of jumping out of bed and going in search of the strangers he has seen, Strieber typically goes back to sleep. [All these patterns are repeated in *Transformation*.—T. D.] . . . Strieber, of course, is convinced of the reality of these experiences. This too is expected. If he was not . . . then the experiences would not be hypnopompic or hallucinatory.

Until this moment I had been skeptical about Baker's theory, which seems designed to give Whitley and other self-styled abductees the benefit of the doubt with regard to their good faith. The internal evidence of *Communion* suggests to me that even if Whitley's aliens had their origins in his waking dreams, they have long since been assimilated into a wholly conscious hoax. Whitley can bring passionate conviction to the defense of his lies; he even boasts of how he breezes through lie-detector tests (while enjoining "'debunkers' intent on twisting the facts" from contacting his front man, Dr. John Gleidman). But liars characteristically evidence a passionate commitment to their lies. Witness such recent bearers of false witness as Oliver North, Kurt Waldheim, President Reagan, and Jim and Tammy Bakker. The list could be continued for many column inches. The 1980s are the Age of Isuzu. Lying has become a form of entertainment. Surely a large part of Whitley's readership approaches his books in a spirit of connoisseurship rather than credulity, relishing the spectacle of his effrontery as one might the penitential tears of Jimmy Swaggart.

But there is no need for *me* to frame an indictment against Whitley. He did so himself with unforgettable (and uncharacteristic) eloquence on the night of October 13.

"Must you come visiting me in my dreams?" I grumbled at the phantasm of Whitley. "Why can't we just declare a truce?"

"You started this, Disch," it hissed. "No other *respectable* writer thought it worth his while to attack a book about UFOs. There's a gentleman's agreement in the book trade that crackpot ideas are not discussed in highbrow journals."

"Right. Only on *The Tonight Show*, and then only if there's no one there to contradict you."

The disembodied head nodded. "Exactly. I am in the business of founding a new faith, and faiths are, by definition, beyond criticism. It's quite simple, really. In a world of systemic corruption, we must all look the other way. If every Watergate conspirator had had the reticence and decency of G. Gordon Liddy, children might still have some respect for constituted authority."

"Oh, Liddy had great team spirit, I'll give you that. The thing is, Whitley, I'm not on *your* team."

"That makes no difference when religion is at issue. Meeting a Mormon socially, you would not cross-examine him about his honest opinion of the revelations Joseph Smith received from the Angel Moroni. And I claim the same exemption from criticism. As I see it, there's not much difference between the books I've written and the synoptic gospels. Like the witnesses of the resurrection and the other miracles reported in the gospels, all I am saying is that I *saw what I saw*. Impeach my honesty and that of those who have colluded in one or another of my fancies, and you impeach the honesty of all true believers, and so my first priority is to take the moral high ground, along with the author of Proverbs, who wrote, 'Smite a scorner, and the simple will beware.' Or, a verse I like even better, 'Judgments are prepared for scorners, and stripes for the backs of fools.'"

This had the ring of the Whitley whose first, fictional exploration of ufology, a short story called "Pain," had taken the form of soft-core S&M porn; the Whitley who witnesses, in *Transformation*, the following cautionary tableau:

. . . a stone floor with a low stone table in the middle of it. The table was a bit more than waist high, and on it there was a set of iron shackles. A man was led down some steps and attached to these shackles. He was right in front of my face, not two feet from me, looking directly at me with eyes so sad that I almost couldn't bear it. . . . Behind him was a taller person wearing black. . . . The next thing I knew this person was beating the poor man with a terrible whip. Before my eyes this man was being almost torn to pieces by the fury of the beating.

Somebody behind me said, "He failed to get you to obey him and now he must bear the consequences."

"There's one thing I still don't understand," I confided to Whitley's head. "I can see *your* incentive to pile it on. You earn a fortune, and it makes you a kind of celebrity, and there must even be a kind of high-wire thrill to see how far you can go with it. But what's in it for the other Johnny-come-lately abductees? They won't have bestsellers or movie sales; they won't be interviewed by talk-show hosts."

"Ah, but as Jesus said at some point, every little bit counts. Bruce Lee, for instance. His testimony wasn't required of him. He isn't even my editor at Morrow. He simply saw there was an opportunity to do something for his employer, and for me, and pitched in. Talk about team players!"

Whitley was referring to one of the drollest tales in his book, concerning the night that Bruce Lee, a senior editor at Morrow, visited a bookstore on Manhattan's Upper East Side on an evening in January 1987 and witnessed two aliens in winter coats, their faces muffled with scarves. The aliens were paging through the newly released *Communion*, "turning—and apparently speed-reading—the pages at a remarkable rate." Mr. Lee noticed that "behind their dark glasses both the man and the woman had large, black, almond-shaped eyes." Lee, a former reporter and correspondent for *Newsweek* and *Reader's Digest*, "felt decidedly uneasy, deeply shocked." Later, Lee would take a lie-detector test administered by Whitley's own polygraphist, Nat Laurendi, and when asked if he thought the beings he saw in the bookstore were aliens—or, as Whitley prefers, "visitors"—Lee replied yes. Then: "He was asked if I had offered him anything of value to tell his story. He answered 'no' and this answer was evaluated as true."

"Yes," Whitley went on, "Bruce is a peach. But really, *everyone* at Morrow has been wonderful. Sherry Arden, who is the president and publisher, has been quoted in *Publisher's Weekly* as saying, 'We truly believe this happened to Whitley.' And Rena Wolner called me 'one of the most creative people I know.' And then there's Phillipe Mora, who'll be directing the movie of *Communion: he* came out to the cottage and met one of the aliens . . . oops, excuse me, *visitors,* right there where it all began."

"But none of them are exactly disinterested witnesses, are they? I'm surprised that everyone at Morrow isn't required to declare their belief in UFOs as a condition of continued employment. The people I can't understand are the people who imitate you for no obvious mercenary reason."

"Every abductee, within the smaller public sphere of his or her own social circle, is a mini-celebrity, a person important enough to have been taken up into the high-tech heaven of a genuine flying saucer. That should be inducement enough for *millions* of people—once I've got this thing rolling."

"Even though everyone knows they're bull-shitting?"

"And who isn't these days? Why should the right to lie and be respected for one's lies be reserved for televangelists and the highest officials of our government? Indeed, in that regard the situation nowadays is strikingly close to that of the Roman Empire in the early Christian era, when the emperors were officially divine. Caligula claimed to have enjoyed sexual congress with the moon-goddess in a manner not unlike my own spicier moments aboard the UFOs. What could have been more personally satisfying for an ordinary Roman citizen, confronted with such poppycock, than to declare an equivalent demi-divinity? If not Godhead, at least co-immortality with the crucified and resurrected God. So much for the divine pretensions of Caligula, or Pat Robertson, or Nero, or Nixon, or Heliogabalus."

"Whitley, are you trying to suggest that your potboilers are on a par with the gospels?"

Whitley smiled a sly smile. "Did I say that? No, no, you're putting words in my mouth."

Before I could ask him any more questions, Whitley laid a pseudopod aside of his nose, and, with a wink, he disappeared. But I fully expect he will return, in a year or so, with new spiritual revelations from his handpuppet aliens.

Postscript

The attentive reader will have noticed a curious feature in the transcript of Whitley's dialogue with me. Repeatedly he paraphrases or exactly quotes phrases and whole sentences that appear in my essay "UFOs and the Origins of Christianity." At first I could not imagine why he would do this, until it dawned on me that he might have intended these as "evidence" that I was cannibalizing my own writing and not giving an actual transcript of his visitation! How could he have accomplished this? I had to ask myself. The essay in question had not yet appeared in *Foundation*, a British magazine he would be unlikely to have read in any case. Then I realized that he must have made earlier night-journeys and seen me at work on that essay. The force of its argument had, in effect, etched my words on his consciousness, and he was able, perhaps unwittingly, to repeat them in the course of the visitation recorded above.

PART SIX **ON SF** After the Future

The Day of the Living Dead

Coming from someone who has written novels as artful as *Hawksmoor* and *Chatterton*, not to mention a well-received biography of T. S. Eliot, Peter Ackroyd's latest novel, *First Light*, is unfathomably bad. So bad it verges on being a pleasure to read. (Though now I've said it, I foresee a copywriter claiming: "A pleasure to read!"—*The Washington Post*.) There can be a kind of inverse genius to certain bad writing, so that the reader is always discovering some new godawfulness to cringe at. Such genius is most common in poetry; the work of the Scottish bard William McGonaghal is the supreme example, though Julia Moore, the Sweet Singer of Michigan, runs him a close second. Sometimes a memoir can do it, like *The Big Love*, Florence Aadland's systemically gauche account of her teenage daughter's affair with Errol Flynn.

But rarely is a bad novel entertainingly bad for more than a few chapters. To be bad on a grand scale one must aim high, and the premise of *First Light* is nothing less than Miltonic in its sweep, encompassing the farthest reaches of the starry heavens and the lives of English country folk. Millennia ago, just as tabloid readers have suspected, alien beings came to earth to build Stonehenge and other rough-hewn astronomical devices. Now in Dorset's Pilgrin Valley a forest fire has revealed the shape of a large burial tumulus, and archaeologists begin to excavate, uncovering an underground labyrinth. Countless chapters later, it is found to contain a coffin, which after some further flummery is opened to reveal a being who is a cross between Dreyer's Nosferatu and an undead Blakean archetype. In its withered face can be descried "the faces of all those who had come before him. And the faces of all those he [Joey, an elderly music-hall comedian who has been initiated into these ancient mysteries by wise old Farmer Mint] has known. . . . Joey is crying, his tears falling upon the ancient human form."

The ancient human form is then incinerated, and in the smoke of the pyre all the living characters in the novel see all the dead ones and they realize that "no one is ever dead, and at this moment of communion a deep sigh arose from the earth and travelled upward to the stars." The

---

Review of *First Light*, by Peter Ackroyd.

ancient human form returns to Aldebaran whence he had come, after which follows the musings of Damian Fell, an astronomer driven mad by his terrible wisdom: "Why is it that we think of a circular motion as the most perfect? Is it because it has no beginning and no end?"

Though this strikes me as an essentially dumb idea, even dumber ideas have produced commercially viable hack novels, but Ackroyd's execution, sentence by sentence, is what is truly McGonaghalesque. The characters have a genius for unwitting verbal pratfalls and marking time in ways that seem self-referential to the book's longueurs, as when the archaeologist hero, after perusing an article in a scholarly journal (which is written in a style suited to the needs of the reading-impaired), "walked through into his study, a small room at the back of the flat which overlooked the yard of the antiques shop beneath them. And when he saw Jude asleep on the floor, its paws tucked in and its back slightly arched, it occurred to him that this was the way that dogs had always slept; even at that time when the great stone monuments were being erected. As soon as he entered the room the animal sprang into wakefulness and, yawning, jumped onto its hind-legs and leaned its paws against Mark. 'Good boy,' he said. 'There's a good boy.' And the dog barked in return."

Mark is constantly bumbling about through the scenery of the novel, having insights equally momentous, and then reviewing them at length. Chapter 4 exactly reprises the landscapes described in chapters 2 and 3. In chapter 6 the spinster heroine, Evangeline Tupper, visits her father and has tea with him, and the narrative thrust of the scene is that Evangeline and Mr. Tupper have nothing to say to each other. For chapter after chapter nothing happens but what we've been told will happen: the tumulus is excavated with meticulous patience.

Sounds boring? Well, so in synopsis might many novels of Thomas Hardy (to whom Ackroyd makes constant, self-aggrandizing reference). Perhaps Ackroyd intends his dull plot to be foil for other brilliances. Such as witty dialogue, like this:

> The telephone was ringing as they returned to their room in the Blue Dog, and Evangeline rushed to answer it. "It's me," she shouted. "Miss Tupper!"
>
> "Is it really? It sounded like Winston Churchill." Augustine Fraicheur, enjoying a pre-lunch drink, was in playful mood. "Voices can be so deceptive, can't they?"
>
> "Along with everything else."
>
> He smiled at his gin. "Any news?" Augustine accentuated the last word, as if he were anticipating something very shocking indeed.

"Actually," she replied, automatically delving into her handbag for another Woodbine, "I have the most fabulous piece of gossip." She paused to light it. "But I don't know if I should tell you."

"Torturer!" He screamed with pleasure.

"Honestly. You'll have to wait."

"I can't *bear* it."

"But I promise that you'll be among the first to know."

"I think I'm beginning to go mad."

I quote at such length because a briefer snippet could not convey the unrelenting and self-referential awfulness of the text. ("I can't *bear* it," indeed!) The book is peppered with enough such knowing winks that I am persuaded that Peter Ackroyd set out deliberately to produce a novel of exactly the thundering awfulness he's achieved.

Why he would want to do such a thing I can't imagine. Perhaps, having read a number of the more numbskulled sorts of novels that crowd the bestseller lists, he thought to out-Cartland Cartland. But *First Light* lacks the essential ingredients of a lowbrow romantic adventure—sincerity and libidinal energy. Perhaps, more perversely, Ackroyd has written a dreadful book for the sake of dreadfulness, challenged by the form as a poet might be by the form of the villanelle. If so, he has achieved his aim. *First Light* deserves a special niche among the curiosities of literature: it may well be the worst novel ever written by a novelist of certifiable distinction.

The Fairy Tale Kingdom of Baghdad

By a strange sort of serendipity, here is a novel by one of America's best writers that is set, for more than half its hefty length, in Baghdad and the Persian Gulf. As the writer in question is John Barth, and not one of the international press corps' literary camp followers, like Robert Stone or Joan Didion, the Baghdad being presented to us is not that of Saddam Hussein but of Sindbad the Sailor, and even the most ingenious interpreters of allegory would be hard-pressed to discover a topical political relevance in the arabesques of Barth's tale. That the fairy tale kingdom he writes about happens to go by the name of Baghdad only underlines the fact that Barth is, among all contemporary novelists of the first rank, the one who least aspires to timeliness.

Timelessness, rather, is the Barthean element: the misty headlands and oceanic vistas of myth, a land and sea of pure fancy where Greek legends may cohabit freely with the *Arabian Nights* (as in his ineffably clever novel *Chimera*), where the mustard seed of an Aesopean fable can swell into the largest whimsy ever written, which is at the same time a knowing satire on academic life (*Giles Goat-Boy*). This time, the irreconcilables Barth seeks to wed are contemporary realism and the *Arabian Nights*, both territories he's explored before, though not, in the latter case, so exhaustively.

Here is how the novel works: Within a narrative frame set at the banquet table of the original Sindbad, alternating chapters recount (1) the first-person reminiscences of a beggarly guest, the "Somebody" of the title, from his childhood days in 1937 in East Dorset, an imaginary city in tidewater Maryland, and continuing at intervals through his fiftieth year, and (2) the day-by-day intrigues and amorous dalliances of Somebody during the six days and nights he spends chez Sindbad. The two strands of this narrative braid remain quite distinct, both in substance and tone, until, at the touch of the author's wand, the Somebody of Here and Now is transported bodily to There and Then, after the manner of Mark Twain's Connecticut Yankee. There is never to be any science-fictional accounting for this wonderful journey; the machinery that accomplishes

---

Review of *The Last Voyage of Somebody the Sailor*, by John Barth.

it is transparently aesthetic, just as the Baghdad Sindbad resides in is patently fabulous, a city and society of narrative conventions as artificial (and often as tiresome) as High Mass or opera seria.

While Barth's scheme makes for occasional tough sledding, there are corresponding rich rewards. Chief among them is a lapidary prose style that out-Nabokovs Nabokov, whether Barth is painting the scenery or caressing memories of erotic pleasure or evoking the Sensual Sublime, as in this evocation of that borderline between daily life and the Beyond, passage across which is the crux of the plot and (Barth implies) the Secret Meaning of Sex:

> My recent reading in Mrs. Moore's *Arabian Nights* had made me chafe not only at being ineluctably I and here and now but likewise at the iron constraints of nature itself, which made it quite certain that no fish would ever talk and no genie appear from a bottle, nor would Daisy and I be magically transported from Dorset County to Samarkand or Serendib. . . . No, the eerie moments of a true near-ecstasy, whose scary disorientation I had learned to protract and relish, had been . . . [when] I was able in a certain combination of drowsiness and less-than-total darkness to rock myself just beyond all usual and normal sensory cues into a charged suspension, vertiginous, electrically humming, in which the ceiling, the walls, the frames of the doors and the windows, and the very bed beneath me were at once their familiar selves and unspeakably alien, their distance and configuration fluid, and I myself was no longer and not merely I but as it were the very lens of the cosmos.

Even readers who delight in such sonorities and extended cadences (and my excerpt ruthlessly truncates the original) may find themselves surfeited as they read *The Last Voyage*. It is not a novel one reads in a desperate haste to reach the denouement; rather, it is like a two-week voyage on a luxury liner, a steady succession of rich meals, each one thirty or forty pages long and fully satiating.

There is another reason why the book resists quick reading, and that is (to put it bluntly) its pornographic nature. Once Simon William Behler, the Somebody of the title, has exited the purlieus of childhood and begins the account of his "second voyage," at age thirteen, the novel's very nearly exclusive focus becomes sex. Barth writes about sex with a languorous, caressing appreciation, or with a zesty exuberance; he writes about it in B-minor and C-major, with ribald glee and with hieratic pomp. And always the sex he writes about is of that healthy variety commended by such authorities as Dr. Ruth and *The Joy of Sex*. When the plot requires unpleasantnesses like rape and incest, they take place offstage or at an ironic distance.

On the other hand, anyone approaching the book in the spirit of salacious interest will be likely to conclude that Barth's lust for metaphor, particularly in the "Arabian" interchapters, much outweighs lust of the triple-X variety, as in such a (not untypical) passage as this:

> We therefore set to as I had foreseen, and if his dhow was not the first to make a dawhat out of the bi'r next door to my wahat, it was the largest, stoutest, and most fraught. So eloquently did it convey to me his love for Marjanah, and I relay it to her, and her dainty Magharet to speak to my tongue of her love for Sindbad, and I relay it to him, that the three of us all too soon climbed Adam's Peak as one, and I was so provisioned both stern and aft that for some moments I left this world altogether.

There is, behind these shimmering veils, a moral intention or allegorical purpose—or, to give it its most unfashionable name, a Meaning other than the unexceptionable one that sex is real and sex is earnest. Sex can be, like the sea that is Barth's protean, ever-present metaphor, dangerous, and of its many dangers the one that has received the most public scrutiny in recent years, and the one that Barth gingerly treats in the text and subtexts of *The Last Voyage*, is father/daughter child abuse and incest.

Simon Behler's first love, Daisy Moore, is a girl who has been abused by her father, and this adds a sinister undercurrent to the otherwise brilliant erotic set-piece in which the teenage Simon and Daisy make love. In the Arabian chapters there is a parallel suspicion of incest between Sindbad and Yasmin, but though the plot knits the most elaborate arabesques of mystery and ambiguity about this primal sin, it doesn't finally find a catharsis to (in Barth's word) "catharse" it. Barth's own last word on the subject would seem to be as casually dismissive as this summing-up by Daisy's luckier kid sister, Julia:

> It's screwed us up, more or less. But long after I was out of the house and Ma was kaput, Daisy went on taking care of him. I believe she happened to love old Sam more than she loved her other men, and I can't help thinking that in a different world everybody could've shrugged their shoulders and got on with it.

In fairness, that is the moral being drawn by one of the author's characters, and the allegory of the Arabian component of the plot resolves the issue otherwise.

An affection for the *Arabian Nights* in the jewel-crusted translation of Richard Burton is not a prerequisite for enjoying Barth's revision of Sindbad's voyages, but it would help, especially when his scheme obliges him to gild refined gold in lavish emulation. But despite the longueurs of such passages, it's a beautiful book, and one that has the rare good fortune to have a cover that is a fair visual analog for the complex richness of its contents.

The collage by Carol Wald depicts a many-minareted city by a sea that is a Turner in the distance, a photograph close to the shore, while an Ingres odalisque luxuriates in one corner beneath a jeweled tabernacle that is the gate to the city. It is, like the book it illustrates, gorgeous, playful, enigmatic, garish, eclectic, and unlike anything else around.

SF: Guides to the Ghetto

It is Stanislaw Lem's deeply felt and closely argued contention that the field of science fiction has produced only four authors worthy of that genre's rich potential: Verne, Wells, Stapledon, and himself. The proliferation of work by other writers in the genre, especially by Americans, has actually been a morbid condition characterized by "retrogression, degeneration, or at the very least developmental stagnation, typical of populations isolated from the outside world and vitiated by inbreeding" such as obtains in ghettoes. American sf is the "domain of herd creativity," and it "repel[s] the more exigent authors and readers, so that the loss of individuality in science fiction is at once a cause and an effect of ghetto seclusion." Lem charitably makes an exception for Philip K. Dick, on the basis of reading only seven of his novels, from which he is nevertheless able to abstract a "main sequence" comprised of "*The Three Stigmata of Palmer Eldritch, Ubik, Now Wait for Last Year*, and perhaps also *Galactic Pot-Healer*."

As that "sequence" will evidence to any reader well-acquainted with Dick's major novels, the fatuity and self-serving nature of Lem's pronouncements on the field of sf are matched only by the slenderness of the reading on which they are based. Most of the essays in *Microworlds* date from ten to fifteen years ago, and even then Lem's knowledge of sf was based (according to the book's introducer, Franz Rottensteiner, who is also Lem's agent in the West) on French translations chosen by Rottensteiner, a filtering process that provided Lem with a canon of American science fiction that systematically excluded most of the titles that were, even within that time-frame, canonical. Except for his random sampling of Dick's novels, most of the titles he cites are by those writers of the forties and fifties—Asimov, van Vogt, Heinlein, Bradbury—whose appeal is essentially to a juvenile audience. Taxed with having dismissed American sf as "a hopeless case" without having read its best authors, Lem, in a postscript to one of his essays, shifts the blame from himself to criticism in general, which has failed to establish a canon. Lem himself, appar-

---

Review of *Microworlds: Writing on Science Fiction and Fantasy*, by Stanislaw Lem; and *Science Fiction: The 100 Best Novels*, by David Pringle.

ently, as a meta-critic stands above the drudgery of distinguishing between the wheat and the chaff.

And truly, he needn't bother, for it is clear from his treatments of even those texts for which he professes some regard that the only living author who can command his sustained attention is Stanislaw Lem. The first essay in the book, "Reflections on My Life," is an exercise in unwitting self-betrayal as droll as the diaries of the thirteen-and-three-quarters-year-old Adrian Mole. It begins with a ponderous inquiry as to whether the series of events that has led to the crowning achievement of his own work can be ascribed to mere chance or whether Destiny didn't somehow enter into it. He marvels at his own IQ: "mine was over 180, and I was said to have been . . . the most intelligent child in southern Poland." He re-invented the differential gear and "drew many funny things in my thick copybooks, including a bicycle on which one rode moving up and down as on a horse." He proves by deductive logic the radical novelty of his most recent work, and as an afterthought remarks on those books that exhibit not his philosophic achievements but his cavortings in the provinces of the humorous—of satire, irony, and wit—with a touch of Swift and of dry, mischievous Voltairean misanthropy: "As is well known, the great humorists were people who had been driven to despair and anger by the conduct of mankind. In this respect, I am one of those people." In the creation of the figure of Stanislaw Lem, if in nothing else, one must grant that he's one of the great humorists, but in the other essays that follow his little autobiography he comes across more vividly as a great pedant driven to despair and anger by the failure of other writers to follow his own example in adulating Stanislaw Lem.

Concerning science fiction in its non-Lemish aspects, a much better guide is available in *Science Fiction: The 100 Best Novels*. These are by the author's admission a personal selection, but Pringle knows the territory well (since 1980 he has been the editor of *Foundation*, the best critical journal surveying the field) and his selection is judicious, respecting the *monstres sacrée* of the genre without weighting his list with their dinosaur eggs. Omitted are such standard texts as Asimov's *Foundation Trilogy* (it "has always seemed to me to be overrated," Pringle explains) and Heinlein's *Stranger in a Strange Land*, and popular favorites like Anne McCaffery and Marion Zimmer Bradley are dismissed as purveyors of "planetary romance" for which Pringle has no use. In short, Pringle's concern is to single out those books and authors (the one hundred titles are by seventy-three authors) likeliest to appeal to the generally literate reader who wants something better than junk food when her imagination is dining out in the genre. As a checklist of what to stock up on, I don't think this book has a rival. Pringle's summaries of the one hundred chosen novels exactly convey the merits and fascination of each book without spoiling its surprises, and I finished the one hundredth evaluation with my own list of a dozen sure bets that I will be making room for on my shelf of ready-to-read good intentions. As an indication of Pringle's (and my own) taste, here are some of the titles from just the last twelve years that receive his highest encomia: Ballard's *Crash* and *High-Rise*, LeGuin's *The Dispossessed*, Russ's *The Female Man*, Crowley's *Engine Summmer*, Benford's *Timescape*, and Wolfe's *The Book of the New Sun*. Strict honesty obliges me to note that I get three citations, and doubtless that made me better-disposed to the book than if I'd had none, or only one, but I can still aspire to the condition of Ballard and Aldiss, who get four each, and Philip Dick, who gets five and an apology for the omission of further first-rate books. I commend the book to one and all—and particularly to Stanislaw Lem.

Over the River and Through the Wood

Doris Lessing was born eighty years ago in a country, Persia, that no longer exists. At the age of five, her parents brought her to South Africa, and she departed that country for England in 1949, leaving behind two husbands and her two children by her first marriage. With the success of her breakthrough novel, *The Golden Notebook* (1954), Lessing was to become emblematic of the liberated (and alienated) woman of the post-War era. Devoid of humor, a dogmatic believer in the perfect righteousness of her every caprice, a Marxist and a Freudian ideologue when those were the fashion, a feminist *avant la lettre* (if one discounts the legions of "New Women" of the 1890s and after), and, in her mature years, the New Age priestess of a misty melange of Sufism and Save-the-Whale liberalism, Lessing has been there and done that more thoroughly than any living female writer of her generation.

Her new book opens with an "Author's Note" that "*Mara and Dann* is a reworking of a very old tale . . . about an orphaned brother and sister who had all kinds of adventures, suffered a hundred vicissitudes, and ended up living happily ever after. This was the oldest story in Europe." Surely, reading her novel one comes increasingly to feel that we are in familiar territory, as the orphans set off on a journey that will take them the length of Ifrik (Africa) during a new Ice Age some six or seven millennia hence. While "Yerrup" lies blanketed under glaciers, Ifrik has become an ecological and cultural wasteland of parched savannahs and boggy tundra, inhabited by tribes squatting in the ruins of twentieth-century civilization and by a much altered fauna that includes giant man-eating scorpions and downsized elephants.

This landscape will be familiar to all readers of science fiction. There have been a dozen future Ice Ages, from John Christopher's *The World in Winter* to Robert Silverberg's *Time of the Great Freezes* and literally hundreds of novels depicting a devolved humanity trying to puzzle out their own lost history, including such five-star classics as Walter Miller's *A Canticle for Leibowitz* and John Crowley's *Engine Summer*. Lessing herself has already written an earlier New Ice Age novel in her Canopus in Argos

---

Review of *Mara and Dann: An Adventure*, by Doris Lessing.

series, *The Making of the Representative for Planet 8*, but there is no reason why she should not revisit a congenial idea so long as the Muse of the Novel is with her.

Sad to say, that's not the case. The world of *Mara and Dann* is constructed from recycled plots (abduction narratives, bodice-ripper suspense, an *interminable* Tolkien-like Symbolic Journey, and a denouement revealing the orphans to be Princess Shahana and Prince Shahmand of the royal blood) and landscapes uniformly generic and befogged. Thus, a crucial river voyage is described in these terms: "Han was keeping a closer watch than usual. Her eyes were always on the move, first one bank, and beyond it to the savannah, then the other bank, then ahead, as the river turned a bend, and behind, from where they had come."

Imagine four hundred pages of such lackluster travel notes, and imagine a cast of characters all as indistinct as that river, and you will have some sense of the longeurs of *Mara and Dann*. Lessing's admirers might wish to point out that character, plot, and poetic evocations of place were never the author's long suit, that she is a novelist of ideas. Not this time. Lessing's parable decodes as a homily against war (cruel and meaningless), men (cruel if left without a woman's nurturing direction), and "Yerrup" (cruel and doomed, if left without, etc.). The villains are routinely witless, incapable of articulating their own (false) ideas, and the good guys show their stuff by ever and again engaging in a Big Hug. Like this:

> Mara left Dann, and climbed up on Daima's lap and put her arms around her neck. This made Daima cry harder, and Mara cried, and then the little boy began tugging at Mara's legs to be lifted up, and soon both children were on Daima's lap and they were all crying.

Perhaps the most dismaying aspect of *Mara and Dann* is the poverty of its language. It is written as though to accommodate the needs of someone learning to read English as a second language. Few novels of this length can have a more limited vocabulary. In the first chapters, when Mara is only seven and we see the world through her eyes, there is a riddling aspect to this linguistic exigence. Thus, during a wholly improbable flash flood, one to rival Noah's deluge, we are told that "another wall of water was coming down. It was not as high as the others, but enough to push in front of it boulders and dead animals, the big ones with trunks and big ears and tusks." Now what might these big animals be, with their trunks and tusks? Elephants perhaps? Have Mara's people lost the word for elephant while still speaking of trunks and tusks? This is riddling at the level of a bedtime story for preschoolers, and it is typical of Lessing's narrative sophistication throughout.

It may be, to give her benefit of the doubt, that the author never intended the book for adult readers, nor yet for "young adults," in the parlance of publishers who regard teenagers as semi-literate. The only readers I can imagine who would not find the book patently simple-minded would be those age ten and younger. Yet the bodice-ripping passages of the later chapters would not recommend themselves to the very young:

> Here they were, Mara and Dann, with scarcely more between them than they had had when they first set out far away down in the south. They saw the tears running down their faces, and then they were in each other's arms, comforting, stroking, holding hot cheeks together; and this passion of protectiveness became a very different passion and their lips were together in a way that had never happened before. They kissed, like lovers, and clung, like lovers, and what they felt announced how dangerous and powerful a thing this love was.

This is, by any standard of measurement, sorry stuff, and I can think of no other way to account for the book's across-the-board shortcomings than to suppose that Lessing has lost her edge in the way that cruel Father Time has decreed to be the fate of all mankind, and womankind, too. She has, after all, entered her ninth decade. Few writers are ever granted so long a run. Perhaps a veiled caveat emptor should suffice in such cases, as it did for the later, symptomatic novels of Iris Murdoch. But Lessing's determination to add to her oeuvre, come what may, is actually the one interesting aspect of *Mara and Dann*, for hers will surely be a common case as more and more novelists survive into their emeritus years and beyond. Writers do have an advantage relative to dancers, opera singers, and athletes in terms of not being forced into early retirement. Often, of course, they fade away into a twilight of memoirs and moral pronouncements. Those who can teach do, often with distinction. But while there are fingers to type, and the will to persist in an established habit, what better way to defy devouring time than to enter the consoling dreamscapes of a novel?

Caveat emptor.

Measures of Hanging

Cities of the Red Night is a book of limited but, for its own happy few, intense appeal. Opium addicts who are sexually aroused by witnessing and/or enacting garroting and hangings will find *Cities* a veritable gallows of delight. Admittedly, female-hanging buffs and those of the heterosexual persuasion may feel cheated of their due, for the Muse of Strangulation—"Ix Tab" William S. Burroughs calls her in his invocation—seems not to extend her patronage to the fair sex. Guided by Ix Tab, a jealous goddess, Mr. Burroughs has eliminated from his book everything incidental to the central task of spinning and respinning the same yarn—characterization, wit, stylistic graces, anything that might detract from the erotic fascination of death by hanging. Even the romance of heroin addiction, which offered an alternative Universal Metaphor to interpreters of *Naked Lunch*, has dwindled to a few rather pro forma evocations of his new drug of preference, opium. In this book drugs are merely a means to an end, and that end is the gallows.

Impatient readers or those whose attention span cannot encompass the demands of Mr. Burroughs's prose (in the earlier chapters there are sometimes eight or nine pages of continuous, linear narrative!) will want to know where to turn for immediate gratification. Worshippers of Ix Tab should dogear the following pages: 18, 27, 47, 77, 108, 142, 154, 162, 173, 179–83, and about everything thereafter.

Mr. Burroughs's eternal tale is told in varying modes. Sometimes it is a fantasy of life aboard a pirate ship. Sometimes it is the story of a private eye investigating the hanging and decapitation of various attractive young victims. Sometimes his decor derives from sci-fi of the more brain-damaged variety, as in the following account of the transmigration of souls in a utopia of strangulation:

> These hardy Transmigrants, in the full vigor of maturity, after rigorous training in concentration and astral projection, would select two death guides to kill them in front of the copulating parents. The methods of death most commonly employed were hanging and strangula-

---

Review of *Cities of the Red Night*, by William S. Burroughs.

tion, the Transmigrant dying in orgasm, which was considered the most reliable method of ensuring a successful transfer. Drugs were also developed, large doses of which occasioned death in erotic convulsions, smaller doses being used to enhance sexual pleasure. . . . In time, death by natural causes became a rare and rather discreditable occurrence. . . .

Readers who would like to add the thrill of hypocrisy to the other pleasures of the text can take their cue from the jacket copy of *Naked Lunch*, published in 1959, where Mr. Burroughs's achievements as a moralist, satirist, and all-around genius were saluted by John Ciardi, Robert Lowell, and Norman Mailer. Mr. Burroughs himself, however, out-Herods them all in the arts of whitewash: "Certain passages in the book that have been called pornographic were written as a tract against Capital Punishment in the manner of Jonathan Swift's 'A Modest Proposal.' These sections are intended to reveal capital punishment as the obscene, barbaric and disgusting anachronism that it is."

Oh yes, and one might add that Pasolini's movie *Salo* is an indictment of Italian Fascism, Swinburne's obsessive doggerel on the subject of flogging an attack on corporal punishment in schools, and de Sade's *Justine* a Christian allegory after the manner of John Bunyan.

Forget morality! Forget art! What Mr. Burroughs offered the rubes back in 1959 and what he offers them today, in somewhat wearier condition, is entrance to a sideshow where they can view his curious id capering and making faces and confessing to bizarre inclinations. The backdrops are changed every few minutes by lazy stagehands, but the capering id delivers an identical performance before each one. It's grotesque, it's disgusting, but gosh—it's real!

Readers who have never caught Mr. Burroughs's act would do better to read *Naked Lunch* than this rather anemic clone. The twenty-two intervening years have impinged little on Mr. Burroughs's consciousness. He's read, or at least heard of, such books as *Future Shock* and *The Biological Time Bomb*, but even such (one might suppose) congenial events as the Manson murders or the Jonesville massacre cannot divert his imagination from its own perfected self-absorption.

The Secret Code Language of Bright Kids

One of the most enduring stock figures from the repertory company of science fiction is the Bright Kid. He may be only normatively bright, like the young hero of E.T., or a full-fledged juvenile Einstein like the Wunderkind heroes of Theodore Sturgeon's *More Than Human* or John Hersey's *The Child Buyer*. The vicarious appeal of such a protagonist is not to be wondered at. Just think of the first time you beat a grown-up at chess or in some other way demonstrated that older and wiser don't necessarily come as a matched set. The Bright Kid as Hero is not, of course, confined to science fiction (think of Dickens and Twain), but he seems to have a natural tropism for the genre, perhaps because so much of the science fiction audience is comprised of Bright Kids or grown-ups wistful for their Orphan Annie years, when "Tomorrow" was a tune they could completely believe in.

In her first and notably successful science fiction book, *Xorandor*, the English avant-garde novelist Christine Brooke-Rose has created a pair of twin Bright Kids, Jip and Zab, who are among the most credible and engaging in the genre. As their co-star, in the title role, she has given us an Alien Invader (if that's what Xorandor really is) in the form of a sentient rock, whose name derives from computer programming language, a dialect of English that receives in this novel its first sustained literary treatment. Jip and Zab, even before they encounter Xorandor sitting on his cairn on the coast of Cornwall, have developed a private language that incorporates some of the shorthand concision and syntactical clarity that characterizes a language like Basic.

Readers with some knowledge of programming will undoubtedly derive an extra measure of pleasure from *Xorandor*, but computer literacy is by no means required. Basic is Greek to me, but I never felt taken out of my depth, never wanted to skim, never was bored. Miss Brooke-Rose's verbal pyrotechnics are deployed in the interest of heightening and enriching her story, which is always riveting, as sheer verbal tour de force. *Xorandor* is comparable to such polyglot marvels as Anthony Burgess's *Clockwork Orange* or Hoban's *Riddley Walker*, books that poach on the territory of poetry without waxing "poetical."

Review of *Xorandor*, by Christine Brooke-Rose.

The story is as old as the hills, and simple as ABC. Jip and Zab, the computer whiz kids, are sporting with their computer on a rock in Cornwall when the rock begins to talk to them, first on their computer's screen, then aloud. The conversations that ensue, and the twins' and assorted experts' efforts to analyze them and to determine the nature, origins, capabilities, and intentions of this sentient rock, are the story in its entirety. There is almost as little action for the human characters as for Xorandor himself, who sits on his cairn and thinks. Xorandor and his progeny are alpha-phages, or eaters of alpha radiation. The opening of a nuclear waste dump near Xorandor's cairn has stirred him from his centuries-long repose and enabled him to begin to breed baby alpha-phages, which, when *they* leave their nest . . . But to tell more would spoil a good story. Enough to assure you that as with so much science fiction, nothing less than the fate of the earth is at stake.

Often, when an otherwise seasoned writer has a go at science fiction, the result is a botch. The genre's toy box is raided for its gaudy tropes, and an instant universe is fabricated that glitters for a few chapters of surrealistic fun and games until the whole structure collapses from a lack of imaginative rigor. Christine Brooke-Rose, however, maintains that delicate balance between fertility of intervention and strict economy of means that is the science-fictional equivalent of "elegance" in mathematics. This is all the more remarkable an accomplishment in that such virtues don't particularly distinguish her earlier novels, which abound in the kind of Joycean vocalises that only very earnest Ph.D. candidates are likely to mistake for good prose. Coming to her previous novel, *Amalgamemnon* (1985), after *Xorandor*, I found it hard to believe that the same author could have written both books, the former so turgid (and never more so than when it is trying its hardest to be oracular), the latter so readable. Yet the same concerns are evident in both books, the same technophobic dreads, the same delight in the elaboration of a palimpsest text. How to account for the differences? Perhaps it's simply that Miss Brooke-Rose is a born science fiction writer.

Double Talk, Double Dutch, Dutch Chocolate

Even the editors of *Postmodern American Fiction* concede that as a principle of selection or classification "postmodern" is so nebulous as to be virtually without meaning except insofar as it signifies "fairly recent." It can also mean "our gang," but the gang in question can include almost anyone. The editors would have it that, "To a major writer and critic such as John Barth, postmodern American fiction is best represented by a well-established group of formally experimental authors who gained recognition in the 1960s: Barth, Thomas Pynchon, Richard Brautigan, Grace Paley, Donald Barthelme and Robert Coover most prominent among them." If Barth himself cast his net so wide to recruit members of this "well-established group," then his judgment is truly prescient of the era to come, in which "diversity" would become the last common ground. In any case, those six names do appear on PAF's contents page, and probably represent an editorial consensus as to some irreducible postmodern minimum. Even so, Grace Paley would seem the odd woman out (or, here, in), since her stories are not notably experimental, even in their candid self-referentiality, which is rarely tricky in the manner of Barth or Philip Roth, but simply Grace-ful in an old-fashioned, tales-from-my-life way.

"Formally experimental" can serve as a qualification for postmodern status only if one forgets all the ways in which the modernists (not to mention the ancients) have anticipated most postmodern innovations, as represented in PAF. The popular cartoonists Lynda Barry and Art Spiegelman are represented here, but with work that is less innovative than George Herriman's "Krazy Kat" strips of the 1920s. There is a cartoon version of Paul Auster's *City of Glass*, by Paul Karasik and David Mazzucchelli, that isn't a cut above the Classic Comic version of *Toilers of the Sea*, in a technical sense. As to inherent narrative interest, I'd have to give the palm to Victor Hugo. Other contributors to PAF offer innovations that pale by comparison to modernist works by Kafka, Woolf, Gide, Cendrars, Gertrude Stein, and, indeed, hundreds of others now known chiefly to modernist antiquarians—as, doubtless, most of PAF's contributors will be known in due course chiefly to postmodernist antiquarians.

Review of Norton's *Postmodern American Fiction.*

For if the postmodern pigeonhole is a shuck, so is the modernist pigeonhole. James Joyce, Ezra Pound, Thomas Mann, William Faulkner, and all the rest of the modernist Pantheon have as little in common as the politicians of the same era: i.e., celebrity and contemporaneity. Good artists are remarkable rather for their individuality and/or universality than for their adherence to a set of specs drawn up after the fact. The specs are drawn up for the use of epigones and camp followers, and that is surely the case here. The elder presences in *PAF* are writers of distinction and wide popularity, such as Thomas Pynchon, William Burroughs, Kurt Vonnegut, Ntozake Shange, Truman Capote, Norman Mailer, Toni Morrison, Joseph Heller, and Don DeLillo—all represented by excerpts from such well-known full-length works as *In Cold Blood, The Armies of the Night, Breakfast of Champions, Beloved,* and *White Noise.* (So, to anyone whose bookcase is already stocked with those writers, caveat emptor.)

The younger contributors, by contrast, offer fictions of often exiguous brevity that seem to have been written with the official Chicago Manual of Postmodern Post-style before them. Thus, an extract from J. Yellowlees Douglas's hypertext screed offers an impressive, if illegible, reproduction of a flowchart, and then two pages of the fustian being diagrammed. A sample:

When he looks at Jake

he realizes the utter impossibility of his ever having the words to tell him this.
He has no inkling of what they would even sound like.

Yet he knows

that the only person in the world who is going to break the news to Jake is sitting in his chair.

Last night, in the parking lot, a guy with a shitty Saturday Night Special had jumped him. When he found Luke didn't have a shred of fucking paper on him—nothing, nada—he was so disgusted he didn't even try to pistol-whip him. Now, looking at Jake's lips curling up around the tube in an attempt at a smile, he wishes he had fucking bashed his skull to kingdom come. Given him retrograde amnesia. Tossed the coroner another stiff for the fridge.

Readers anxious to catch more of Ms. Douglas's act can find it at the Norton Web site: <http://www.wwnorton.com>. I would submit that the same half-baked hard-boiled piffle, offered as a book, would find no takers and that it is only within the protective confines of the postmodern label that such stuff could see its way to print. But is Douglas ever a member of the club and proud possessor of the official encoding ring! Her attached resume informs us the author, born in 1962, was "formerly director of the Program in Professional Writing at Lehman College, the City University of New York. Douglas is now director of the Center for Written and Oral Communication at the University of Florida, where she is also assistant professor of English. Her critical work on hypertext has appeared in journals and collections in the United States, the United Kingdom, and Australia, focusing on the applicability of literary theory, narratology, and esthetics to hypertext environments."

That is typical in its institutional bonafides of the resumes of the younger contributors to PAF, as the excerpt from "I Have Said Nothing" is typical in its choppiness and effortless inexpressivity of their style. When they are not writing botched genre, they favor lame stand-up comedy, as in this intro by performance artist Laurie Anderson (born 1947):

> Good evening. Now I'm no mathematician but I'd like to talk about just a couple of numbers that have really been bothering me lately, and they are zero and one. Now first, let's take a look at zero. Now nobody wants to be a zero. To be a zero means to be a nothing, a nobody, a has-been, a zilch.
> On the other hand, just about everybody wants to be number one. To be number one means to be a winner, top of the heap, the acme.

To heighten the hilarity, Anderson accompanies the script of "Talkshow" (which is a section of "Stories from the Nerve Bible," which is taken from her book of 1986, *Lower Mathematics*) with a picture of herself on stage in a white suit and mask.

Want more? Here's some schtick from Mark Leyner (born 1956), who prefaces this excerpt from *Tooth Imprints from a Corn Dog* (1995) with a statement of intent: "My work isn't animated by a desire to be experimental or post-modernist or aesthetically subversive or even 'innovative'—it is animated by a desire to craft a kind of writing that is at every single moment exhilarating for the reader, where each phrase, each sentence is an event." Like this:

> I have programmed the television in my bedroom to awaken me, and at six o'clock I'm roused by CNN. I mute the news and telephone room service for a sweetbreads burrito and a thermos of black coffee.
> Several lines of verse have emerged intact from my hypnopompic state, and I scrawl them on a pad before they can evaporate:

In a drawing room at Armani Kids,
I found the dead body of a policewoman.
I sucked her toe and she came to life.

There are also two fragments. The neo-Keatsian

Beads of mercury bubble from
the mouths of hemorrhaging androids . . .

and the evocative

Tooth imprints on a corn dog.

After momentarily considering revising the initial lines to read: "At a counterfeit hair-care products lab, / I found the dead body of a police-woman. / I sucked her toe and she came to life," and then not (there's something so much more febrile and chthonic about discovering this sleeping-beauty-in-blue at a juvenile couturier), I decided against incorporating any of this material into the poem.

These samplings are sophomoric not only in their humor (big words are thought to be innately funny; likewise, body fluids, brand names, and unfamiliar food) but in their a priori hostility toward all forms of life other than sophomores. The message of postmodernism (as of Dada, back when) is that the Past is an oppressive burden that is best dealt with by inept parody that will show how dumb the past was. Thus, Duchamps's urinal; thus, Douglas's *faux noir*. Such barings of the artistic bum have become rituals of the avant-garde by this point: Yoko Ono made a movie featuring nothing but celebrity asses. PAF is often the prose equivalent.

"Postmodern" may also be the literary equivalent for that favorite euphemism of the politically correct, "diversity." Those parts of the introduction in which the editors explain why writers who are women, gays, lesbians, African Americans, or other hyphenates are postmodern in their very nature are classic persiflage and worth close study by anyone intending a career in academia. It all boils down to why the once margin-alized Other should become the canonical Author, as she has in PAF. Admittedly, of the fifty-nine authors of fiction, a preponderance are still male (thirty-five men, twenty-four women), but of *those* twenty-four women, two are Asian American, three African American, three Hispanic American, and two Native American. (There are, additionally, four males in these categories.) This would suggest that women writers of color might be sympathetically disposed toward postmodernism as an arena of equal opportunities, but bell hooks (born 1955) in her essay "Postmodern Blackness," included in PAF's critical appendix, expresses mainly her sense of grievance and exclusion:

> The failure to recognize a critical black presence in the culture and in most scholarship and writing on postmodernism compels a black reader, particularly a black female reader, to interrogate her interest in a subject where those who discuss and write about it seem not to know black women exist or even to consider the possibility that we might be somewhere writing or saying something that should be listened to, or producing art that should be seen, heard, approached with intellectual seriousness.
>
> . . . Music is the cultural product created by African-Americans that has most attracted postmodern theorists. It is rarely acknowledged that there is far greater censorship and restriction of other forms of cultural production by black folks—literary, critical writing, etc. Attempts on the part of editors and publishing houses to control and manipulate the representation of black culture, as well as the desire to promote the creation of products that will attract the widest audience, limit in a crippling and stifling way the kind of work many black folks feel we can do and still receive recognition. Using myself as an example, that creative writing I do which I consider to be most reflective of a postmodern oppositional sensibility, work that is abstract, fragmented, non-linear narrative, is constantly rejected by editors and publishers. It does not conform to the type of writing they think black women should be doing or the type of writing they believe will sell.

I daresay that bell hooks speaks in this essay not only for many African American women writers, but for virtually all writers who have been discriminated against by editors and publishing houses solely on the basis of whether someone might want to read their work. Innumerable times I have been crippled and stifled myself in the same way as bell hooks, and I agree with her that "postmodern thinkers and philosophers [should] constitute themselves as an audience for such work" and open up the field so that it will be more inclusive. It seems a pity in the light of such advocacy that the editors could not have opened up their own pages to offer us a sampling from one of hooks's abstract, fragmented, nonlinear narratives. Her nonfiction whets my appetite for more.

My estimate of the amount of material included in *Postmodern American Fiction* solely to meet affirmative action quotas would be eleven out of fifty-seven pieces. As many more stories by writers of distinction or at least with name-recognition value might be present for diversity's sake as much as for merit, and as many more again are by writers with solid postmodern credentials, such as William Vollman, Susan Daitch, and the nine other PAF contributors whose work is also to be found in *After Yesterday's Crash: The Avant-Pop Anthology*, edited by Larry McCaffery (1995).

The practical consequence of using an anthology as a means of achieving "gender and racial balance" may well be the opposite of what its editors intended, for the dead and elderly white males who make the cut are generally not editorial "discoveries" but recognizable brand names whose presence will enhance the book's general sales prospects—Pynchon, Burroughs, Barthelme, et al.—and whose blatant talent tends to overshadow those who made the cut by virtue of the quota system. And there is no middle ground between them, for the white male mediocrities who might have counterbalanced mediocrities of diversity don't make the cut. The result is a seeming gulf between Menu A and Menu B, visible to all and never to be mentioned aloud.

This gulf can absorb any amount of criticism, since the disparity between the two menus—between, that is, the books people actually have enjoyed reading and those they should have enjoyed reading but don't or won't or haven't heard of—is the kind of aesthetic scandal that is grist for the critical mill.

Critics are happiest with texts that allow them to display their full toolkit, texts that are either dense, opaque, or occluded, and so can only be traversed with a guide's assistance, or else seem stupefyingly simple, like Warhol's movie of the Empire State Building. As yet, there is little published fiction of the latter, minimalist tendency. Is this only because of the efforts of editors and publishers, noted by bell hooks, to "promote the creation of products that will attract the widest audience"? She generously allows as how she is not "the only black person engaged in forms of cultural production, especially experimental ones, who is constrained by a lack of an audience for such work." One could go further and say she is not the only person of whatever race, sex, or gender preference to feel such constraints, and that almost everyone already in the postmodern club she is anxious to join shares her frustration with editors, publishers, and the lack of attentive critics and readers.

The situation with regard to criticism must be especially galling, when the critics who should be paying attention so often prefer to write about Elvis and Madonna rather than (as she notes herself) about bell hooks. In PAF's concluding eighty-page "Casebook of Postmodern Theory" there is little apparent connection between the preceding 580 pages of fiction and what the critics are concerned with. Jean Baudrillard takes a keen interest in Disneyland, but then he's French and can't be expected to *read* postmodern American fiction. The same holds true for Hélène Cixous, who does, however, mention Mallarmé, and cites Plato, Hegel, and Nietzsche, whom she excoriates for "the repression, repudiation, distancing of woman; a murder that is mixed up with history as the manifestation and representation of masculine power" in a footnote of only three and a half lines. The opening scenes of the excerpt from Cixous's *Stories: Out and Out: Attacks/Ways Out, Foray* will be an inspiration to all students who've been required to buy PAF as a required text (and that is surely the book's *raison d'être*), for they are a model of how, postmodernly, to finesse any term paper or exam:

Where is she?
Activity/passivity
Sun Moon
Culture! Nature
Day! Night

Father! Mother
Head! Heart
Intelligible! Palpable
Logos! Pathos
Form, convex, step, advance, semen, progress.
Matter, concave ground—where steps are taken,
holding- and dumping-ground.
Man
Woman

How is one to answer this new, non-hegemonic style of discourse? Donna Haraway (born 1944), an American theorist who teaches at the History of Consciousness Program at the University of California in Santa Cruz, offers her answer to that in a key passage from *A Cyborg Manifesto: Science, Technology, and Socialist-Feminism in the Late Twentieth Century*. (In PAF this title is footnoted, in part: "Research was funded by an Academic Senate Faculty Research Grant from the University of California, Santa Cruz." The footnote goes on to trace the complex evolution of Haraway's manifesto to a paper delivered at Barnard in 1983.)

Representation	Simulation
Bourgeois novel, realism	Science fiction, postmodernism
Organism	Biotic component

Depth, integrity	Surface, boundary
Heat	Noise

And so on for twenty-seven more dichotomies, concluding with:

Sex	Genetic engineering
Labour	Robotics
Mind	Artificial Intelligence
Second World War	Star Wars
White Capitalist Patriarchy	Informatics of Domination

It would not be fair to oppose the mind-privileging language of White Capitalist Patriarchy to a schemata inspired by a feminist-Lacanian discourse, so let me reply in kind to Haraway, Cixous, and the triad of editorial personnel engaged in the issuance of this cultural product:

Masculine	Feminine
He	She
They (male)	We (female)
Atomic bomb	Hug
New York Times bestseller list	Hug

Double talk, double dutch, dutch chocolate
Postmodern, Hostess Cupcakes, hostage taking

Hostage taking, not in the sense advanced by Sherman Alexie in his story in PAF, "Captivity," inspired by a seventeenth-century Indian captivity narrative, but in the sense that the many good writers in PAF act as a kind of human shield for the many more mediocre and lousy writers. None of these good writers are to be blamed for going along for the ride. New readers are born every minute, and what better way to find them than to have a chapter of one's most popular novel assigned as homework? Those who've already read it will be grateful to be spared the task, and among the vast majority who haven't some might want to read the rest of the book. As to keeping company with no-accounts, it is an accepted ritual of literary life to share the podium with lesser luminaries, and so long as they can be counted on not to look cleverer, what harm can come from it? So, even with the inevitable turn-downs from those whose agents or publishers demanded bigger fees than Norton's advance would accommodate (and there are some odd omissions that that might account for), a phalanx of A-menu writers would have been a snap to recruit. The rest of the seats would be as easy to fill as lifeboats on the *Titanic*.

In the *New York Times* of November 1, 1997, six scholars were asked what was the Most Overrated Idea of the present day. The philosopher Richard Rorty replied, "The first thing that comes to mind is postmodernism. It's one of those terms that has been used so much that nobody has the foggiest idea what it means. It means one thing in philosophy, another thing in architecture and nothing in literature. It would be nice to get rid of it."

Anyone required to read *Postmodern American Fiction* would surely agree.

Acknowledgments

The essays and articles in this book originally appeared in the following publications, sometimes in earlier versions and under previous titles.

"The Embarrassments of Science Fiction" appeared in *Science Fiction in Dimension*, edited by Peter Nicholls (Harper & Row, 1976).

Foundation published "Ideas: A Popular Misconception," "A Different Different World," "UFOs and the Origins of Christianity," "Science Fiction as a Church," and "A Closer Look at *Close Encounters.*"

"Mythology and Science Fiction" appeared as the introduction to *New Constellations*, edited by Thomas M. Disch (HarperCollins, 1976).

"Big Ideas and Dead-End Thrills: The Further Embarrassments of Science Fiction" appeared in the *Atlantic Monthly* 269, no. 2 (1992).

The *Los Angeles Times* published "Poe's Appalling Life" and "Time, Space, the Limitlessness of the Imagination—and Abs to Die For."

"Luncheon in the Sepulcher: Poe and the Gothic Tradition" appeared as the introduction to *Strangeness*, edited by Thomas M. Disch and Charles Naylor (Avon, 1983).

"*Brave New World* Revisited Once Again" appeared in *Omni.*

The *New York Times Book Review* published "A Tableful of Twinkies" under the title "Our Wild Future in Space," "The Champion of Cyberpunk: On Two Works by William Gibson," "Queen Victoria's Computers," and "Measures of Hanging."

The *Times Literary Supplement* published "Sic, Sic, Sic," "A Bus Trip to Heaven," "Jokes across the Generation Gap," "SF: Guides to the Ghetto," and "The Secret Code Language of Bright Kids."

"The Doldrums of Space" appeared in *Inquiry.*

"Isaac Asimov (1920–1992)" appeared in *Entertainment Weekly.*

"The King and His Minions: Thoughts of a *Twilight Zone* Reviewer" and "The Feast of St. Bradbury" appeared in *Twilight Zone.*

Fantasy and Science Fiction published "Talking with Jesus," "The Labor Day Group," and "1979: Fluff and Fizzles."

The *Washington Post Book World* published "Crowley's Poetry," "Wolfe's New Sun," and "The Day of the Living Dead."

"Dick's First Novel" appeared as the introduction to *Solar Lottery*, by Philip K. Dick (Gregg Press, 1976).

"In the Mold of 1964" appeared as the afterword to *The Penultimate Truth*, by Philip K. Dick (Bluejay, 1984).

The *Nation* published "The Village Alien" (244, no. 10); "The Road to Heaven: Science Fiction and the Militarization of Space" (242, no. 18); "Speaker Moonbeam: Newt's Futurist Brain Trust" (260, no. 8); and "Primal Hooting" (247, no. 14).

The *Hudson Review* published "The Evidence of Things Not Seen" and "Double Talk, Double Dutch, Dutch Chocolate."

"The Fairy Tale Kingdom of Baghdad" appeared in the *Chicago Tribune* (February 3, 1991).

"Over the River and Through the Wood" appeared in the *Wall Street Journal* (January 15, 1995).

Index